# BREAKAWAY

# BREAKAWAY

## HOCKEY AND THE YEARS BEYOND

## CHARLES WILKINS

M&S

**Canadian Cataloguing in Publication Data**
Wilkins, Charles
Breakaway: hockey and the years beyond

ISBN 0-7710-8840-X

1. Hockey players – Canada – Retirement. 2. National Hockey
League – Biography. 3. Hockey players – Canada – Biography.
I. Title.

GV848.5.A1W55 1995     796.962'092'2     C95-931918-2

The publishers acknowledge the support of the Canada Council
and the Ontario Arts Council for their publishing program.

Typesetting by M&S, Toronto

Printed and bound in Canada on acid-free paper.

McClelland & Stewart Inc.
*The Canadian Publishers*
481 University Avenue
Toronto, Ontario
M5G 2E9

1  2  3  4  5     99  98  97  96  95

# CONTENTS

*for my father, Hume Wilkins,*
*and to the memory of my mother, Norma,*
*who shared my pleasure in the game*

# INTRODUCTION

IT HAS OCCURRED to me in rare moments – some would say deluded moments – that the careers of professional writers and NHL hockey players have a commonality that is largely hidden by the vast differences in their fan base, physiques, and bank accounts – and, of course, their respective talents. Like many Canadian men (and perhaps women), I have sometimes reflected on what it must be like to make a living in the National Hockey League. As a kid, I frequently imagined myself doing so. My fantasies ranged across the roar of the crowd, the raging glory of winning the Stanley Cup, and, more persistently, my own prodigious skating and scoring. Somehow, those fantasies never included the frightful intimidation and brutality – the broken bones, torn eyeballs, and bashed kidneys – that are as much a part of the NHL game as brilliant skating and scoring.

In the years since my childhood, it has been driven home to me in countless ways that I could never have done the job of a professional hockey player – I cannot think of a single writer who could. And I can think of few hockey players who would want to do the job of a professional writer. So, when I speak of a commonality between the vocations I am be no means speculating on any real or imagined interchangeability of roles. I am commenting, rather, on the endless hours of preparation and practice that make a career in either calling possible; on the marginalized life style, the bohemian work hours, and the degree to which both endeavours make social and psychological outsiders of their practitioners.

The writer Wallace Stegner wrote that a commitment to words pushes a writer irreversibly towards the edges of his society, at the same time disqualifying him for that society's mainstream work. Eric Nesterenko and others have told me that big-league hockey, with it intense passions and ongoing adrenaline highs – its physicality and theatre and camaraderie – has much the same effect on a hockey player.

During the writing of this book, I have found my subjects remarkably forthcoming in telling me their stories. In some cases, they have taken me into their confidence with an almost painful honesty. I believe that, at least in part, this willingness to talk is a result of the players themselves having recognized in the hollow-eyed writer who arrives on their doorstep not so much an inquisitor or clinician as another of life's irregulars, in front of whom they can safely unpack their treasures and trunks.

This book, as a result, is as much about vulnerability and survival, both physical and psychological, as it is about the game of hockey. More simply, it's about well-known hockey players, now retired from the game, speaking with honesty and directness about who they are, where they've been, and what they've seen. It is Bobby Smith on obsession; Eric Nesterenko on fear, humiliation, and his epochal fight with John Ferguson; Reggie Leach on his astonishing boyhood and the Dionysian partying that shortened his career. It is Randy Gregg on both the glories and the unseen tensions of the great years of the Edmonton Oilers.

In writing the book, I have done my best to station myself in the gap between the lionizing mythology that surrounds and even traps our professional athletes and the seldom-witnessed realities of their lives.

As always, the process of researching and writing has been both exciting and instructive, and I trust that the chapters that follow will be as engaging and enjoyable to read as they have been to write.

It hardly needs saying that book-length manuscripts do not come together without the advice and assistance of many people. This one is no exception. For their generosity and kindness during my travels around the continent, I would like the thank Adele and Kevin Parkinson, Elizabeth Yip and Jim Carpick, Rosemary and Gerry Waldron, and Larry Krotz. For their helpful suggestions and information, Karen Pappin, Susan Carpick, David Ranta, Jake MacDonald, Bill Hay, John Halligan, and especially Phil Pritchard, whose assistance at the Hockey Hall of Fame went well beyond the call of duty. My thanks also go to Dan Diamond for his guidance, generosity, and friendship; to my publisher, Doug Gibson, for suggesting the project and supporting it along the way; to my editor, Dinah Forbes, whose goodwill has been a lesson throughout; and to my copy editor, Peter Buck. As ever, I also wish to thank my wife, Betty Carpick, for her love, tolerance, and frequent editorial assistance. I might add that Betty's latest pregnancy corresponded exactly with the gestation of this book, and that, even as I write, her suitcase is packed in readiness for a trip to the Port Arthur General Hospital. She has occasionally commented on the coincidence of our "being pregnant" at the same time, I with my book, she with our third child. May our offspring, both literal and literary, prosper on the planet.

# IN THE FORESTS OF THE NIGHT

THE BRITISH PROPERTIES IN West Vancouver are the most radiant residential district in a city as radiant as any on earth. The affluent suburb, whose name hints at privilege if not downright snobbery, rises in a precipitous sprawl off the Upper Levels Highway, due north of the Lions' Gate Bridge. In varying measure it offers a breathtaking southward view of the lower B.C. mainland, the Georgia Strait, and, in the near distance, downtown Vancouver, stretched out along the Burrard Inlet as tidy as Lego.

If you ascend through the lush streets of this extraordinary quarter, past the driveways with their BMWs and Mercedes-Benzes, past the holly hedges and the million-dollar digs, you come eventually to the edge of the wilderness, to the deep coastal rainforest, where the urban paradise stops and the planetary paradise begins.

Here, on the upper cusp of the city, ravens, hawks, and bears share acreage with stock promoters, corporate executives, and the mavens of the tea-time aristocracy. The air is thinner up here on the border between dream and dream, but the insulation from the harsher lessons of urban life is infinitely thicker.

If you travel to the highest reaches of this West Coast *Zona Rosa*, and you know what you're looking for (and care), you just might happen upon the residence of a rather unlikely member of the local gentry, a survivor of the NHL jungles and the all-time penalty king of big-league hockey, David "Tiger" Williams.

Tiger and his wife, Brenda, have owned their splendid mountainside home for some fourteen years, and on this particular afternoon in mid-August, Tiger and a visitor are relaxing barefoot on the back deck, looking out over the family pool and a thousand square kilometres of city and seascape. The sky is cloudless, the air rich with hemlock and fir, and a moist soft breeze is rising off the Pacific, holding the temperature to a tolerably balmy twenty-five Celsius.

With its sculpted trees, well-worked gardens, and magnificent view, the Williams home is decidedly in sync with the tony suburb that cascades down the mountain below it. But the same can hardly be said for the redoubtable personality and habits of the man of the house. Indeed, Tiger's deportment is a vivid foil, a kind of wacky-house mirror, for the generally staid *gestalt* of the neighbourhood. Consider, for instance, that in this enclave of relative gentility he keeps 128 guns locked in a gun safe in the basement of his home: antique Colts and Winchesters, as well as the latest in shotguns and rifles. Or that on evenings in January or February, he will occasionally choose a hunting bow from among the several he owns and, wrapped against the cold, take to the street for target practice. "I open the garage door," he says casually, "turn on the light, and shoot at a target inside." The arrows, he neglects to mention, cross the public thoroughfare behind the house at some three hundred kilometres per hour. In warmer weather, he hones his shooting skills on an archery range that he has laid out on the property's lower terrace, below the pool.

Tiger chews tobacco, eats cougar and bear meat, and, in striking contrast to wealthy urbanites from West Vancouver to West Berlin, is a model of almost Thoreauvian self-sufficiency. He does all his own landscaping and yard work – prunes the trees, grooms the terraces, and nourishes the soil (the flowers are Brenda's domain). Twice a year, he undertakes the meticulous task of shaving sixteen ornamental cedars that at some point in the past have been sculpted into eight-foot upright spheroids, aesthetic masterpieces as smooth and plump as goose eggs. He lays flooring, pours concrete, and is perfectly capable of doing any home renovation, or even of building a house. (Asked if he does drywall, he responds perfunctorily, "I do, but I hate it, so I don't.")

Every year, he smokes a winter's supply of B.C. salmon in his homemade smoker. ("Smoked anything is my fave!") He marinates the fish using his own recipe, and professes to have learned much of what he knows about the culinary wilds from West Coast Indians with whom he hunts and fishes.

He loads his own rifle and shotgun shells and makes all his own hunting arrows, deadly missiles with razored tips that can penetrate the thorax of a moose at a distance of forty metres.

Lest anyone get the wrong impression, Tiger is by no means living out his retirement from hockey in quirky isolation, an eccentric warrior indulging in the spoils of a career in pro sport. In fact, on this very afternoon, he is pouring heart and soul into a rambling conversation about the manifold facets of his phenomenally busy work life – his priorities and passions, the bridges he has built and those he has burned.

By his own rather liberal estimate, Tiger has "a million irons in the fire." Business. Charity. Stock market. Property development. Family. Sport. More business. More investment. He seldom works fewer than seventy hours a week and winnows more business propositions in a year than the average financier would be called upon to sort in a decade. "People come up to me constantly, anywhere, trying to get me involved in this, that, and the other," he says with a dismissive flick of his hand. "All I can tell them is if they wanta see me, they've gotta do it on my time, and I don't have any time."

The fact is, Tiger has become a celebrity of such stature on B.C.'s lower mainland that his mere endorsement of an idea or endeavour, the sniff of his presence, can be enough to raise the profile of that endeavour into sharp public focus. And he is successful enough that he can afford to turn his back on even the most promising of propositions if they do not meet his fancy. He is a living caricature not just of sporting and business success but of the underlying constructs – the ambition, self-confidence, and relentless hard work – on which his successes have been founded.

Even though he has not played professional hockey in the city for more than ten years, he is greeted left and right by passersby on the street, is sought out for autographs and photos, and is interviewed regularly in the press and on radio and television. Energy pours off him like heat off a stove, and the people around him are, in turn, energized by that heat. "He's forever interacting with people, giving to them, lighting them up," says Brenda. "It's one of the things I like most about Dave and, ironically, one of the things I dislike most. I'll be waiting for him in, say, a restaurant, and he'll be chatting away with someone he doesn't even know, and I'll think, *Arrghh, TIGER, come and sit down and . . . well . . . let's* just say it can be tiring keeping up to him."

Mike Condon, a former editor of the Vancouver tabloid *Sports Vue*, submits that Tiger is considerably more popular in Vancouver today than he was during his days as a player. Which is not to say he was anything less than a hit when he arrived from Toronto to play for the Vancouver Canucks in 1979. "At that time, the team was pretty laid back, even self-satisfied," says Condon. "And suddenly here was this ferocious prairie pug who put everything he had into *every minute he was on the ice!* He'd *skate* and *check* and play to the crowd, and of course he thought nothing of taking on the toughest thugs on the toughest teams in the league. The fans out here had never seen anything like him. You'd catch him on television before a game, belting out the national anthem while the guys beside him stood stone-faced waiting for the game to start. Oh, he was a character. He hated apathy, and he hated losing, and everybody, including the media, ate it up."

Tiger still hates losing. At anything. "In my dreams," he says, working a fleck of tobacco off his lower incisor, "I always come out on top – win the game, win the fight, shoot the animal – I never lose."

It is a measure of his popularity, not to mention his promotional capabilities, that his 1984 autobiography sold more than 100,000 copies, three or four times as many as most hockey biographies. Predictably, a large portion of those sales were in Vancouver and British Columbia. Now ten years out of print, the book covers Tiger's boyhood, youth, and his first ten years in pro hockey. But it is a nonetheless telling primer on the bridling contentiousness, the refusal to accept the unacceptable, that still marks his personality and circumscribes his life beyond the game.

What the book does *not* reveal is the profound degree to which Tiger made use of his years in hockey not only to broaden his sensitivities, but to prepare for his eventual entry into retirement and business. Part of that preparation lay in educating himself in the subtleties of investment, taxation, and property development. To that end, he consorted with corporate executives, consumed countless business and financial reports, and became friendly with wealthy free-wheelers such as Barrie Sali, president of the billion-dollar Tim Br Mart corporation, and rock impresario Bruce Allen, best known as the agent of rock star Bryan Adams.

In ironic contrast to his public image, Tiger's business activities have tended to be anonymous. "A couple of years ago," he smiles, "my son Ben said to me, 'Dad, people are always asking me what you're doing these days. And I'm always telling them I don't really know. What *are* ya doing, anyway?'"

Pressed on the point, Tiger allows that, during the past decade, he has built up extensive property holdings, including several residences in southern British Columbia and hotels in Alberta and Saskatchewan, and part control of a fifteen-acre chunk of land on the Vancouver waterfront. He has also been involved in a variety of land development and construction endeavours, most notably the financing and construction of two sizable condominium projects in the Vancouver area. "On the bigger of those projects," he says, "I not only raised capital and acted as site manager while the thing was being built, I ended up selling some of the units."

What's more, he is a veteran player on the Toronto, New York, and Vancouver stock exchanges, the activities of which he studies with the tenacity of a scholarship student preparing for a final exam. He makes most of his own buying and selling decisions, never takes market advice from friends, and discreetly confides that the Toronto and New York markets have been "very good" to him.

His axiom for business involvement is as level as the Saskatchewan prairie: "I've gotta like what it is I'm getting into. It's gotta look profitable, and I've gotta have full control – I want my finger on the switch at all times."

In 1993, Tiger clarified his employment picture by hitching up his garters as a major shareholder and coach of

the Vancouver Voodoo, a professional roller-hockey team
that he has moulded in his own image and guided through
three successful seasons on the Roller Hockey International
circuit.

I met Tiger for the first time on a Saturday morning in
August 1994. He had just put the Voodoo through their
game-day licks and chops in preparation for a game that
night against the Sacramento River Rats, and, when I
caught up with him, he was sitting, feet on the desk, in the
Voodoo's Lilliputian training room, dictating onto tape a
weekly column that he "writes" for a local newspaper. The
team's home at that time was the Vancouver Agridome, a
four-thousand-seat arena on the Pacific National Exhibition grounds, a stone's throw from the Pacific Coliseum,
where the team now plays and where Tiger performed as a
Canuck. As its name suggests, the arena is an agricultural
building, a cow palace, which on warm days in summer is
distinctly redolent of past four-legged occupants. "The
smell," said one of Tiger's associates, "is *not* the
Vancouver Voodoo."

As players came and went from the room, consulting
the trainer about a variety of traumas and ailments, Tiger
held forth on the difficulties of establishing a franchise in
a new sport, particularly in Vancouver, where the sports
fan's dollar is already stretched to transparency by the NHL,
the CFL, and a variety of attractions such as Indy-Car
Racing, professional soccer, and baseball (the stretch will
be significantly greater after the imminent arrival of the
NBA). He offered views on the obligations and exigencies of
coaching, and, more forcefully, on his expectations of the
young turks who play on his team: "The bottom line with
me is, if I don't think you're giving me an honest day's
effort, I'm gonna make it tough for you, whether we're
playing roller hockey or banging nails on a construction
site. Life's too short for half-assed efforts."

Considering his reputation for toughness, Tiger is by no means a big man – in fact, he is surprisingly compact. But he has the body of a weight-lifter, densely muscled and almost perfectly proportioned. His neck is thick, his cheekbones broad and flat, and his nose has been compressed into a knotty metaphor for the irrepressible violence that is a fact of life in professional hockey.

Despite the baldness that has claimed the top of his pate, his face is youthful, and his remaining curls are an undiluted black. On the day I met him, his hairline was concealed beneath a black leather baseball hat that had been pressed onto his head in a manner that suggested the habberdashery of the Confederate army. He wore snug black jeans, moccasin-style shoes without socks, and a white cotton polo shirt bearing a miniature crest of the Vancouver Voodoo. His eyes are an intense Mediterranean blue.

Even at age forty-one, there is an impudence about Tiger, a street-punk sauciness, that goes back to his boyhood and is well understood by anyone familiar with his reputation as a hockey player. But as our conversation blossomed, this particular aspect of his personality subsided beneath his meticulous attention to the business at hand and a curious, almost charming geniality that I had not anticipated. The latter, it seemed, rose out of his apparent respect for the fact that I had travelled thousands of kilometres to meet him, that like him I was another human being with a peculiar set of challenges to overcome, and, just possibly, I imagined, out of some unspoken notion (partly justified) that I shared his contempt for the proverbial half-assed effort. Every question, every detail of our conversation, drew his utmost concern and attention. It also drew the full force of his seemingly boundless aptitude for instructing those around him in everything from morals to money management to the politics of the environment – from the importance of a positive attitude to the preferred method for gutting and dressing an elk.

Despite Tiger's feline monicker, the conceptual model for his personality lies less in the sleek jungle cat than in some radically ambitious hybrid of bull terrier and non-stop pedagogue. He is endlessly tenacious, endlessly analytical, endlessly instructive. Unshakable certainty would seem to be his hedge against the corrosive chaos and confusion that, he knows as well as anyone, lie thinly veiled beneath even the surest of regimens and most orderly precepts for living.

"The ability to work hard every day is a talent," he told me within minutes of shaking my hand. "If you know how to go to work you'll always have a job."

And a few minutes later: "When something goes wrong, don't dwell on the problem, dwell on the solution. And make sure it doesn't happen again."

And shortly after that: "Never let *anybody* push you around. When I was playing for the Maple Leafs, Mr. Ballard used to give some of the guys a bad time, and I'd say, 'Don't take it! Tell him what you think of him! That's the only way he'll respect you.' The thing to do with the schoolyard bully is kick him where it hurts the first day of school. You may take a beating, but he'll never come near you again."

As our conversation veered from sport to business to books (Tiger is, after all, an author), I made what I thought was an innocuous observation on the uncertainties and challenges of the literary trade. After brief consideration of the point, he said, "A lot of people don't see it this way, but as far as I'm concerned you have two choices in life: quit complaining about what you're doing and get on with it, or for heaven's sake do something else."

At noon sharp, we left the Agridome and did something else – drove across the Second Narrows Bridge to a funky waterside restaurant called the Bellair Café. As he tucked into a mastodon's helping of eggs Benedict and fries, Tiger offered up a painstaking description of his method for smoking salmon. The process involves, among other things, salt, sugar, charcoal briquettes, tiny cubes of dried alder, a coffee can, a steel drum, a free-standing plywood smoking closet, and of course fresh, boneless salmon fillets.

He next told me how, one evening, as he was driving along the Gardiner Expressway in Toronto during the seventies, he saw another driver roll down his window and throw a piece of garbage out onto the pavement. Incensed by the heedlessness of the act, Tiger rolled down his own window and told the driver what he thought of him. "The guy gave me the finger," says Tiger, "so, I followed him off the expressway and started chasing him through downtown Toronto." The chase went on for some ten minutes, until suddenly the frantic driver screeched to a stop in front of a police sub-station and ran inside, hollering at the desk sergeant that some maniac was trying to kill him. At that moment, Tiger himself appeared in the station and announced to the sergeant that he had caught the man littering and was placing him under citizen's arrest. "It turned out the guy had about a hundred unpaid traffic tickets in his name, so they arrested him anyway, locked him up, and thanked me for bringing him in."

From the restaurant, we took the Upper Levels Highway to West Vancouver and the British Properties. As we pursued our conversation on the deck of the Williams home, Tiger lamented that the summer schedule of roller hockey had entirely routed his cherished fishing activities, not to mention the hunt for bighorned sheep that he traditionally undertakes during the first week in August. "As soon as the schedule's over," he brightened, "I'll be gone for three weeks' hunting up north."

No matter what Tiger says about *anything*, it is not until he begins to talk about hunting that the richness and contour of his personality come fully into view. He revels in both the high drama and the smallest details of the art, and can speculate knowledgeably on the intelligence of elk, the honour of grizzlies, and the mystic riddle of the cougar. His favourite meal, bar none, is fresh liver, taken straight from the gut of a newly killed deer. "You get your fire going as you're doing your gutting, and as soon as the liver comes out, you plop it in the pan."

As a boy, he hunted deer with his father to provide a treat for the family table. He also hunted waterfowl, and to this day speaks wistfully of prairie sloughs and of the bracing clarity of cold mornings in autumn when the ducks and geese were on the wing.

So in love is he with hunting that, for several months of the year, he carries booklets of hunting regulations amid the business papers and contracts in his briefcase. "I'm not much of a reader," he shrugs, "but every chance I get, I take out these booklets and I study them, line by line, and I imagine what it's going to be like."

He typically hunts three months a year and, like all true hunters, is humbly, profoundly aware that, were it not for the efficiencies of his weaponry, the clay-footed hunter would be decidedly overmatched by cougar, bighorn, and elk. Which is largely why Tiger, ever solicitous of challenge, has all but forsaken rifles for the more primitive and exacting demands of the hunting bow. In the battle of wiles between hunter and animal, the bow, as Tiger puts it, "tilts the advantage back toward the animal."

Whatever the weapon, the rewards of his hunting are by no means limited to the bagging of prey. On four occasions during a recent hunting trip, he found himself within whispering distance of a grizzly but declined to reach for an arrow. "I shot one fifteen years ago," he says, "and so far haven't found a good enough reason to shoot another."

He takes as much pleasure in describing the animals that have eluded him as the ones that have not, and takes particular relish in the details of his recent stand-off with an elk that eventually outwitted him, leaving him stranded in the wilderness of northern B.C., in impenetrable darkness. "This was way up near Fort Nelson, in the mountains," he explains. "I'd gone up with a couple of guys, but I was out on my own, on horseback, and I spotted a great big bull elk. I dismounted and stalked him for maybe ten or fifteen minutes, until he ran out beyond a little brush thicket where I couldn't see him, and just waited there. This was late in the afternoon, and the only way I was going to get a shot at him was if I could get in close."

Over a period of a couple of hours Tiger crept to within thirty metres of where he knew the bull was sheltering. "By now it was dusk," he says.

As he tells the story, he takes an empty Sprite can and cuts the top off it with what appears to be a gutting knife. He slips a fingerload of smokeless tobacco under his lower lip and as the juices begin to accumulate – tea-coloured and flecked – he ejects them, with barely a pucker, into the makeshift spittoon.

"I waited a little longer," he continues, "and by the time I stood up to get my bearings, I realized I could hardly see a thing, including my horse. I groped around, looking for him, calling him, listening, until finally it was so dark I just had to accept that I wasn't going to find him. I was maybe ten miles from camp. I woulda stayed out there all night, no problem, but by this time it was getting cold, and all I had on was a light shirt. Besides, I figured the other guys would be worried if I didn't show up, so I set out hiking." (As Tiger relates this part of his adventure, my mind wanders, with an absurd determination of its own, to William Blake's famous lines: "Tyger, Tyger, burning bright/In the forests of the night . . .")

After tramping until 3 or 4 a.m. along a mountain trail, Tiger arrived at camp, slept for several hours and got up at dawn, returning to the hunting site to retrieve his horse, which was tied where he'd left it.

"Now to most guys," enthuses Tiger, "that'd be a lousy hunting experience; they'd hate it. But as far as I was concerned it was just great. I mean, how often in a lifetime do you get a chance to test yourself in that way?"

A glance at Tiger's past would suggest that he has had more than his share of opportunities to test himself against the capricious inflictions of fate. He was born during the depths of winter, 1954, the fourth of eight children, in a tiny house in Weyburn, Saskatchewan. His father, "Taffy," a Welsh immigrant with the physique and demeanour of a bulldog, worked as a painter at the local mental hospital and at any odd job that allowed him to add a few dollars to his meagre income. Betty Williams patched clothes, stretched recipes to the limit, and, on Sundays, marched her entire flock to the local Anglican church for the lessons that, in large part, Tiger and his brothers repudiated during the week.

"We had no luxuries, very little sports equipment, never had Cokes or chips or any of the sorts of things that other kids took for granted," says Tiger. "When I could get one, I'd bring home a broken hockey stick, and my dad would get special nails from the hospital workshop, and I'd patch it up and glue it and tape it, and hope it didn't fall apart in my hands when I got to the rink."

One thing the Williams kids did have was an almost preternatural enthusiasm for conquest. For the most part, they inherited it from their father, who taught that winning was not merely desirable but necessary, and could often best be achieved with the effective use of a quick pair of fists. "Always get the first punch in," was one of his adages, and his boys became masters at it. Hugh, the oldest and fiercest (now a school principal in Weyburn), generally set the example for Tiger and his brothers. "From our point of view, no one in Weyburn was tougher than we were," says Tiger, "and if we heard about someone who was, our attitude was, let's go find 'im and we'll get things sorted out."

Craig Jordan, the best man at Tiger's wedding, admits that, as a kid, he'd have done anything rather than walk past the Williams house on Bison Avenue, and that a lot of other kids shared his trepidation. "We were a bunch of guys who wanted to run everything," says Tiger. "And nobody anywhere was going to stand in our way."

Tiger's dreams were as vivid as his reputation, and by the time he was ten years old his chief fantasy was that one day he would transcend the humiliations of poverty and do so in such a way that the people of Weyburn, particularly his detractors, would swoon with envy at his success. Hockey, he realized, was his ramp to the future, and even as a peewee he showed the competitive ferocity that would eventually transport him from small-town Saskatchewan to the big-league arenas of his imagination.

"Originally, I was a goalie," he explains, "but I wasn't very good and I wouldn't wear a mask. Johnny Bower didn't wear one – why should I? I used to whack guys when they came around the net, and sometimes I'd just get fed up with being in goal and I'd head up ice after the puck."

Coach Johnny Norman conferred the name "Tiger" on the indomitable pipsqueak and, sensing that his young goalie's capacities could be used to better advantage on unrestricted ice, eventually turned him loose as a forward.

"There were always kids with more natural talent than

I had," recalls Tiger, "and they'd laugh at me when I told them I was going to make it to the NHL, and it'd drive me crazy. I'd tell them about the Cadillac I was going to own and the big fancy house beside the rink (so that I wouldn't have to walk too far in bad weather), and I guess at a certain point I really started to believe this stuff. I've always felt that if you put your heart into something and don't listen to the pessimists, you'll eventually get what you want."

The death of his mother from cancer when he was four-teen left Tiger angry, frustrated, and increasingly inclined to violence. "I went through a phase," he says, "where I'd just as soon have punched somebody in the face as shaken their hand."

By the following hockey season, his exploits on and off the ice had earned him the scorn of some and the down-right enmity of others who believed he should be removed from the Weyburn bantams as a dangerous social defec-tive. But his coach, Jerry Murray, stuck with him, encour-aging his skill development and stressing the importance of persistence and effort. The team travelled in an old school bus that was occasionally driven by Tiger's father. "If we lost," says Tiger, "he'd be so mad he wouldn't put the heater on on the way home and we'd be half-frozen by the time we got back to Weyburn." When teammates com-plained, Tiger would remind them of what they had to do to get heat.

If his dreams of a career in pro hockey needed added impetus, they got them during the winter of his sixteenth year, when, desperate for money, and having quit school for good, he took a job in the oil fields near Weyburn. "I'd go to hockey practice during the day," he recalls, "then I'd work all night driving a D-8 Cat, scraping away frozen soil to make a mud pit for drilling. Sometimes it'd be forty below. As the months passed I had a good chance to look at the guys I worked with, guys with no hope, busting their guts all day and drinking till closing time in the bars. It was a hard education for me, but a good one, too, in that I learned what it is to come home from work with your back breaking; I learned how hard most guys have to work to make a living or to get a little extra for the wife and kids. I'd get home after an all-night shift, and get into bed in the empty house, and I'd say to myself, 'There has to be more to life than this.'"

If there *was* more, it was not to be found in Weyburn, and the following year Tiger crossed the province and signed on with the Swift Current Broncos, a junior team with a blossoming nucleus of players that included future pros Terry Ruskowski, Ron Delorme, and Bryan Trottier. Tiger's hyper-aggressive play quickly ingratiated him with coach Stan Dunn, and, within a year, Dunn was touting him as an NHL prospect, despite his lack of God-given talent.

The one aspect of Tiger's behaviour that did *not* please Dunn was his courting of a local teenager named Brenda Dyck, who entered Tiger's life during his second year in Swift Current and has been at the centre of it ever since. "It wasn't that he had anything against her personally," says Tiger. "He just felt girls were a distraction to a player. And, besides, they had parents who said things like, 'Oh, you might not make it in hockey. Maybe you ought to go to university,' and that might set a guy thinking."

Brenda and Tiger had been introduced by mutual friends, and although Tiger was charmed by the intelligent, red-haired high school student, Brenda admits that, at first brush, Tiger "really didn't make any impression" on her. "Then a week later, I met him again. He and I and some others sat and had coffee, and I think I was in love before the evening was over. He was so different, so self-confident. He just seemed to know exactly what he wanted out of life and exactly how to get it – not at all like most eighteen-year-olds, who are pretty much aimless. Plus, he'd been on his own for three years, ever since his mother died, so he was very self-sufficient for a kid that age."

In Brenda, whose parents operated a wheat farm outside Weyburn, Tiger discovered an anchor against the ongoing maelstrom that pretty much defines junior hockey: the endless practices, the frenzied games and diabolically long bus trips. "When she met me she didn't even know hockey existed," he says. "It was a new experience for me, being around people who couldn't have cared less about the game. But I liked the feel of it. I liked her family life and the quiet of their home."

By the time Tiger was drafted by the Toronto Maple Leafs in 1974, he and Brenda were married and, before long, were expecting their first child (son Ben was born in 1975, daughter Clancy in 1977). The story is still told in Weyburn – indeed might have been lifted whole off the pages of a W.O. Mitchell novel – of how Tiger took the $30,000 cheque he received as a signing bonus and, during a trip home to visit his dad, walked into a Weyburn bank and took the entire amount in ten-dollar bills. His next stop was the pool hall where, with savage inner joy, he showed the money around, each bill a kind of flag above the doubts and insults he had endured back in peewee and bantam and midget hockey. "I had a lot of bitterness in me," he allows, "and here was the evidence that people had been wrong about me. Really, I *had* been going somewhere."

But, in spite of a contract that promised him $100,000 a year if he stuck with the Leafs, Tiger's welcome into pro hockey was by no means amicable or unconditional. Indeed, all along, there had been those who felt he was ill-equipped for the demands of the NHL. "I'd been watching him pretty carefully through junior," says Johnny Bower, who, at the time, was a Maple Leaf scout. "We knew he had toughness and character, but we weren't sure whether his skating was good enough. I spoke up for him more than anyone on the scouting staff, and one day, not long before the amateur draft, our owner called me aside and said, 'John, if we take him and he's no good, your job's on the line.' So, I had a lot at stake personally. And when we voted among ourselves on whether to draft him, he passed by one vote, and we went ahead."

Initially, Bower had little cause to feel secure. Training camp was a nightmare for the young Westerner and ended with an assignment to the Leafs' farm team in Oklahoma. "He not only can't skate, he can't fight," snarled Leaf general manager, Jim Gregory, whose assessment of Tiger's scrapping abilities was based largely on his having been stunned by a sucker punch thrown by Chicago's Keith Magnuson.

But the same methods and attitude that had served him in Weyburn and Swift Current served him equally well in purgatory. The rock'em and sock'em brought confidence, and the confidence brought scoring. And by early January he was back in the NHL, this time to stay.


Tiger's NHL career is remembered as one of the most flagrantly defiant on record. He was testiness incarnate, and the disdain he showed for the rules and for his opponents extended to anyone who offended him anywhere, and even to the behavioural weaknesses of some of his teammates. Within days of arriving in Toronto, he spoke out against the prodigious boozing that was dragging down a number of Leaf players and hurting the team on the ice. "Why," he said at the time, "should the efforts of some guys be wasted because others are too hungover to do their jobs?"

He could be equally outspoken where NHL managers and owners were concerned. "I had every respect for [Leaf owner] Harold Ballard, but if he called me a stubble-jumper, I told him that he was a fat old man and that he was fulla crap. A lot of owners want you to be competitive and combative every second of the day, except when you're talking to them. Then you're supposed to take your hat off, fold your hands, and take what's coming. I'm not like that. Life's too short. I don't care if the guy owns the whole world, if he confronts me, I'm not gonna back down – unless I feel I've screwed up; then I'll take it."

On the ice, Tiger did everything he could to help a Maple Leaf team that was decidedly lacking in hard edges. He pummelled and yapped and scrapped, providing a kind of spinal conscience for many of his less adamant team-mates. In 1977, after a protracted court battle, he was acquitted of assault charges brought against him by the Attorney General of Ontario over a stick infraction that put a forty-six-stitch cut in the head of Dennis Owchar of the Pittsburgh Penguins.

What's more, he scored goals, often playing on a line with the Leafs' star centre, Darryl Sittler, one of Tiger's closest friends.

By the end of his fourth year, he had helped shape the Leafs into a respectable team. However, with Harold Ballard's ill-advised hiring of retread manager Punch Imlach in 1979, the franchise entered a phase of cata-strophic trades, unaccountable hirings and firings, and unproductive draft choices. Despite his commitment to the franchise, Tiger quickly fell out of favour with the petulant, mule-driving Imlach, and in early 1980 he was traded to the Vancouver Canucks.

Although he would eventually be traded three more times, the move to Vancouver began a love affair with the West Coast which thrives to this day. Shortly after their arrival, the Williamses bought an expansive mountainside home in the British Properties. "If you're going to live out here and you can afford it," says Tiger, "you might as well have a view."

A subsequent move took them further up the mountain into the house they occupy today. However, they had barely got comfortable at their new address when Tiger was traded to Detroit and they were again on the move. The catalyst for the trade was reported to have been the upcoming publication of Tiger's autobiography, which, it was assumed, would be an embarrassment to the Canucks. "But that's nonsense," says Tiger. "I was traded because I wanted a new contract, and they didn't wanta give it to me."

During the ten seasons that had elapsed since Tiger and Brenda had left Swift Current, Brenda had remained both a still point and a rallying point at the centre of Tiger's life. "My salvation," she says, "was that I never got caught up in the highs and lows, never got angry about this coach or that general manager, or that person sitting behind me at a game, or even the outcome of a game. It's not really important. Not that I haven't gotten briefly aggravated at times – for example, about things I'd read in the press, things critical to Dave. I'd think, well, I know Dave better than this guy, and I probably know hockey better, too, and what they're saying just isn't true."

Brenda allows that she suffered more protracted irritation in the aftermath of the trades in which her husband was involved. "He'd be gone immediately, received with open arms in his new city, playing the game, dining out, and so on, while I'd be back home, packing up, doing paperwork, cleaning, raising kids – for weeks sometimes! And, I mean, in that situation, you're in a town where you don't care about the team anymore, and perhaps the only people you know are others connected to that team.

"One thing I appreciate about Dave's hockey career is

that it's made me very independent. A player isn't going to take a day off just because his wife or children are sick, for instance. Hockey's just too competitive for that. And of course you're alone a lot because of the travel. I've always said that as a hockey wife you have to be schizophrenic: when your husband's gone you've got to *do* everything, *run* everything, make all the decisions. And when he's home, you go to the rink, shut up, look good, sit in your seat, and try to be unobtrusive. Then when the game's over, you pick up where you left off. I mean, it's nice to support your husband and everything, but you can drive yourself crazy; you can pull so much of their hockey into your life that you wake up hoping *they've* had a good sleep, instead of you. And it really doesn't change the outcome of the game. Which is why I've tended to detach myself."

From Detroit, Tiger was traded to the Los Angeles Kings, with whom he played for three seasons. He made a brief final stop in Hartford in 1988, and then he and Brenda and the kids headed back to Canada.

It is symmetrically appropriate that the family's first stop on returning to their homeland was in Weyburn, to be with Tiger's dad, who was suffering from cancer. "We spent the summer there," says Tiger. "I was with him every day until he died in September."

Tiger and his father had been extraordinarily close and remarkably alike in temperament. "Dave's discipline and self-reliance come straight from his dad," says Brenda.

"I never knew anybody who hated losing as much as he did," says Tiger, "except maybe me."

Tiger also ascribes his love of the outdoors and of gardening to his dad. "When I was a kid, we had the best gardens in Weyburn," he says. "I knew what a hoe was."

During the early 1980s, Taffy Williams had been a frequent visitor at the Williams home in Vancouver. Tiger and his dad would often go out into the wilds, sometimes picking berries as they had done in the past in Saskatchewan. "I used to carry him across the Capilano River on my back to a big blueberry patch that nobody knew about," says Tiger. "He'd get over there, and every time he'd see a big berry, you had to go over and look at it before he picked it. We'd end up doing more looking than picking. He just loved it out here. In 1984, I fixed up a room for him, all nicely renovated. But just when it was ready, I got traded, so he never got to use it."

Tiger and the family returned to Vancouver after Taffy Williams' funeral, and within days Tiger turned passionately to hunting. "But at the end of hunting season," he says, "the fact that I had no hockey in my life started getting to me, and, a few weeks before Christmas, I got unbelievably depressed, something that had never happened to me."

"When players quit," reflects Brenda, "everything they've thought about since they were four or five years old is suddenly gone. They're not only not doing what they love, they're out of a job. It's a complete life-style change. There's no easing out."

Tiger acknowledges that his spirits were temporarily lifted by the activities of the Christmas season. "Because of hockey," he says, "I hadn't been to a Christmas party in twenty years." He was further buoyed by a mid-winter trip to northern Manitoba, where he and a team of former NHL players toured small towns and Native reserves, playing local hockey teams and kibitzing with the northern fans. "But when the playoffs started, I was worse than ever," he says. "I didn't want to get out of bed, didn't want to talk to anybody, see anybody. I'd get up and read the stock market reports, but, really, I couldn't have cared less."

Four years earlier, Tiger and a business partner had built a twenty-four-unit townhouse in the Vancouver suburbs. Throughout his depression, he had been a passive investor in a sixty-eight-unit structure that the same partner was preparing to build. "I hadn't planned on doing *anything* at the site," says Tiger. "But when construction began in the late spring, I didn't have anything else to keep me outa trouble, so I started going over, doing this and that, and gradually got involved to the point where it just made sense for me to become construction manager. I spent every day there for months. I was so busy, I didn't have time to be depressed."

Before the project was complete, however, Tiger might well have had cause for a relapse. Interest rates went up, the housing market cooled, and he and his partner were unable to sell the units at anything like the pace they had anticipated. "We ran into financial pressures," explains Tiger, "and I took the thing over, so that, in effect, I had the most to gain from it, but also the most to lose if I couldn't put it back on its feet. I already had $350,000 of my own money in it, and I'll tell ya, there was a time when I wasn't sure I was gonna get it back out. The Royal Bank put the screws to me; I wouldn't deal with them again if they were the last outhouse in the world."

In a desperate final move, Tiger put in another $200,000 of his own money and, in his own words, "worked like a dog, dawn to dusk – building, selling, whatever I had to do to make it work. In the end, the thing not only got built, it returned twenty-eight per cent on the original investment – twice the bank rate."


"C'mon," says Tiger, "lemme show ya around the house," and he rises from his chair on the patio, leading me in through the kitchen to the living room, the walls of which are hung with mounted heads of stone sheep, bighorn sheep, and mountain goat. A moose rack some six feet across hangs on one wall and, on the floor, lies a spent black bear with bared fangs of the sort that tend to come alive in dreams. Taxidermy notwithstanding, the room is a modestly decorated gallery of low furniture, large windows, and several items of Haida and Inuit art. The books in evidence are largely about wildlife and the natural world, and on a low shelf sits a commemorative plate bearing likenesses of Tiger in Maple Leaf and Canuck uniforms.

"Come on in here," he says, leading the way into a small business-like room, where he directs my attention to an antique wooden postal bureau, with dozens of compartments and drawers. The piece, a relic of the Weyburn post office, belonged to his dad, who loved stamps, and collected them so assiduously that in his later years he won awards in both Canadian and European philatelic competitions. "When he'd visit me in Toronto," says Tiger, who owns and cherishes his dad's massive collection, "I'd take him to the dealers and buy him all sorts of rare stamps."

On the lower floor of the house is the room Tiger built for his father in 1984 and newly renovated bedrooms belonging to Ben, who is in his third year of junior hockey, and to Clancy, who recently began studies at a private junior college in Tokyo, Japan.

In all, there are surprisingly few reminders of hockey in the house – no trophies or photos, no commemorative pucks or sticks. On the other hand, there is a sense in which the entire place is a reminder of hockey – and of the psychological subsoil in which Tiger's exceptional career took root. The evidence of his intense compulsion to succeed is certainly less obvious these days than it was when it could be calculated in goals scored and punches thrown. But it exists nonetheless as a kind of back-beat to prosperity and recognition, and, perhaps less directly, as a facet of Tiger's arcane private morality and the paradoxical arc of his personality. Despite his reputation as a scrapper and a matinee villain, he is a concerned and generous man, a smart man, often misunderstood because his opinionated views and dockside mannerisms do not translate well into the petty orthodoxies of politically correct society. He possesses, for instance, an irrepressible sense of community. "If you're in trouble on the street," says Brenda, "Dave is the guy you want to come along. Because he'll help. Anybody. He's not afraid to get involved. He doesn't like injustice."

Tiger is a long-time friend of disadvantaged children, raises money for the B.C. Special Olympics through his annual charity golf tournament, and over the years has made countless hospital visits, primarily to bolster the spirits of chronically ill or dying children. "I look at those kids, and I look at what I'm up against, and I feel very fortunate," he says. "It used to drive me crazy to see athletes or celebrities, people with every advantage, go into a hospital, spend a few minutes, then drive off in their big, fancy cars. That's not good enough. Of course, some of them just can't do it; it's too hard on them."

Tiger supports friends and family, both morally and financially – or, in some cases, *doesn't* support them, ostensibly for their own good. "If you help people too much," he reasons, "they never learn to stand on their own feet."

On this day, in particular, he is bothered by what he perceives as a kind of degenerative societal sickness – people's willingness to renounce responsibilities and renege on promises, both personal and professional. "They commit to something, make an agreement," he laments, "and before you know it they've bailed out. A little bit of rough weather and they jump ship. You see it in business, sport, families, everywhere. When I make a deal, I'm in no

25

matter what happens. I stick it out. I mean, if people don't honour their commitments, what's left? – of the whole society?"

There are days, Tiger admits, when he gets so weary of the world he wants nothing more than to jump in his truck and head for the wilderness with his bow and arrow. "Before too long, I hope to pack it all in and hunt year-round," he says. "I'll go all over the globe, wherever the season is open." ("When the buffalo are gone we will hunt mice," said the legendary Sioux chief, Sitting Bull, "for we are hunters and we love our freedom.")

But even as Tiger talks of year-round hunting, he is ambitiously padding his portfolio of business and professional responsibilities – as well as expressing concern over what he calls his "enormous" personal overhead: children to educate; expensive properties to maintain; four family vehicles; exorbitant taxes. At the moment he and Mike King are considering bringing a retail sporting-wear chain under the wing of Voodoo Ventures, the public company that owns the Vancouver Voodoo and in which Tiger and Mike have controlling interests. The pair also want to introduce roller hockey to Washington State, where Voodoo owns the franchise rights. What's more, Tiger is dabbling with the idea of building a roller-hockey arena somewhere on B.C.'s lower mainland.

And of course there is the team: a schedule to play, promotion to generate, a championship to gain.

Tiger is not only "unable to relax," to use Brenda's words, he is contemptuous of the very idea. "A couple of years ago, Brenda and I went to Hawaii," he explains. "I made her a deal that I wouldn't move for fourteen days. After four days I'd had enough. I ran into a guy who told me he had a friend who took people hunting for wild pigs and goats. I said, 'I'm in.' The guy picked me up at 4 in the morning, and away we went. I shot a goat and speared a pig.

That was the fifth day. On the sixth day, I said to Brenda, 'I'm outa here, I'm going home.' I didn't last fourteen days, but I did pretty well to last six."

Beyond hunting year-round, Tiger has a retirement fantasy that would see him and Brenda installed in an isolated cabin in a remote part of the northern B.C. wilderness – for one year? two years? three years? "There'd be no TV, no phone, no luxuries at all," he says cheerfully. "The only trouble is I don't think Brenda could stand it."

"I don't think you could either," laughs Brenda, who has been listening to his commentary.

"Why do you say that?" he demands.

"Not enough action."

"I'll make my own action!" scoffs Tiger, who has built a career around making his own action.

He stares up the mountain that rises sharply behind the house. "We'll put in a helicopter pad so you can go into Prince George and shop," he says.

"Sounds idyllic," says Brenda.

"You've gotta have dreams," he shrugs.

And few know it better than he.

# FREE OF THE BURDEN OF GRAVITY

IN MID-NOVEMBER 1994, I travelled to Vail, Colorado, for a three-day visit with Eric Nesterenko, who has lived in Vail since 1980. Toward the end of my stay, Eric and I took a late-evening stroll through the narrow, car-free streets of this exotic resort community in the Rocky Mountains. Snow was falling and beyond the streetlights the surrounding peaks and ski runs were lost in darkness.

We walked up into the heart of Vail Village, walked back down, and stopped on a bridge that crosses Gore Creek. As we stood looking into the water, Eric said, "I've lived a very simple life, and I've probably succeeded somewhat on my own terms. Some people might consider me a failure, and that's their prerogative. But I spent fifteen years living the bourgeois life, and then I didn't want to do it any more, so I bailed out. As a consequence I've gone through periods where I didn't have any money. But I've found if you don't own anything and you're not addicted to anything (I gave my family everything I had), you don't really need any money. I'm pretty well educated and fairly worldly, so something always comes up. There's always a way to get along financially. Of course, most people aren't interested in that. They're interested in acquiring things, owning things, taking care of things, and as a result they need a lot of money. I've tried never to trade on my career as a hockey player. It never interested me. I don't know if it's admirable, and I don't care if other guys do it. It's just that if you do it, you imprison yourself in the past. I prefer the present. I get the odd offer to go sign hockey cards somewhere, but not very often because nobody knows where I am. I do it for the money if I can, but it's a very hollow role, an empty way to live."

There is a conspicuous diversity to Eric Nesterenko's curriculum vitae. As a career map, it suggests a man of renegade imagination, a man who, somewhere on the road to somewhere, hung a right-angled turn and accelerated not just off the pavement, but across the shoulder, the ditch, the right-of-way, and off on his own through the wilderness. He has been a disk jockey, a stockbroker, and the caretaker of an estate in Aspen, Colorado. He has been a high school hockey coach and an Air Canada travel broker, selling what he calls "northern hunting and fishing packages to Americans."

"One of my crazier jobs," he says, "was laying decals on tractor trailers one summer in Texas. The trucks would come in, and I'd take off the old decal design and put new ones on. I'd work round the clock on the weekend, and had the rest of the week free." At one point, the job required him to place decals on six thousand metal signs, four by six feet, for "some sort of cattlemen's association," a job that was expected to take months of manual labour and was contracted as such. "But I found an old press in the plant," he says, "and did it ten times faster than they expected. I made pisspots of money, because they still had to pay me what we agreed on."

He made more money yet when, for two six-month periods during the early eighties, he worked for an American company named Federal Electric on the Arctic DEW Line. "As a kid," he muses, "I used to dream about the Arctic – vivid, primal dreams, with great expanses of ice and water and tundra. Then I got this chance to go up there as a utility operator, driving a loader and a diesel Cat. My job was clearing snow and transporting fuel oil from storage tanks by the ocean to various radar sites. It was light all the time, and at night I'd go out walking on my own – for miles! I'd see peregrines, caribou, giant Arctic hare. The caribou would come up and stare at me – they'd never seen a human being. It's a crazy bunch of people that work the Arctic: misfits, dropouts from regular life. I guess I'm the type."

Eric has been a freelance writer, a university professor, and a construction worker. By his own admission, he has also been an alcoholic, an amphetamine popper, and a beneficiary of the psychiatrist's couch. Although it will never appear on his c.v., he is one of a small number of people to have been present in the courtroom for the 1969 trial of the Chicago Seven anti-war demonstrators.

He is the subject not only of a novel entitled *The Drubbing of Nesterenko* but of a chapter in Studs Terkel's bestselling book *Working*, about the work lives of Americans.

Today, at sixty-two, he is a ski instructor in Vail, where he works approximately a hundred days a year, earning a set fee of $380 a day for teaching groups of up to seven skiers, or sometimes individuals. He skis an additional eighty days for pleasure, travelling as far as Oregon and Whistler, B.C., to indulge his love of the sport. When he talks about skiing, he does so with rhapsodic intensity, ascending at times into something close to free-form poetry: "The speed and the tremendous sensation of motion, way out there on the edge of control, are extraordinarily exciting," he says. "One of the thrills of skiing is going back to the rich feelings you had as a kid. There's a joy and an openness to it. This area really has some terrain and some of the best powder snow anywhere. I'm up early when it's coming down, a little kid looking out the window; I've got butterflies. I like going out when it's really storming, and there's nobody on the mountain. Your normal tourist doesn't ski much in the snowstorms. But the hard-cores are out there. You let go; you invent a whole new version of yourself, a better version, free of the burden of gravity. I think human beings are meant to be in motion. Dancing. I go with my son into the back areas. I've seen him pop an eighty-foot cliff out there. On a big powder day, I'll go off a fifteen-footer – land in something soft, so it doesn't matter if you fall. We walk in. There's always the danger of avalanche, which adds a dimension. You end up on the highway somewhere, hitchhiking. Somebody stops, curious about what these guys are doing out there."

Eric is best-known, of course, as an NHL hockey player, a gracefully loping defensive specialist whose pro career began in 1951 with the Toronto Maple Leafs and ended twenty-one years later with the Chicago Blackhawks.

In hockey, as elsewhere, he was a radical, a sceptic, a spit in the eye of conformity. Even under the absurdly submissive code that governed the conduct of players in the old six-team NHL, he found ways of expressing not only his contempt for owners and management, but his personal preferences for living. When he joined the Blackhawks in 1956, for example, he insisted that he be allowed to attend university full-time in Toronto, joining the Blackhawks for games only. The team bent its standards to accommodate him. The following season, he attended the University of Western Ontario, in London, flying to Blackhawk games a few hours before faceoff and returning immediately afterwards. "The management didn't like it one bit," he says. "They tried to tell me the players didn't either, that they'd never accept me, but it was nonsense. I did take some ragging, but I held my own on the ice, and that's what mattered to the guys. I could just never see why playing hockey should rob you of your right to an education."

Inspired by the late Lloyd Percival, Toronto's celebrated fitness pioneer, Eric espoused equally unorthodox ideas about nutrition and conditioning. During the early fifties, when pro hockey players routinely – ritualistically – gobbled a pound or more of rare beef within a few hours of game time ("most of them dismissed salads and vegetables as 'rabbit food,'" says Eric), he turned largely to carbohydrates, fruits and whole grains . . . and rabbit food. "I still ate a little meat," he allows, "but before a game I'd have pasta, a salad, a couple of baked potatoes, the sort of things all the players eat nowadays. And I ate yogurt – a Toronto newspaper once referred to me as 'the yogurt kid.'"

Percival also introduced Eric to aerobic training, mostly in the form of running, as a method of getting and staying fit. "I'd go forty, fifty miles a week," he recalls. "In those days it was unheard-of. The guys 'played' themselves into shape."

During the early sixties, some twenty years ahead of his time, Eric discovered that, under certain circumstances, even walking was an effective approach to high-level fitness, not to mention mental equanimity. "I've always had a very strong identification with mountains," he says, "and as I got into mid-career – I was in Chicago by this time – I started taking a couple of weeks before training camp every year and going up into northern Wyoming, the Wind River area, big-time mountains, and hiking hundreds of miles with a seventy-five-pound pack on my back. I'd lose eight or ten pounds, and of course at ten thousand feet the heart and lungs get working pretty efficiently."

His attachment to the area deepened to the point where, during the seventies and eighties, he would make the trek not so much for physical as for spiritual and psychological conditioning. "I really believe human beings need a lot of silence," he says. "We spend half our lives surrounded by electronic distractions and entertainments – television, radio, recordings. They create a reality, a very superficial one, that doesn't demand any effort, so that you end up getting lost in them, with no real sense of time or focus. Out there in the back country, by yourself, you're really forced to deal with who and what you are; you have to create your own reality, in a sense create yourself. And as you do that, things take on a magical quality. When I'm out there, I always have extraordinary dreams."

Even today, Eric heads for the Wyoming mountains when the spirit moves him. "I spent twenty-five days up there this year," he notes. "Two trips. I go with an old buddy from the sixties, Billy Stevenson, who used to play football with the Calgary Stampeders. I always come back energized."


On my first full day in Vail, I met Eric for lunch and for a lengthy afternoon of conversation, followed by a two-hour drive up and down the Vail Valley in his black four-by-four pick-up. He is a big man, with long arms and legs, and when I walked into the lobby of the hotel where we had arranged to rendezvous, he was not so much *seated* on the low couch as folded onto it, like a collapsible ruler. He was wearing red-framed reading glasses and was so thoroughly absorbed in the *Denver Post* that he didn't acknowledge my approach until I was virtually on top of him. When I said his name, he threw his head back, smiled, and unfolded, throwing out a hand that by rough estimate was twice the size of my own.

As a child and teenager, I had watched Eric play dozens of games on television, and had seen him several times in person at Maple Leaf Gardens. But in thirty-odd years my recollections of his presence on the ice had been reduced to a blur. As I followed him from the hotel, however, I experienced a sudden *déjà vu*, an almost cinematic recall of his skating and checking style, summoned uncannily by the shambling slide of his walk, the slouch of his shoulders, the marionette hang of his arms, his head thrown slightly forward. He was a player who, at times, seemed to have no bones.

At the Sweet Basil restaurant, he exchanged greetings with a number of acquaintances, folded himself into a banquette, and ordered expansively. He ate with unselfconscious gusto. He is handsome in a craggy sort of way; the overall appeal of his face is greater than might be expected from the state of its components. His eyes are small, his lips large, and his nose is in a shocking state of disfigurement. It is not so much a nose, in fact, as a twisted ridge of skin and gristle, a mangled caterpillar, appliquéd more or less to the centre of his face where a nose ought to be. He has a full head of greying hair, and there is something in the configuration of his mouth and jaw that creates an expression of slight but constant surprise.

We warmed quickly to one another, and in the hours that elapsed between our first appetizer (gingered shrimp and squid) and our fifth or sixth cup of coffee, the conversation ranged across a panoply of subjects that included wealth, poverty, fear, art, mortality, the oppressive politics of the New Right, and the novels of Michigan writer Jim Harrison, whom we both admire. And of course hockey.

But before he got to any of that, he told me about his family; he has a daughter, aged thirty-two, in Chicago, a son, twenty-nine, in San Francisco, and a son, thirty, in Vail, with whom he sometimes skis. He has been divorced from his wife, Barbara McKechnie, for nearly twenty years, and in early 1994 split up with Kaye Ferry, a Vail restaurateur with whom he had lived since 1987. He described his wife at various points in our conversation as "an opera lover," "a genuine intellectual," and "one of the most intelligent people" he has ever met. "I used to study her books on human behaviour when she was working on her M.A. in social work," he says, "so she's partly responsible for my education, such as it is. Compared to her I'm just a dilettante. . . . We're still good friends." (He is still good friends with Kaye Ferry.) At the moment, he is living at the home of his friend Kevin Cooke, a former tight end with the Oakland Raiders, who now works as a contractor in Vail.

By his own assessment, Eric seldom talks or even thinks about hockey – "I have no reason to out here. Most people in Vail don't even know I played." Perhaps on that account, there is a freshness about his reflections on his one-time occupation, a sense that they are coming to life like spring bulbs, having gathered energy during a lengthy period of interment. He speaks lyrically and philosophically about the game, and possesses a rare ability to conceptualize his impressions of it (and seemingly of anything else that falls into the focus of his intelligence), to see the shape of the tornado where others see only flying trees and rooftops.

And he is honest. Strikingly. He says without a trace of misgiving, for instance, that he played hockey "in constant fear."

"So much so," he says, "that fear became an old friend. It's a tremendous stimulus; you have to court it at the same time as you try to dispel it. Fear of being humiliated, fear of losing, fear of getting hurt. Those are the big three."

He summons the waiter, orders a bowl of fresh raspberries, and says, "Picture it. There are twenty thousand people at the game, and if you act badly or play badly, there's no place to hide. You can't talk it down or bullshit it; it's there for everyone to see. You are what you are. It's a killer. You have to be ready to hold your own. It took everything I had in terms of my physicality and intelligence. Sure, it's a goofy way to live, but there's nothing like it for excitement."

Typically, Eric's methods for dealing with his fear, of transforming and redirecting it into something useful to him, were twenty years ahead of their time, and are now commonly applied by sports psychologists. "One of my tricks," he explains, "was simply to *let the fear in*, imagine the worst thing that could happen to me. Fear doesn't stay around long if you give in to it; it's when you resist it that it stays with you. You let it in, allow it to have its way, and before long it leaves you in what I call a cold calculating rage. Fear and rage are corollaries of one another. So instead of being terrified, you're completely focused and stimulated."

Like all NHL hockey players, Eric had ample reason to fear the worst of his chosen profession. His poetic nature and various unorthodoxies attracted no particular antipathy from rival players, but nor did they provide even a smidgin of dispensation from the commonplace brutalities of NHL life. "A lotta guys gave it to me when I was starting out," he says. "Bert Olmstead gave me a stick in the gut, knocked my wind out, brought me to my knees. He said, 'Welcome to the league, kid.' Ted Lindsay knocked out a couple of my front teeth with his stick and laughed at me. Same with Milt Schmidt. He practically put me through the boards one night, and stood there laughing as I staggered up. Mind you, I could get prickly, too. In hockey, if somebody sticks you and you don't retaliate in some way, word gets out on you, and you get more trouble down the line. But I never tried to take anybody's head off. If I threw a forearm, I'd aim into the area between the waist and the shoulders. I wasn't looking for enemies."

Eric views his old foes with remarkable detachment, seeming to bear no grudge against even the most virulent of them. If anything, he harbours an inflated respect for many of them, tending almost to romanticize their capabilities, attributing to them a kind of primitive nobility of the sort that is sometimes ascribed to prehistoric tribesmen. "A lot of these guys were very smart, very intuitive," he says. "They didn't have words, but the game is beyond language, so they communicated in older ways, the ways in which hunters and warriors communicate. Some of the best hockey players I knew were great poker players. They had that ability to intuit, even though their lack of language limited their ability to articulate who they were and their feelings about life. I guess if you don't have words, your intelligence is narrowed. But within the range of intelligence required on the ice, there's no politics, no rhetoric, so the guy with words has no advantage. The smartest guys, period, survive."

His respect notwithstanding, Eric is scornful of any societal tendency to make heroes or role models of professional athletes, past or present. "It's bogus!" he says. "They're not heroes at all. There's still the odd one who does the right thing, but most of the ones I've known lead very flawed lives. Some of them are *totally* screwed up. And the most venerated of them are often the worst. When I played, the relationship between the players and fans was probably a little more honest than it is now; for one thing, we didn't have as much money, so we were more accessible to them. Wealth isolates today's players to the point where their perceived relationship with the public, the implied kinship, is even more hypocritical than it would be otherwise."

Eric harbours particular contempt for NHL owners, characterizing most of those he met over the years as "really nasty, vicious, greedy, self-serving people. You have no idea how we were exploited by them. Completely locked in. If an owner or manager decided he didn't want you – or worse still, didn't like you – you were dead, finished. By the terms of our contracts, we were the property of one team only; we couldn't move unless they wanted to move us – no free agency. They buried some guys so deep, they never surfaced. And we were grossly underpaid, made to feel we were lucky to be playing the game. . . . Of course there were wonderful rewards and compensations for what we did, too. For an adrenaline junkie like myself, the games themselves could be extremely exciting. I remember games with twenty thousand people and the place going crazy with sound and action and colour, the enormous energy the crowd produces all coming in on the ice, focusing directly on the players. It's pretty hard to resist that. I remember a game during the semi-finals of the year we won the Stanley Cup in Chicago, in '61. It was the sixth game against Montreal. They were the big club; they'd won five Cups in a row. We were the Cinderella team. The score was 3–0, for us, with five minutes to play. As a spontaneous gesture, twenty thousand people stood up. I was on the ice. I remember seeing that whole stadium, just solid, row on row, from the balcony to the boxes, standing. These people were turned on by us. We came off the ice three feet in the air."

The emotional transcendence of such moments was something Eric at times achieved quite independently of the fickle attentions of the crowd. "One of the things I really loved about the game," he enthuses, "was the possibility it afforded for what I guess you could call 'peak experience phenomenon.' I probably spent twenty-five per cent of my time on the ice in a kind of elevated state of being. I guess it was a function of the motion and energy and so on. Time would just slow right down for me; I'd feel terrific joy and well-being, totally disappear into the moment; I couldn't seem to get hurt. Sometimes I experience it when I'm skiing or backpacking. I've talked to other players who seem to know what I mean. I guess the better players achieve it more often. The Eastern religions have explored the human capability to get into such states. Meditation can apparently do it, but it was the game that did it for me. In fact, it helped me *survive* the game. I felt as if I was somebody else, a remarkable feeling. It's one of the things I've always lived for."

He muses for a moment, and notes rather sullenly that of course the games could go badly, too – and often did. "Sometimes, I could hardly wait for them to end. Then as soon as they were over," he laughs, "I couldn't wait for the next one to begin."

When we had talked for perhaps two hours, had finished our dessert, and were on our third or fourth cup of coffee, I asked Eric casually if he knew he was the subject of a novel. He is widely read and possesses an unusually diverse curiosity, in particular about matters that concern himself, and I was all but certain he'd be familiar with the book, written by Canadian Hanford Woods and published in Montreal during the early seventies. I was not so certain he would be entirely open to discussing it. Indeed, I had hesitated until that point to bring it up – and even then was doing so in a most tangential way, avoiding the book's title, for instance – because it deals with an extremely unpleasant incident from Eric's past and is somewhat untoward in its presentation of him (the book's title, *The Drubbing of Nesterenko*, did not pass my lips during the entire time I spent with him).

He looked at me with incredulity and said, "Whaddaya mean I'm the subject of a novel?"

"You're a non-fiction character in a fictional book," I

said, proceeding to explain as delicately as I could that, basically, the novel was a kind of loss-of-innocence story set during the mid-sixties, and that its protagonist, a Montreal teenager, a shoplifter, was a passionate fan of the Chicago Blackhawks and especially of Eric Nesterenko.

The novel is fine-textured, intelligent and, in parts, highly poetic. And anyone who has read it will understand my reluctance to elaborate too fully on its contents in front of Eric.

The event around which the book revolves (an actual event transported to a fictional world and worried into metaphor) is an epochally vicious thrashing laid on Eric by the Montreal Canadiens' legendary thumper John Ferguson. For the teenage protagonist, the thrashing is a rage-inducing cataclysm, a mindlessly brutal introduction to the world of experience and cynicism. And when I first made reference to the brutality in front of Eric – the fight as opposed to merely the book – I do not believe I am exaggerating in saying that, for the briefest of moments, he seemed stricken, even panicked, leading me to believe (perhaps falsely) that I had triggered some long unresolved anxiety or rage of his own. As if in a parody of such moments, his hand, containing a coffee cup, stood momentarily paralyzed a few inches in front of his lips.

As he put the cup down, the faintest of inscrutable smiles transformed his face. "That's bizarre," he said quietly, "it's totally bizarre."

The "fight," if it can be called that (in reality it was a mugging), was thought by many, including Hanford Woods, to be a symbolic threshold in the 1965 final between the Canadiens and Blackhawks, a series the Blackhawks were perhaps good enough to have won but ended up losing. Certainly, to the Blackhawks it must have been a distressing, ill-omened event – likewise to Hawks' fans of the era, most of whom have never forgotten it. "Ferguson's fists hammered at him, hard, even after the annihilation of what became nothing more than butchered meat," writes Woods. "Nesterenko slumped to his knees, his arms dangled at his sides, he was asleep before he hit the ice. On the television his blood was the deepest black."

Eric was helped from the ice with a towel wrapped around his face. "Later," says Woods, "he returned to the game. He skated from the clinic at the south end of the Forum to the Chicago player's bench, skated through the swaggering contempt of the Canadiens on the ice, Ferguson one of them, impatiently circling, his anger unappeasable, those on the bench malevolently alert to the signal defeat of Nesterenko's broken posture; skated through the resignation of his teammates who with eyes lowered were already fixing him as the scapegoat of the defeat inevitably settling upon them; dragged himself listlessly through the gate, took his seat on the bench."

One of the most appalling things about the incident was the apparent randomness with which Ferguson had inflicted the beating. Although Ferguson has always maintained that Eric provoked the carnage by "clipping" him on the head, film of the occurrence supports the belief that it sprang from some merciless causal void, unprovoked, at least in any direct sense.

"I read the Montreal papers the next day with an avid loathing," continues Woods. "The columnists probed the wound pitilessly, brought down their verdict: Nesterenko had been guilty of some indefensible incursion into Fergy's domain, he should never have been there, Fergy had acted within his rights. The writers drew strength for the pronouncement from its utter inexplicability. Talk on the streets was only of the fight, the fans vaunted Fergy's prowess as their own. The entire city revelled in their mean, stupid triumph. . . . Let all weak men die and obloquy be heaped upon their bones."


Eric was obviously unable to discuss the book, but he was by no means reluctant to discuss the fight and its ramifications for his career and image. In fact, he did so with surprising candour and, after his initial agitation had subsided (it took all of a few seconds), impressive equanimity.

"Most people made a lot more of the incident than I did," he said. "Some of them even saw it as an indictment of me, gave me a hard time over it, razzed me during games, that sort of thing, and I had to live with that. But really it was no big deal. I got suckered. The guy nailed me. Our line had been shutting down their big line, the Béliveau line, throughout the series. Just before it happened, we'd been scrambling very hard in the corner, and the whistle blew. I stopped, turned around, and skated into his punch. The only reason I know that is that I've seen the films of it; at the time I didn't know what happened. Ferguson's a strong guy, and as I went to my knees he got me with a few more pretty heavy punches. I wasn't badly hurt – picked up fifteen stitches in the face. But I played the next game. In fact, we won the next two games in Chicago, so it's nonsense to suggest that the fight ended the series. In the end they beat us because they had a better team, no other reason."

According to Eric, what did affect him powerfully about the episode was neither the beating itself nor the reaction of the fans or other players, but the realization that his "perceptive skills" were beginning to wane and that he had been unprepared for the ambush. "I was thirty-five years old by this time," he says, "and I wasn't as focused as I had been earlier in my career. I should have been able to see it coming. Given that we were doing a number on the Canadiens and that Ferguson was out there, I should have been aware that he was going to get me one of these times. A big part of intelligence in hockey is preparing for what *might* happen, and I wasn't prepared, and in the aftermath it scared me. But I'll tell ya, I was a lot more aware after that. I played six more years. Actually, I had five or six more go-rounds with Fergy. But of course I was ready for him; I carried my stick a lot higher around him from that point on. He never really got the better of me again."

If Eric has not entirely forgiven himself for his consequential lapse of awareness, he has apparently forgiven Ferguson for his attack, and is at peace with the egregious allowances of the sport that made such an attack possible. "I respect Ferguson," he says with no apparent irony. "The arena is a survival place. I know he had no personal interest in hurting me; he was just knocking me out of the game. It was his way of getting rid of me."

That Eric could, at this point, speak with such control about the mugging and its consequences moved me to wonder out loud why his initial response to my bringing it up had been one of such seeming agitation?

He reflected for a moment, shrugged, and said, "I don't know. Probably on some level there's still a trace of humiliation. I got beaten up pretty badly; at the time I was humiliated. I guess it kinda caught me off guard that it's still around after all these years."

The incident was certainly still around the following season when, as Eric puts it, "every thug on every team" took a run at him. "It went on till Christmas," he says. "The shark mentality – one guy'd taken a bite outa me, they all wanted a bite." After fifteen years in the NHL, he was obliged to re-establish what he refers to as "his space."

"If you can't re-establish it," he says, "they can end up intimidating you to the point where you can't function.

They wanta see if you can still play; it's part of hockey. But my sensitivity had been entirely re-honed by the incident, so that before every game I'd go to the kid who I figured might try to stick me and I'd say, 'I know you're coming after me, and if you do I'm going to hit you over the head as hard as I can with my stick.'"


Eric was born in 1932 in the mining town of Flin Flon, Manitoba, some six hundred kilometres north of Winnipeg. His parents were Ukrainian political refugees, who had fled to Czechoslovakia after the Russian Revolution, and had emigrated from there to Canada. His father, a chemist at the mining smelter in Flin Flon, spoke six languages and, for Eric and his sister, was a ready model for the value of education. "We read a lot," says Eric. "I loved school; I was good at it. But I *lived* for hockey. My dad bought me a pair of skates when I was four or five. That's how I got started. We lived across the street from an outdoor rink in Jubilee Park. I played every day and night after school. Our *de facto* coaches were the older boys. If they let you join their game that was a thrill. We didn't have any equipment, so the skills were all stick skills – the ability to take the puck away from somebody with a poke check, or to keep it if you were good enough. It was a never-ending game, shifting personnel, sometimes three kids to a team, sometimes fifteen – or a few games going on at once, so that you had to work at avoiding people."

Eric recalls with an air of wistful relinquishment what he refers to as "the best nights" in Flin Flon. "They were clear, not too cold, maybe ten or fifteen below, with the northern lights and no wind. The ice was hard and fast, and you'd be so engrossed in the game that time would stop. . . . The kids don't play the way we did any more; it's all organized, indoors. They may be stronger and better conditioned, but they don't have the skills because they don't put the hours in."

At the age of eleven, Eric moved with his family to Toronto, where his dad had been offered a better job in industrial chemistry. In his new city, Eric played for top-level peewee and bantam teams. Then as a teenager he was drawn into the feeder system of the Toronto Maple Leafs. "I was a skinny, ratty kid with a terrible case of acne," he told Studs Terkel in 1970. "I moved pretty well, but I never really looked like much."

He looked sufficiently impressive to the Maple Leaf organization that, by 1949, he had been selected to play for the Toronto Marlboroughs, the Leafs' top junior club. With the Marlies, he scored a goal a game during his final year and was among the top junior players in Canada. When the Montreal Canadiens signed Jean Béliveau to a contract in 1950, Leaf owner Conn Smythe bragged to the press that he had his own emerging star, a kid named Nesterenko, who would one day make the hockey world forget about Béliveau.

With a year of junior eligibility remaining, Eric was offered a four-year hockey scholarship at the University of Michigan. "Then the Leafs offered me $6,000 under the table to reject the scholarship and turn pro with their farm team in Pittsburgh," he says.

He took the money. But instead of sending him to Pittsburgh for seasoning, the Leafs put their own uniform on him and kept him in Toronto. "The problem was they tied my game down," says Eric. "They wouldn't allow any free-wheeling. No imagination. You had to stick on your wing. Detroit and Montreal were playing much more imaginatively. Toronto had been a great team in the past, but at that point they weren't doing much."

Eric did get a chance to exercise his imagination by moonlighting as a jazz disk jockey at broadcaster Foster Hewitt's radio station in Toronto. But under the Leafs' uninspired regime, he never became the offensive sparkler that Smythe had imagined. "I guess ultimately I disappointed the old man," he says. "But I don't care. He was an exploitive old son-of-a-bitch. I had no use for him. . . . Eventually I got into a big fight with the Leafs about how they were playing me. In those days you didn't question management at all, and in 1954 they got rid of me, sold my rights to Chicago."

Thinking his career was over, Eric enrolled in the physical education program at the University of Toronto and went out for the football team; he had been a football star at North Toronto Collegiate. But the Blackhawks, the NHL's perennial bottom-feeders, were determined to sign him, imagining that with his size and skating ability (they may even have recognized his intelligence), he could be converted into a penalty-killing defensive expert who could be deployed against the league's best forwards.

"I made a lot of trips to Toronto that summer," says Tommy Ivan, who at the time was the Blackhawks' general manager. "But I didn't have much luck. There I'd be, as the university's bus carrying the football team to camp pulled away, waving goodbye to Nesterenko, who would be looking out the back window."

Ivan finally bagged his quarry in January, and Eric became the NHL's first, and perhaps last, full-time university student, a distinction he would enjoy for the next year and a half, at which point he became a full-time hockey player.

When he had contract problems in Chicago in 1956, he decamped not to university but for a try-out with the Toronto Argonauts, a professional football team that, after assessing his skills, offered him a contract. Fearing he would abandon them, the Blackhawks stepped forward with an improved contract of their own, which he signed.

By the late fifties, Eric had not only accepted his defensive role, as he never really had in Toronto, but had become an exemplar among defensive forwards, potting a sluggish stream of goals (he averaged thirteen or fourteen a season) but for the most part committing himself to preventing them. "I'm a survivor," he says today. "If I was going to stay in the league, that was the way to do it. And I learned to do it pretty well. I had a good reach, I could skate, and I was willing to scruff around in the corners. I wouldn't give up. But, more importantly, I could control the space around me. I always played against the other teams' top lines, and I got to a point where I could often keep a guy in check without even touching him, just by playing the angles and leverage. Mind you, it got harder as I got older and my skills started waning. But by that time a couple of waves of expansion players had come into the league, and that tended to balance things off. A lot of the new players weren't very smart; they were easy to control. They shouldn't even have been there." Eric pauses at this point and his voice takes on the timbre of scriptural conviction: "Hockey is a very simple game," he says. "You control the space and don't let the other team play. If you have enough skilled forwards to take advantage of the openings, you'll always be competitive."

When we had finished lunch, we took a spin in Eric's pick-up, out I-70 toward Beaver Creek, a glaringly affluent housing and ski development, where until a year ago Eric shared rented accommodation with Kaye Ferry. As we sat at a stoplight in West Vail, I asked him about the roots of his non-conformity.

"I guess I've always marched to my own drummer," he said. "Never cared what others thought. Certainly, my parents were conformists. I just know that by my early teens I'd started realizing I was an individual. I was a very high-level player even as a child, so the coaches let me do pretty much as I pleased. I imagine that reinforced my sense of individualism."

By the late sixties, he had begun to pass along his habit of mind to his three children, born in '62, '65, and '66. "Every June," he says, "we'd close shop in Chicago, pack up the van, and go on the road for ten weeks. We'd find places to stay, sometimes on ranches in Wyoming and Montana. We'd car camp and hike and fish. These are things my father had exposed me to in Flin Flon. We did this for five years or so. The kids all remember it, and they've all become back-country types themselves. My son, in particular, is an Indian. He's so at home in the woods and mountains, it's scary."

Chicago, on the other hand, had become a kind of Xanadu for Eric, a pleasure dome of artistic and intellectual stimulation. "I saw a *lot* of theatre in those days," he recalls, "a lot of experimental and esoteric stuff. And Barbara and I would go to the opera; I developed my taste for it through her." The Nesterenkos were also patrons of the Chicago Symphony, and Eric spent numerous hours exploring the Chicago Art Institute, with its hoardings of work by Picasso, Kandinsky, Gauguin, Chagall, and van Gogh. In the meantime, he took university literature courses and read authors as diverse as John le Carré, Peter Mathiesson, and Henry David Thoreau. "There's a great bookstore in Chicago called Kroch's and Brentano's," he says. "I used to like to hang around there – in fact anywhere writers were. I always valued words. It's very difficult to understand anything if you don't have words. . . . When the Blackhawks were in New York to play the Rangers, I'd go to the Lion's Head pub on the edge of the Village, where the writers hung out. I met Norman Mailer there and Jimmy Breslin. And I knew the newspaper writers. I loved hearing their b.s. They were fun to be around. Some of them were wonderful story-tellers. I guess at some level I was making up for things I'd cut myself off from as a young guy. The game was all-consuming back then; it pretty well had to be if you were going to make it. I know a lot of pro athletes who had the capacity for broader experience, but they wanted to be champions, so they narrowed their focus right down to their sport. It can be pretty dehumanizing. Later, if they didn't have the means or words to deal with things such as art or literature or ideas, they just moved away from them. I didn't want to do that; I was far too curious. That's one of the reasons I lived right on the edge of downtown Chicago – at least until my children were born. Most of the guys lived way out in the far suburbs."

When the Democratic Convention came to Chicago in 1968, Eric was on hand for the now-famous anti-war demonstrations. "I saw the cops beating kids up," he says. "It was extremely depressing." And when the most famous of the demonstrators, the so-called Chicago Seven, were put on trial for sedition the following year, a lawyer friend provided Eric with access to Judge Hoffman's court-room. "I was fascinated by the free-speech thing," he says. "Like a lot of other people, I'd always assumed free speech was a right in America. But for some, it apparently wasn't. I was amazed at how primitive it all was. Judge Hoffman was a very limited mainstream guy; he had no way of dealing with these people like Jerry Rubin and Abbie Hoffman and Bobby Seale – either judicially *or* intellectu-ally. They taped Seale's mouth shut so that he wouldn't be able to disrupt the proceedings! . . . As hockey players, we

49

were expected to shut up," he laughs, "but they never went so far as to tape our mouths."

By 1970, Eric's hockey skills were, by his own estimate, "in pretty severe decline." So too was his interest in the game. "I should have quit earlier," he says. "I was doing it for the money. I was in pain a lot. I stopped taking risks, reduced my game. I'd get beat. It was awful. Besides that, the kids were getting meaner and tougher. I'd come up against some hard twenty-one-year-old stud who wanted the puck, and I'd be inclined to give it to him. And that's not a good sign for a professional hockey player."

Eric's physical decline was accompanied by an increasing restlessness with the psychological imperatives imposed by the game. "The role of the professional athlete is one I learned to play pretty well," he says. "Laughing with strangers, signing autographs, shaking hands, accepting people's good wishes, indulging the adulation. It doesn't take much; it has its built-in moves, responses. But it's all quite meaningless in the end, and I got fed up with it. More and more when somebody I didn't know came up to me and said, 'Hello, Eric!' I'd be inclined to brush them off. It's exhausting."

He got equally fed up with the restrictions and fatigue of the lengthy road trips. "I'm not wild about living in hotels, plane travel, having to spend time in a room, sometimes a whole day, waiting for a game. I didn't mind killing time when I was younger, but I grew to resent it. I didn't want to *kill* time. I wanted to *do* something with it."

Yet like most professional athletes, Eric harboured a fear of relinquishing what he refers to as "the thrill of the game," the drama and motion, the adrenaline high, of which he speaks with such eloquence. "When you've done it for twenty years in the NHL, and for fifteen years before that," he says, "ordinary life just isn't very exciting by comparison. It's a very rare athlete who finds another all-encompassing action to sustain him when he quits." During the early and mid-sixties, Eric had tried off-season work both as a travel-package salesman and as a stock-broker and had found both jobs stiflingly unappealing.

When he was invited to become playing coach of a team in Lausanne, Switzerland, a few months after his retirement in 1972, he leapt at the opportunity, packing up the family and taking off for Europe. "It was great," says Eric. "The hockey life was relatively relaxed; we had all that exposure to another culture; learned some French; and I was introduced to skiing."

At the end of the year, however, his wife, Barbara, was offered what Eric describes as "a really good job" back in Evanston, and the family came home.

For Eric, it was the beginning of a five- or six-year period of restless emotional transience and, at times, outright dissipation. Within a year of returning home, he had separated from Barbara and taken an apartment of his own in Evanston, where he could be close to his children. "Barb and I had had some wonderful times," he allows. "But it wasn't working at that point, and we couldn't see any way of keeping it together."

Eric played briefly for the Chicago Cougars of the WHA, then in 1975 took a job coaching semi-pro hockey in Trail, B.C.

Although the position itself was ultimately of little consequence to him it afforded him an opportunity to ski in the Rockies and to work part-time on the ski patrol at Rossland. "It was kind of a threshold year for me," he says. "Skiing was the first thing I'd done that gave me anywhere near the thrill that hockey had given me. And it put a notion in my head that just maybe I could eventually make some sort of a life out of it."

He returned to Evanston and attempted unsuccessfully to put his marriage back together. "About this time," he says, "I got in with a really goofy bunch of people – people in the media and advertising. They were very heavy drinkers, into drugs and so on. It was the seventies – even forty- and fifty-year-olds were playing some heavy-duty games. Basically, I was drunk for three years, during and after my break-up. Alcoholic. I'd drink beer and wine, occasional hard stuff. Chicago's a twenty-four-hour town, and I'd go two or three days straight, putting back a couple of drinks an hour. I was strong then. I'd toss back some amphetamines and keep going. I wasn't into drugs; I just wanted to stay awake. I put on fifty pounds. Needless to say, I didn't have a job at that point. Couldn't keep one."

Inclusion in Studs Terkel's bestselling book in 1971 had raised Eric's profile somewhat and thrown light on his poetic sensibilities, and at the height of his alcoholic binge, a Toronto publisher, Fitzhenry and Whiteside, suggested he write an autobiography. They sent him an advance of $5,000. "I got thirty thousand words into it, all the stuff about growing up in Canada," he says, "and I bogged down – didn't send them anything for months. It's a miracle I got as far into the book as I did, the way I was living. . . . It was practically a cliché: the bad winters, dreams of success, and so on. I really had no idea that writing was so hard. Anyway, I never finished it. They ended up publishing what I wrote as a kids' book."

When, in Eric's words, he was "close to bottoming out," he was offered a position coaching the hockey team at New Trier West High School in Chicago's wealthy north-shore suburbs. For a man of Eric's intellect and athletic experience, such a job could hardly have been seen as a significant challenge. He took it anyway, unaware that it would be an important catalyst in his rehabilitation.

"I had twelve rich kids on the team," he says. "Some of

Tiger Williams in 1984 with the Vancouver Canucks. (*Courtesy of Dan Diamond*)

Tiger behind the bench of the Vancouver Voodoo, 1995. (*C. J. Relke*)

Eric Nesterenko in his prime, with the Chicago Blackhawks.

Eric flies down the slope
at Vail, Colorado, 1995.

John Ferguson (right) and linemate Ralph Backstrom with the Prince of Wales Trophy, awarded to the Canadiens for their first-place finish in John's rookie season, 1963-64.

Fergy with coach Toe Blake and teammates Ralph Backstrom, Jean Béliveau, and J. C. Tremblay, after defeating the New York Rangers in the first game of the 1967 semifinals.

Fergy with
Claude Provost,
Jean-Guy Talbot,
and Gump
Worsley. Fergy
is holding the
good luck charm
that helped the
Canadiens win
the Stanley Cup
in 1969.

The Fergusons at "Pony-rama," Richelieu Park,
1970. Left to right: Chris, Cathy, Joan, John
Jr., John, and Joanne. Uncle William Ferguson
is at top left.

John and Joan
showing off the
silver medal won by
Team Canada at the
World Hockey
Championship
in Stockholm,
Sweden, 1989.

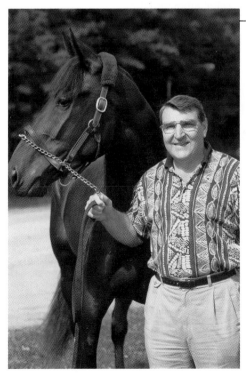

John with Hardie
Hanover, the North
American champion
three-year-old pacing
filly for 1994.
(*Michael Burns*)

Reggie Leach with
the Flyers during
their 1974–75
Cup-winning season.

Reg and his son, Jamie, in 1982. Jamie has played for four NHL
teams and is currently with the Buffalo Sabres. He was a member
of the Stanley Cup champion Pittsburgh Penguins in 1991.

Reg and Jamie at Arnes,
Manitoba, near Reg's
home town of Riverton.

Reg and his fiancée, Debbie Copper, in Switzerland in 1993.

Brandon (Debbie's son) and Brandie (Reg's daughter). Brandie played for the Canadian Women's National lacrosse team in 1992. She is a student at Rowan Community College in Glassboro, New Jersey. Brandon attends elementary school near Sewell, New Jersey.

Reg with the Flyers Alumni team, on tour in Switzerland in 1993. At left is former Flyer Rick MacLeish, at right Al Secord.

them were into drugs and booze. They'd played hockey since they were little, but they'd never won anything, never been properly coached. My only rule was: Show up for practices straight and sober."

Not surprisingly, Eric's coaching reflected the studied defensive tactics that he had employed so effectively as a player. "I took the emphasis off scoring goals, and put it on preventing them," he says. "We had no complicated plays, no break-out patterns or anything like that. Everything very simple. It took me a third of the season to convince them that this was a way to win, but once I did, we ended up so clean in our own end that teams just couldn't set up against us."

In that orderly manner, Eric guided the team to the state high school championship.

"But really," he says, "the kids gave me a lot more than I gave them." Most importantly, he explains, they triggered a baleful realization that if he was going to be around them and be respected by them, he could not, in his words, be "a fat drunk."

He weaned himself gradually from the bottle and lost weight. He began to see a psychiatrist. "I told him my problems," says Eric, "and over the course of a year, he persuaded me that I had to quit lying to myself – that I was just going to fool myself if I settled into some normal middle-management job, or, worse, took the typical path of the ex-professional athlete, trading off my past as some sort of sales or public-relations-type person. A lot of players have done that and made the transition very comfortably. But, intuitively, I was resisting it, which was probably responsible for the heavy drinking. In the end, the guy told me, 'Look, you've obviously got to find another life for yourself, something that turns you on. What do you like to do?'"

Eric notes that, for one thing, he knew he'd be best off

with physical work, preferably something outdoors. "I've always loved the physicality, the sensuality of life," he says, "particularly in my interactions with the landscape and elements." He knew, too, that sooner or later he would have to leave Chicago. "If I'd stayed," he explains, "I'd have been an ex-Blackhawk forever, perpetually recognized and defined in that role. I don't have any need to be acknowledged by people I don't know. The people who know me in Vail know me for who I am here, not as a hockey player."

Gradually, it became clear to him that skiing would make a healthy focus for his future, though at that stage he had no idea how he would go about making a living at it, if at all. Given his love of mountains, Colorado seemed an ideal destination, particularly in its proximity to his beloved Wyoming. "So, in 1978," he says, "when my older kids had reached university, I came out here and started life as a ski bum."

He went first to Aspen, where (ever a man of his roots) he started an adult recreational hockey program. "I had a job as a caretaker on a wealthy Texan's estate," he says. "But we had a disagreement, and he fired me, so I went over to Summit County." There, for a lark, he attended a three-day trial for jobs in a local ski school. "I never figured they'd hire me," he laughs. "I just wanted to enjoy some free skiing. But they ended up giving me a job that I kept for a couple of years, before moving on to Vail."

For a man who has chosen the present as his psycho-philosophic domain, Vail is perhaps the perfect earthly locale; it has no history. On the other hand, it is a somewhat unlikely location for someone who has foresworn luxury and affluence. For it is not so much a town as an indulgence on a grand scale, an almost unseemly aggregation of wealth. "We're not rich," Eric says of his fellow ski instructors and joyriders (some of whom are forty years his junior), "but we live off the rich."

Vail was founded in 1962 and first came to the attention of the mass of North Americans when President Gerald Ford began taking well-publicized winter vacations there during the early seventies (he is reported to have been given a luxurious chalet by the town as a public-relations gesture). But the place did not hit its stride as a resort until roughly 1980, when, as Eric puts it, "the building boom started," and what was essentially a pleasant winter hide-away exploded into one of the largest and most lavish ski resorts anywhere.

The town and its contiguous real-estate developments stretch for some twenty miles along I-70, 120 miles west of Denver, in the trough of what is frequently referred to as "Happy Valley." Vail's year-round population of approximately 8,000 is swollen by 5,000 seasonal employees in winter and, on some days, up to 50,000 skiers. "The amazing thing," says Eric, "is that, even with that influx, the town works." As well it might. Its sole reason for existing is, and has always been, skiing; and millions upon millions of dollars have been spent converting the seven-mile-wide bosom of Vail Mountain into a lacy topography of more than a hundred ski runs serviced by twenty-five lifts and an army of attendants and instructors.

At one remove from those attendants is a second army of hoteliers, restaurateurs, and high-end retailers of ski-wear, furs, and exotic bric-a-brac. (Provided one has the money, it is easier to buy a fur coat or a $2,000 skiing outfit in Vail than to track down a loaf of bread or a quart of milk.) "When I need everyday clothes, that sort of thing," says Eric, "I'll drive in to Denver."

Many of the town's seventy-five hotels bear the trappings of Tyrolean lodges, while the restaurants (there are a hundred or more) are festooned with ersatz remembrances of the Alps. An inordinate proportion of the town's dwellings are multimillion-dollar chalets; and, for the most part, the people who occupy them are short-term out-patients from the high-life of cities such as New York, Chicago, Los Angeles, Dallas, and San Francisco. The local TV channel is a kind of ongoing "infomercial" for ski-wear, real estate, dining, and fashion. (A televised advertisement for a Vail plastic surgeon contends that "a well-constructed face" [i.e., reconstructed] is a "work of fine art.")

Vail has no poverty, no racism, and no serious crime. Seen otherwise, the insidious racism of economic exclusion has kept blacks away, and the crimes on which many of the town's fortunes are founded – the graft and exploitation and environmental plundering – have been committed somewhere else. The social problems, for a change, are those of the desperate rich, not the desperate poor. "We've had a few Wall Street criminals build out here," said Eric as we drove through Beaver Creek just west of Vail. "See that house over there? It was built by Mexican gangsters. They sold it for $7 million, twenty-five thousand square feet. Jack Nicklaus has a place here. We get a lot of actors and entertainers."

On a symbolic level, it hardly seems surprising that many people, on visiting Vail for the first time, suffer intense lightheadedness and nausea – and, often, difficulty in breathing – brought on by an inability to adjust rapidly enough to the altitude, with its low levels of available oxygen.

Beyond any cynicism that might be inspired by Vail and its ethos, it is an extraordinarily beautiful place. The peaks of its namesake mountain rise to nineteen thousand feet, and the glistening ski trails descend off the slopes like mile-long streamers at some magnificent winter Saturnalia. At night, it is alive with what its promotional pamphlet refers to as "a hundred thousand glittering lights." "In winter," says Eric, "it's just magical. I probably tend to take the beauty for granted. But when I'm away I miss it; there's a hole in my life."

After fourteen years in Vail, Eric is a well-known figure about town. During the time I spent with him, he was greeted warmly everywhere we went – by restaurant and hotel people, by shop owners, and by other ski instructors and patrol members. He is connected to them in a multiplicity of ways: sends his ski students to a particular ski shop, for example, and in return is given preferential treatment as a customer; frequents this restaurant, that café, this bookstore; visits the library for its periodicals, the post office for his NHL pension cheques. His posture is somewhat droopy, and as he strides through the "Tyrolean" heart of the community, dressed in his Wolverine shoes and brown leather jacket, his aura is that of a slightly impatient curmudgeon, sceptical of the glitz but so well acquainted with it that, for the most part, he barely seems to notice. His low-key antipathy toward Vail's obvious materialism and socially privileged smugness is implicit in his democratic spirit and lean preferences for living, but otherwise it tends to be obscured by his outspoken affection for the local skiing and topography. For the most part, he seems to like the town just as it is. He clearly takes pleasure in its better restaurants and hotels – a throwback to what he calls "the big fat times" he had as an NHL hockey player. To be sure, Vail is a long way from the workaday grind that he loathes.

It is perhaps an indication of his true valences with the town that his friends tend to be other free spirits like himself, often other "ski bums," rather than members of the local power elite or bulwarks of the social register. He is so poorly connected in any conventional sense that, during the mid-eighties, when he founded a hockey team – high-level amateurs that drew sell-out crowds to exhibition games at the local arena – he was shunned by the town's administration when he went to them asking for support. "I was providing an obviously popular entertainment in a community that exists for such things," he says. "I was working hard at it, and I thought they could at least provide me with some money to help support myself – God knows they've got lots of it. But they wouldn't, so I stopped doing it."

On another occasion he suggested to a Vail lawyer prominent in the local minor-hockey program that, for a fraction of the typical lawyer's hourly fee, he would coach the boys in proper hockey techniques, make winners of them as he had done with the boys at New Trier West. "I never heard from the guy," laughs Eric.

Vail gets an astounding thirty feet of snow a year, and in some years – 1993, for example – as much as forty feet. The first serious snowfalls come in early November, and by American Thanksgiving Eric is spending as many as thirty hours a week on the mountain. "Early in the season I teach three or four week-long classes," he says. "Then I have my own clientele, often people who've skied with me before, mid-level skiers who don't so much want help as they want a kind of athletic confidant, a decent skier with whom they can share their experiences on the mountain and perhaps move into some new territory where they're not quite sure of themselves. It's pretty lighthearted, a lot of fun. And I'm connecting with them in a nice way, at times a very imme-diate way, because one of the things I have to help them face is their physical fear. I try to show them ways of dealing with it and still take some risk. I'm on a pretty inti-mate level with these people right away. A lot of them don't even know that I was in the NHL for twenty-one years. And that's good, because my old life is a distraction. They just see an older guy who tends to go for it, and I tend to pull them along. It's not the greatest job in terms of saving the world or creating anything, but I'm not doing anybody any harm, and I guess I help people live in the moment and forget their problems."

Eric's best days on the slopes are those in which he can cut loose, "recreate" himself, as he puts it, sometimes with his son, sometimes with an adventurous client. Sometimes by himself. "On a good powder day," he says, "you give yourself up to the motion and speed; and for that brief time on the mountain you're in the wonderful state of being free of your own mortality."

In lesser moments, Eric admits to being increasingly aware of his mortality. "I think about it a lot," he says. "I feel I have to if I'm going to come to terms with it."

He is reminded of it by, among other things, the arthritis in his back and limbs. "I live a lot with Advil," he says. "I can't bend my wrist because the cartilage is all worn out from decades of handling the puck. The knees are sore. The joints work, but they ache. I've gotta stay active, or I'm afraid everything'll seize up."

During the summer, Eric golfs, hikes, and fishes. One summer, he skied in Australia. Since moving to Colorado, he has augmented his winter income with a variety of summer jobs that include his two sessions in the Arctic during the early eighties and his time in Texas applying decals to trucks. He played the role of a coach in a hockey film called *Youngblood*.

This past summer, he worked as a carpenter's assistant for his friend Kevin Cooke, in whose home he lives. "I hated it," he says. "I only did it because he's my friend and because he asked me to. Half days, that was it."

In Eric's domain, *play* has always been a far more important consideration than work. And he has well-developed thoughts on the subject, many of them formulated during the summer of 1983, when he was invited to the University of Guelph for a term, to lecture on the psychology, philosophy, and sociology of play. "What a lot of people don't seem to realize," he says, "is that play – and by extension finding new forms of play – is almost as important for adults as for kids. Higher animals and human beings really can't live without it. If we could renew and reinvent ourselves through our work, that'd be terrific. But most people can't, because most work is more about conformity, obeying the law, colouring within the lines, than using the imagination. Too many forms of kids' play these days fall into that category, too – too much of it is overly structured. I'm told the outdoor rinks are empty. . . . I've been lucky, or at least persistent; for the most part, I've been able to 'play' at making a living, as I do when I ski."

The last time Eric played hockey was in 1993, in a tournament of NHL oldtimers, staged in the Canadian Maritimes. "There were five of us over fifty," he says (Eric was over sixty): "Billy Harris, Alex Delvecchio, myself, and a couple of guys from the Bruins. That's where I realized it was completely and utterly over for me. I really didn't belong."

It can't be said, however, that "it is completely and utterly over" for Eric's fans. Every year for the past two decades, a long-suffering follower of the Blackhawks, a Chicago resident, has petitioned the Hockey Hall of Fame in Toronto, pleading the case not only for Eric's unique talents but for his nomination and election to hockey's permanent shrine.

The petitioning is almost certainly in vain. Hanford Woods described Eric's career as "a minor legend of uncelebrated works." And minor it may be. But it is a legend nonetheless – one far more resonant than those of many of the game's Paul Bunyans.

"I've heard about the petitions," smiles Eric. "Apparently I was nominated one time, but didn't get in. I guess it'd be nice to be recognized by my peers, but it's so

far removed from my life now, it doesn't make much difference; I don't really give a damn."

As Eric and I walked through Vail, on the last night of
my visit, he said: "I don't think many people would term
my life a success – no wife, no money; I don't own or run
anything. I could have handled my money and my personal
situation a little better. But, ya know, I've made the choices
I wanted to make. It's cost me, sure, but it's also allowed
me to go in search of meaningful things. I'm still trying to
discover who I am, why I'm doing what I'm doing. I seem
to be following some inner voice."

As for the future, Eric is planning "a low-key, contem-
plative life," with lots of reading. "I hope to stay healthy,"
he says.

He also plans to spend a summer or two in Alaska,
financing his trips with the benefits that are likely to
accrue to him when the well-documented NHL pension
debacle is resolved. "I was up in Alaska a couple of years
ago," he says, "and I had a very strong feeling of sublimi-
nal connection to the place. And I like northern British
Columbia. I'd like to float some of the great rivers that are
up there. If I can't get anybody to go with me, I'll go alone."

Some twenty-five years ago, during the last days of his
career with the Blackhawks, Eric described to a writer how
one day he had been driving along the shore of Lake
Michigan in Chicago when he spotted a vast expanse of
natural ice. "It was a clear, crisp afternoon," he said. "And
dammit if I didn't pull over and put on my skates. I carry a
pair in the car. I took off my camel-hair coat; I was just in
a suit jacket; nobody was there. The wind was blowing
from the north. With the wind behind you, you can wheel
and dive and turn; you can lay yourself into impossible
angles that you never could walking or running. You lay
yourself at a forty-five-degree angle, your elbow virtually
touching the ice as you're in a turn. I flew. I was free as a

bird. Really happy. That goes back to when I was a kid. You're breaking the bounds of gravity. I have a feeling that's the innate desire of man."

It is a feeling that dies hard. And, at times, lives hard. "Now I satisfy it mostly on skis," says Eric.

But on the off-chance that ice and wind and innate desire should ever reconvene in quite the way they did that day in Chicago, he will, like the Boy Scouts, be prepared. For in the small back seat of his pick-up, he carries a pair of aging skates.

"Oh, those," he says when asked about them. "They're always there. You never know . . ."

He stops short of finishing the thought, but the gist of the message is clear.

You never know when you might feel an urge to break the bounds of gravity.

# BALLET AND MURDER

EARLY IN HIS CAREER with the Montreal Canadiens, John Ferguson announced his desire to be the meanest, rottenest, most despicably miserable cuss ever to skate in the NHL. Which, as hockey desires go, was extravagant but not extraordinary. Long before Conn Smythe prophesied that if you couldn't beat 'em in the alley, you couldn't beat 'em on the ice, NHL aspirants realized that success in pro hockey had almost as much to do with belligerence as with beauty (poet Al Purdy called the game "a combination of ballet and murder").

The difference between Ferguson's desires and those of the young terror-mongers who might have shared them was that Ferguson had the power – a remarkable combination of physical strength and competitive malfeasance – actually to *be* the meanest, rottenest, most despicably miserable cuss ever to score a knockout (or a goal) in the dramatic burlesque that is our national game.

Only twelve seconds had elapsed in Fergy's first NHL engagement, in 1963, when he took on "Terrible Ted" Green, the Boston Bruins' house vigilante, "going right over top of him," as Ferguson describes it, and placing a big red floribunda on his kisser.

Ferguson and students of his career are dutiful in pointing out that he also scored two goals that night, and a few days later was named NHL Player of the Week – the point being, of course, that he had not learned his hockey in a boxing ring and that he was far more than a headknocker. And he was! But it was not the news of his goal-scoring that put the rest of the league on nervous alert over the arrival of the young left winger. What caught their attention was the impressive report that he had dusted off Terrible Ted, had done so with gusto, and just might be the meanest, rottenest, et cetera, ever to arrive in the NHL.

In fact, during the eight years that followed, Ferguson was *exactly* that, a free-ranging locus of vehemence and ill will, a kind of anti-Franciscan, sowing despair where there was hope, darkness where there was light, a broken nose and five loose teeth where, once, there was facial integrity.

It is one of those anomalies understood best by bag ladies and poets that, away from hockey, Ferguson has always been a paragon of discretion, a shy and considerate man, as avuncular as Wiggily, as obliging as Pooh. He was once referred to as "a real sweetie" by no less a witness than Nancy Bower, wife of Johnny Bower, the fabled Maple Leaf goaltender who knew Fergy's wrath as well as anyone during the years of their combatantcy. Which isn't to say that Ferguson has never betrayed social or personal raw edges, or that he has ever been taken for Casper Milquetoast, even in a dark room (Casper doesn't smoke cigars). But, away from the rink, he does indeed possess an unassuming mien, an innocence and sensitivity that, over the years, has revealed only traces of the professional animosity on which he founded his reputation as a player.

Discretion has figured so significantly in the composite of Ferguson's off-ice personality that, when it came time to write his autobiography in 1986, there were aspects of his life – thoughts, reminiscences, reflections on people and events – that he simply did not feel comfortable committing to print, for fear that some person or organization might somehow, somewhere, be offended.

"There are things you just can't *put* in a book," says Joan Ferguson, John's wife of thirty-seven years.

"Like what?" she and John are asked as they sit at the dining table of their home in Amherstburg, Ontario, on a mild mid-winter day.

"Well," John says circumspectly, and within seconds he has begun to explain how, for example, it has always been assumed that his retirement from hockey in 1971 was predicated strictly on the lure of opportunities in the knitwear and restaurant trades and at Blue Bonnet Raceway in Montreal. (He doesn't mention that that assumption has been perpetuated by the book itself.) "What I didn't discuss in the book," he continues, "what I've *never* discussed publicly, is that at a point during my second-to-last season, I felt . . . well . . . I guess you could say *betrayed* by the Canadiens, an organization to which I'd given everything possible, and then some, for seven seasons."

At the root of John's comments is an injury he received just before Christmas, 1969, when in a game against the Minnesota North Stars, in Minneapolis, a puck struck him so violently in the face that it detached the retina of his right eye and crushed the occipital bone beneath the eyeball. "I had emergency surgery in Minneapolis to correct the detached retina," he says, "but I didn't want to stay in the hospital there, so the next day I checked myself out and went to the airport to get a flight to Chicago. But before I could get one, the pain in my face worsened to where it was as if my whole head was being torn off. And my eye had begun to drop in its socket. At that point, it was all I could do to get back to the hospital in Minneapolis."

A day or two later, Ferguson reached Montreal and again entered hospital, this time to have the damaged bone beneath his eye replaced with a plastic implant. "For six days over the Christmas holidays, I lay there in the Montreal General, either freezing to death in the hallway, waiting for the operation, or in excruciating pain after the drugs wore off. And during that time, not one member of the Canadiens' ownership or management or coaching staff came to visit me, or even sent flowers or a card. In fact, only one of them even phoned – Toe Blake. Once. And I'll tell ya, it soured me, lying there, realizing that apparently none of them cared. It was probably nothing personal, but it told me something, and while I was in hospital I promised that if I ever ran a hockey club I'd never *ever* let such a thing happen to one of my players. And I didn't. When I was general manager of the Rangers, then the Jets, we did everything we could for injured players – visited them, sent flowers, helped their families, anything to make them more comfortable."

It is typical of his personality, and of his commitment to team stability, that John has never mentioned his resentment to the Canadiens. Yet he is adamant that it led directly to his retirement in 1970. "I did make a comeback for half a season in '71," he says, "and Sam Pollock offered me the captaincy if I'd stay on longer, but even that didn't sway me."

If John needed added incentive to convert his blades into ploughshares, he got it in spades from business partners with whom he'd gone into knitwear manufacturing earlier in the year, and who now managed to persuade him that he was about make his fortune in the *schmata* trade. And initially their prediction seemed sound. "Within a year or two of my getting there we went from sixty employees to twelve hundred," says John. "We were going twenty-four hours a day, turning out everything from sweaters to dresses to pants."

While the knitting machines were turning yarn into golf shirts and profit projections, John's primary job was to get the company dub, Butternut Enterprises, through the doors of department stores such as Eaton's and the Bay. "But I was also an investor, a buyer, a designer," he says. "I'd go to Florida and California and bring back sample items, whatever was hot, and we'd do knock-offs and fire 'em out the door."

At the same time, the company opened "Fergy's" restaurant on Decarie Street beneath the garment factory. "I'd start the day at the factory," says John, "then I'd go down to the restaurant, check things out, keep things moving." In early afternoon, with a pickle and a smoked-meat sandwich behind his belt buckle, he would leave the restaurant and head to Blue Bonnet Raceway, where for years he'd been indulging the longest-standing love of his life, horse racing, and where a short time hence he would be named assistant director of racing.

The impression is created, both in talking to John and in his book, that retirement at this point was one great swirl of productive activity, and that hockey, by comparison, was a rather bleary memory seen through the reducing end of a peepscope.

Joan Ferguson is considerably less idealistic in her view of the period, although painstaking in her determination not to tarnish the off-ice accomplishments of the man she loves. "I guess I'm a realist," she smiles, "and it seems to me, looking back, that John's business partners had an agenda that wasn't always conceived in John's best interests. They persuaded him, for example, that the Canadiens weren't giving him the money or respect he deserved, even though he was working himself to the bone for them. Of course, *they* wanted him full time, to represent the company. His popularity in Montreal was a real benefit to them. At the same time, they more or less used his knowledge of horses to get into the racing business themselves. He worked with them for five or six years – we had money in the business – and only later, in thinking back, did he realize that he never did get a salary from them, even though he was president of the company."

Asked what John *did* get from the business, Joan responds bluntly, "Being busy. He was extremely busy. When it was over and the business sold, he certainly didn't come out of it with anything to speak of. And yet, being the man he is, he wouldn't breathe a word against these guys! Even after twenty years! I guess you could say he felt the same way about them that he felt about Mr. Selke [long-time general manager of the Canadiens], whose first contract with John was a handshake and a little piece of torn-off paper that said, 'I will pay you $7,500 for the season – F.J. Selke.' John carried it around in his wallet.

"If somebody is willing to shake hands with John, he feels they'll be as honest as he is about their agreement. . . . Really, I don't want to say too much more about the clothing business, except that I think we got out of it lucky, with ourselves intact and our family still functioning very well." Now Joan is laughing. "We had John's past lives analyzed one night for fun, and, as I figured, he's on his first life. He can be so trusting and naive. And yet he's so shrewd in other ways – with his horses and hockey, for instance."

It was John's shrewdness as a hockey man that, a year after his retirement from the Canadiens, led to what he calls his "greatest thrill in sport," surpassing five Stanley Cup victories and a handful of Executive of the Year awards won during his term as general manager of the Winnipeg Jets. For Canadians, the story of the Soviet–Canada hockey summit in 1972 has taken on Biblical dimensions, dwarfing even the heroic victories of Canadians during the First and Second World Wars. And there are few parts of this seminal national story that are not well known even to casual fans of the game. However, one detail that has generally escaped codification is that if Harry Sinden, the team's general manager, had had his way, the Canadian contingent of left wingers – an iconographic cast featuring the likes of Frank Mahovlich and Paul Henderson – would have included the perhaps unlikely name of John Bowie Ferguson. "He asked me to play, and the only reason I didn't," says Fergy, "was that there'd already been an ugly drawn-out debate over the exclusion of Bobby Hull from the team, because he'd left the NHL, and I felt my participation as a player, after more than a year of retirement, would probably have opened up another controversy that would have detracted from the focus on the series."

Fergy went on to take a proud and significant role in the selection, coaching, and management of the team and has never regretted his decision not to participate as a player. What does bother him are the infrequent but lingering questions – "they still come up" – concerning what a player such as he might have contributed to the Canadian effort should he have decided to put on a uniform. "People always saw me merely as a fighter," he laments. "They don't realize that I was all-star in junior, an all-star in the American League, that one year I led the Canadiens in goal-scoring [twenty-nine goals in 1968–69], that twice I was the Canadiens' top-scoring left winger – what's a guy have to do? Everybody seemed to suggest that World War Three was going to break out if I played in that series. As a player I had other things to offer as well as toughness. And I knew that."

And Harry Sinden knew it; and so did Toe Blake, Frank Selke, and Sam Pollock – and a slew of rival coaches and players, not to mention anyone who ever played alongside John. "When I became coach of the Bruins," Harry Sinden once said, "I would have taken Ferguson over anybody else in the league. *Anybody*. He had the kind of aggressiveness that could lift an entire team and keep it hitting and fighting, long after it had passed the point of exhaustion."

It is hardly a coincidence that after his arrival in Montreal in 1963, the Canadiens, who had not won a championship in three years, went on to win Stanley Cups in four of the next six years, three times in the absence of their grand potentate, Jean Béliveau, who missed the finals because of injuries. Nor is it a coincidence that in some fifteen years of junior and professional hockey, John was never traded (who in possession of such a weapon would put it in the arsenal of a rival army?).

"It's a kind of chicken-and-egg thing," says Joan. "John was never traded because of his attitude, and his attitude was partly a result of him never having been traded. If he'd bounced around from one team to another like so many players do, he'd probably have gotten cynical, and his commitment would have wavered."

The annals of the era shiver with tales of his intensity and dedication: how once as a minor-leaguer he fired a puck at the head of a teammate who was kibitzing with a rival player during the warm-up for a game. ("I missed," he says matter-of-factly.) How he once stormed out of George's restaurant in Toronto, leaving an untouched steak on the table, because his teammate Dick Duff struck up a conversation with John's arch-rival, Eddie Shack, who happened to come in ("I couldn't stand being in the same room with the guy, let alone seeing a teammate talking to him!"). How he would turn his contemptuous stare on any teammate who showed even the slightest sign of flippancy before or during a game ("He was as intimidating to our own guys as to the opposition," says Jean Béliveau).

"Where hockey was concerned," says Joan, "there was only one word to describe John – 'possessed.' His only fear was losing, and wherever he could he passed that along to his teammates."

It hardly needs saying that Fergy was not a deft puck-handler or skater (he didn't don skates until the age of twelve), but he is quite justified in pointing out that his contribution as a player was by no means confined to adrenaline and ice boxing. Besides getting to the net when it counted and scoring his share of goals, he was an avid student of positional play and was a ferociously successful checker. In eight years of personally checking Gordie Howe, he didn't once permit Howe a goal. In all, Fergy himself scored 145 goals in a 500-game career (the ratio extrapolated to a career the length of Howe's – 2,186 games – would give him 634 goals). More remarkably, he averaged only 2.4 minutes per game in penalties (compared to, say, Tiger Williams, who averaged more than four minutes per game).

But no matter how the lily is gilded, or the record book interpreted, John will inevitably be remembered best as the man he wanted to be – the meanest, rottenest, most despicably miserable cuss ever to lace on skates. And as a five-star slugger. In a jingoistic exercise orchestrated by *Canadian* magazine during the late sixties, boxer George Chuvalo picked the top ten fighters in hockey and, not surprisingly, chose Ferguson as the heavyweight champion of the lot. A short time later, Fergy was more than willing to participate in a proposed exhibition bout with Chuvalo. However, the Canadiens nixed the idea for fear that Ferguson would be hurt – or perhaps that Chuvalo would. It may even have occurred to them that if Fergy scored well against the famous boxer (he had, after all, taken boxing lessons as a teenager) he might, in the flush of victory, be tempted to abandon hockey for a more lucrative career in the ring. "I was so cocky, I just never believed I'd lose to *anybody*," Ferguson says with a shrug. "When Imlach was in Toronto, he'd often say he was bringing some guy up from the minors who was gonna do a number on me, and I'd skate by the Toronto bench, and I'd say, 'Who ya got this week, Punch? Send him out now!'"

"Fergy was the most formidable player of the decade, if not in the Canadiens' history," says Jean Béliveau. "He'd do what he had to to win, and he had to win; he wouldn't stand for anything less."

It was this indefatigable will to dispose of his opposition – as well as his success with Team Canada and with a professional lacrosse team he ran in Montreal during the early seventies – that, in 1975, brought Fergy to the attention of the floundering New York Rangers, who sent him a distress call and, within days, hired him as coach and general manager. Their hope was that he would imbue the team – a gang Ferguson characterizes as having massive salaries and massive hypochondria – with much-needed discipline and direction. Not surprisingly, one of Fergy's earliest moves in New York was to acquire Nick Fotiu, a 220-pound practitioner of hockey's darker arts. He also cleared the dressing room of its coterie of fawning doctors, hired a fitness expert, and began purging the roster of high-priced players who weren't pulling their (sometimes ample) weight.

But the book on Fergy's tenure on Broadway is by no means a slavish testament to discipline or old-style management. He was the first, for instance, to allow female reporters into the dressing room at Madison Square Garden, declaring an unequivocal belief in what he calls "the practice of equal rights." He also responded to changes in the game, indeed influenced those changes, by advancing the boundaries of conventional scouting, chiefly in Europe, and by recognizing the talents of Scandinavian and American college players, who many in the game still viewed as fancy-skating, light-hitting irregulars. One of his last acts as Ranger general manager was to acquire Swedish stars Ulf Nilsson and Anders Hedberg from the Winnipeg Jets of the WHA.

Fergy's unexpected downfall in New York began four years after his arrival when he eased long-time Ranger hero Rod Gilbert, whom he considered overpaid and significantly overripe, out of the line-up and into a minor executive job with the club. Gilbert worked from behind the scenes to turn Sonny Werblin, a senior Garden executive, against Ferguson, and one morning in the spring of 1979 Fergy and the rest of the city awoke to a headline in the New York *Daily News* informing them that Fergy was no longer an employee of the Rangers.

The bitter turn of events was repeated in Winnipeg nine years later, after Ferguson's lengthy and successful term as general manager of the Jets. But this time the betrayal was perpetrated not by an obvious foe such as Gilbert but by Mike Smith, whom Ferguson had first hired in New York and had groomed as his assistant in Winnipeg. The duplicitous assistant convinced team owner Barry Shenkarow, a one-time business partner of Ferguson's, that Fergy was no longer right for the job, and Shenkarow fired the man who had led the Jets from the WHA into the NHL and had established them as a respectable and entertaining franchise.

"When John was fired in New York," says Joan, "I just told him, 'Don't worry about it – it's their loss.' I know it was painful for him, but it wasn't as if he'd been diagnosed with some fatal disease. Same in Winnipeg, really. It hurt him, and it's not at all like somebody getting laid off from a factory. It's headline news! You've given your heart and brains to this thing for so long, and it's over, and there's nothing you can do about it."

"And for that reason," says John, "we've never wasted

any time thinking about the disappointments and disloyal-
ties of the past. They come along, you deal with them, then
it's on to the next challenge."

Asked if there are disappointments he has not dispelled
so easily, Fergy thinks for a moment and gives a most
unexpected answer on yet another topic that does not
appear in his autobiography. "Quite a few years back," he
reflects, "I was nominated for the Hockey Hall of Fame,
and I heard from somebody close to the selection process
that my nomination had gone through and I was in. Then
when the new inductees were announced, my name wasn't
among them. It's a very political process, and apparently
there'd been a slight shift among the committee members
at the last moment – enough to turn things against me. I
wouldn't have felt so badly, except that I'd heard that I was
in. It was very disappointing."

When it is suggested in jest that perhaps at some point
in the past Fergy had beaten up someone he shouldn't have
– a committee member? a committee member's friend or
teammate? – his face broadens into a smile. "If I did," he
says quietly, "he probably deserved it."


Considering the proclivities of his early years, Fergy's face,
at age fifty-six, is remarkably free of scars, and even of
wrinkles. And despite the many injuries he suffered in the
NHL trenches – inflictions of the sort that, for many NHL
survivors, have led to debilitating arthritis – there is
nothing about his gait or physical mannerisms that betrays
even a hint of stiffness or incapacitation. He has an extraordinarily long nose with the contour of a flaying knife,
thick brown hair, and the physique of a Kodiak bear. You
cannot look at him without suspecting that at least part of
his success as a pugilist must have come from his robust
thighs and low centre of gravity.

Fergy also possesses a less obvious pugilistic asset that, in the arcane realm of hockey warfare, may have cost him as much as it earned: "He was very slow to bleed," says Joan. "He could get clobbered on the head with, say, a stick, and he'd go to show the ref to prove it, and there wouldn't be a trace of blood, because his scalp, even the flesh on his forehead, is so extremely supple. You can pick it up between your fingers. He's like a shar-pei dog. A barber in Nanaimo once told him that, with a scalp like his, he'd never lose his hair."

Fergy has not punched anybody out in nearly twenty-four years, and he has no plans to do so. Yet when you ask him to show you the famous fists, the efficacious jackhammers that rearranged so many noses and jaws during his years in the NHL, he doesn't hesitate to fold them and raise them. And even though it's only for show – and despite the smile on his face – you sense in the way he strikes the pose, elbows tucked, neck slightly scrunched, that way down deep, in the regions where the nerves think for themselves, he has not entirely forgotten the adrenaline thrill of vanquishing the many challengers who faced him.

Fergy once said the *size* of his hands was a significant factor in his stunning success as a fighter. And his hands are indeed large, the palms as thick as steak-house filets. But they are not so much big in breadth or length as they are *stout* hands, muscular hands, each a kind of mortar shell faced with knuckles an inch in diameter. As fists, they give the impression of being unarticulated extensions of his daunting arms and shoulders – and perhaps, more significantly, of the Draconian competitive temperament that, where sport is concerned, still lurks in the backwaters of his personality. On this particular afternoon, the old sensibility reveals itself in his low-key bridling over the buttery hockey being played by Wayne Gretzky and his band of all-stars, on tour in Europe while NHL owners and players consume themselves and their season in wearisome labour negotiations. "That's not hockey they're playing over there!" Fergy scoffs. "There's absolutely no bloody intensity to it! When I played, we had pride! We did what we had to to win!"

For Fergy more than others, winning at any cost is an article of competitive faith. "As a hockey man," he says, "there's nothing worse than having to sit there and watch players float around and smile at one another and chit-chat during faceoffs. Our own NHL all-star games are awful – imagine scores like 17–16!" He leans toward his visitor and taps his forefinger on the coffee table. "I'll tell ya something," he says, peering across the top of his reading glasses. "When they take the animosity out of the game, they can all go on strike, and nobody will miss them."

While her attitude toward hockey is somewhat less assertive than her husband's, Joan Ferguson, too, takes the view that pacifism is getting the upper hand in the game and is eventually going to give hockey a black eye. "What's the point if there's no drive to win?" she asks. "You might just as well draw straws and say, okay, your team wins tonight, ours'll win another night!"

Joan is a slim, insightful woman with an expressive face and an abundance of upbeat energy. Her outlook and attentiveness are a testimony to the range of domestic and psychological capabilities that must have been required to raise four children, often in John's absence, and to attend to John's hockey career as assiduously as she has. "He worked hard and I did, too," she says. "But I must say that I've genuinely enjoyed the hockey." During John's twenty-five years as a professional player, coach, and manager, she missed only a handful of the thousand-odd home games his teams played. Behind the scenes, she acted as dietician, chauffeur, morale booster, archivist, and family ambassador to local charities and schools. "There were times when I even played doctor," she says. "I'd change dressings, make hospital visits, snip out sutures, whatever needed doing."

Today, she and Fergy occupy a stylish townhouse condominium in a newly developed section of Amherstburg, an historic town of ten thousand inhabitants, in the extreme southwest corner of Ontario, where the Detroit River flows into Lake Erie some thirty kilometres south of Windsor and Detroit. Within a kilometre of their front door, ocean-going vessels carrying grain and potash and wood pulp make their way up and down the St. Lawrence Seaway, while on the surrounding flatlands farmers and market gardeners grow tomatoes and vegetables for the canning factories in nearby Leamington and Chatham. The town's streets are gracious and verdant, its tax base solid, and, like the rest of Essex County, its topography is as flat as a sheet of gyprock. Amherstburg is, in large part, a retirement community – "a mini-Victoria" as resident Gerry Waldron describes it – and beyond its preponderance of medical clinics and retirement homes, there is little in the way of visible industry. The town's history and character are perhaps best represented by the partially restored (and eminently sedate) Fort Malden, a seventeenth-century British stronghold, which occupies a large waterfront park on the main street, attracting a quiet flow of tourists during the warm weather.

At the Ferguson home, large ground-floor windows look out past hardwoods and birdfeeders onto the expansive fairways of the Pointe West Golf Club. Inside, despite the comfy furniture and potted plants, the open-style ground floor is less a living room than a kind of indoor paddock for porcelain and bronze horses. There are *dozens* of them – trophies, mementoes, antiques – some so small they could curl comfortably in a tea cup, others as big as border collies: thoroughbreds, standardbreds, Belgians, Lippezanners,

Welsh ponies, jumpers, RCMP mounts, cart and sleigh horses. On a table in the corner shines a large Tiffany-style lamp, whose base is a bronze trotter and whose shade depicts another trotter in bright primary colours. Not ten feet away, by the piano, stands a knee-high likeness of a rearing stallion cast in icy green glass (and protected from galloping grandchildren by a strategically placed plant). On the walls and on available shelving are more horses, some in framed paintings, others fired onto ceramic commemorative plates.

"C'mon downstairs," says Fergy, and he turns up the lights on yet another level of the family equine museum: racing trophies, track citations, horses in paintings and in an extensive grouping of equine postage stamps arranged in a framed collage; horses on a tapestry and in photos, several of which show Fergy and Joan in the winner's circles of various racetracks, with some of the hundreds of winners they have raised and owned over the years. By comparison, there are few reminders of hockey: a couple of photos from the 1972 Soviet series, a Tex Coulter painting of John as a Canadien, and a brace of executive awards from the years in Winnipeg. Asked about his replica Stanley Cup trophies, John responds casually that they're "in a box in the garage somewhere."

The Fergusons would not *be* in Amherstburg were it not for horses. In 1988, after John was released as general manager of the Winnipeg Jets, he accepted a job as president and CEO of the Windsor Raceway, twenty-five kilometres north of Amherstburg on Highway 18. Joan, too, went to work at the track, running the gift shop and handling a variety of public-relations responsibilities.

For both of them, but particularly for John, it was a return to a cherished past. Fergy has had the smell of horses in his nostrils almost since he was born. Indeed, horse racing, perhaps more than hockey, has been the sustaining passion of his life.

John's dad, a Scottish immigrant, was an assistant trainer at Old Hastings Park, a Vancouver track, and John spent the summer of 1939, his first on the planet, in a bassinet at Willows Racetrack in Victoria, with his mom and dad. The Fergusons lived on Clark Drive in Hastings East, a rough (now derelict) section of downtown Vancouver, and long before he started school, John was making the daily streetcar ride with his dad either to Old Hastings Park or to Lansdowne Park, another racetrack. "Back then," he explains, "the tracks used to print what they called a 'green sheet' that carried all the past performances of the horses racing that day. I learned to read off that sheet. By the time I was five I knew practically every racehorse in Vancouver."

Although his dad died in 1949, John's affection for the horses never wavered. Even as an elementary-school student he would scoot promptly to the track after school, beg a program from someone who was leaving early, and be in the grandstand by post time for the third race. "Then I started working as an exercise boy," he says, "walking the horses in the morning, and hot-walking them after they'd run."

It was in the horse barns and on the turf of Old Hastings Park that Fergy gained his earliest appreciation of thoroughbred bloodlines and physical attributes and of the subtle equation that connects those factors to performance on the track – an appreciation that he has refined and expanded throughout his adult life. As a senior elementary-school student, he also picked up a hockey stick for the first time. "I could barely skate," he recalls, "but because I'd played a lot of soccer and lacrosse, I understood the patterns of the game, and, at thirteen, I made my first hockey team, the Lamoreux Concessions. I even scored a goal in my first game."

"One day in I guess the summer of 1952," says Joan, "I was on my way to figure-skating practice at the Vancouver Forum at eight o'clock in the morning. I was at the streetcar stop, and along came John – my friend Arlene McFarlane introduced us. I've always said John was on his way home from hot-walking horses. He says he was coming from rink-ratting at the Forum."

Throughout their early teens, the two saw one another regularly at social and sporting events. By 1953, they were attending rival high schools, John playing football, Joan performing on her school's cheerleading team. "We used to play Joan's school," smiles John. "It was the only time in my life that I ever fraternized with the enemy after a game."

By this time, Joan was training year-round as a figure skater, with hopes of becoming a professional. When the opportunity presented itself, in 1955, she tried out for the Ice Follies, made the grade, and at the age of sixteen was off to Los Angeles to learn her routines. Her mother, who had encouraged her skating, died in an accident without ever seeing her perform.

"Professional skating wasn't nearly as glamorous as you might think," says Joan. "It could be exciting, mind you, but there were endless hours of practice and touring, and as teenage girls it always seemed we were fighting off strange men."

After a year of it, she left the Follies and returned to Vancouver, where she and John were married in 1958.

The two spent their first year of marriage in a drafty apartment in Melville, Saskatchewan, where John was finishing his junior career, then spent a year in Fort Wayne, Indiana, John's first stop as a pro. In 1960, after a summer in Vancouver, they moved on to Cleveland, where, for three years, John refined his skills, and his increasingly frosty reputation, with the Cleveland Barons of the American Hockey League.

"When you're in the minors," says Joan, "you never completely lose the thought of making it to the NHL. But in those days, even very good players could spend their entire careers down there, and I don't *really* think we believed we'd ever get out. All we were doing was going day to day. We had the first of our children to raise, and John was doing what he wanted to do."

Joan describes their eventual move to Montreal as "sort of scary," in that the pressures and expectations, as well as the calibre of hockey, were suddenly "so much more intense."

But while the uniforms and calibre of hockey changed, John's obsession with horses remained constant. Whenever possible, wherever he happened to be, he would head almost instinctively to the track. "I'll never forget my first trip to Louisville with the Fort Wayne Komets," he says. "All my life I'd dreamed about going to Churchill Downs; I just couldn't wait to walk into the grandstand, go into the tunnel under the track and out onto the infield." Unfortunately, when John arrived at the renowned facility early in the morning, it was not yet open. "And I couldn't wait around," he says. "But just being there was a thrill."

On his next visit to Louisville, Fergy made another pilgrimage, this time to the famous Calumet Farms, where, during the late fifties, legendary horses such as Citation and Iron Liege were the farm's ranking studs. "I stood there for a long time watching the mares and foals," says John, "thinking about how much I'd eventually like to breed and race horses of my own."

In Montreal, Fergy soon became a regular at Blue Bonnet Raceway. But it was not until late in his years with the Canadiens that he and Joan found the capital to begin buying horses of their own – thoroughbreds and standard-breds at first, then gradually, exclusively, standardbred trotters and pacers.

Since then, they have *always* owned horses, as few as seven or eight, as many as forty-four during the mid-seventies in Montreal. Sometimes they have had owner-ship partners, sometimes not. "We always seem to own a hundred percent of the ones that don't make any money," laughs Joan, "and only a share of those that do." At the moment, they have ten horses, some owned outright, some co-owned, all stabled in Toronto. "We have a trainer and a groom, and I stop by as often as I can to talk to them, see how things are going," says John. "I don't get to the races very often, but I try to watch them by satellite."

An esteemed judge of pacers and trotters, John is per-petually on the lookout for promising yearlings and, to that end, makes annual spring treks to farms and sales in Kentucky and Pennsylvania, as well as regular visits to Canadian farms such as Armstrong Brothers in Brampton, Ontario. He keeps a microscopic eye on the intersections of established bloodlines and, in the barns and paddocks, is an obsessive observer of the minutest details of growth and balance, knees and hocks, all in the interest of gaining a split-second advantage somewhere down the line.

"We've put a lot of money into horses over the years," confides Joan. "My guess is that we haven't taken as much out as we've put in, but we've sure supported a mini-economy of blacksmiths, vets, trainers, grooms, track employees, feed companies, sales people, government people. At one time I was paying bills in nineteen direc-tions. The bad horses eat as much as the good ones. Of course, it's not that we didn't know it'd *be* that way. You have to be slightly mad to get into racing in the first place. And totally dedicated."

Fergy admits that, although the horses are supposed to

be financially self-sustaining, even profitable, he and Joan have often been obliged to cover the high costs of the breeding and racing operation with money earned in hockey. "We've had terrible years, and we've had wonderful years," he says.

And they have had terrible and wonderful days. Fergy compares the reversals of the horse-racing world with those of hockey. "There's nothing like going into the Meadowlands with the best horse, the favourite, in a major stake race, being 1 to 9 on the board, with John Campbell on your horse, and the horse going offstride before it gets out of the gate and not getting into the race. That happened to us last August with our filly Hardie Hanover, and it was a horrible low! Thank goodness there was a consolation race the next week, which she won."

Largely because of Hardie Hanover (Canada's top two-year-old filly pacer in 1993), the racing year as a whole has been what John calls "a remarkable success." The prized filly won both the 1994 Fan Hanover Cup in Toronto and the Cadillac Breeders' Stakes at Garden State Raceway outside Philadelphia. "She earned $600,000 in total," says John, "and when we broke up the business relationship with her co-owners in November, we ended up selling her for half a million dollars."

By his own estimate, John "pays attention" to his horses about a hundred days a year. He would spend more time than he does with them except that, in 1991, when his friend Tom Joy, who had brought him to Windsor in the first place, was about to sell the Windsor Raceway, he weighed his prospects for the future and accepted a job as director of player personnel with the Ottawa Senators. As an indication of his priorities, it is worth considering that during his years at the track he turned down three offers to manage established NHL clubs.

He started with the Senators six months before their

first draft of players and now spends as many as two hundred days a year on the road, scouting prospects, attending meetings, and supervising scouts in every corner of the hockey-playing world. A condition of his taking the job was that he be allowed to work from Amherstburg, where he is comfortably established and has drivable access to hundreds of college, junior, and minor-pro games in southern Ontario and the north-central U.S.A. "Besides," he says "We can see NHL hockey in Detroit."

His professional bible is a well-thumbed tome, published annually, which, as Fergy puts it, "lists every scheduled game in every upper-level league in every part of the world. I can go through it at the beginning of the year and co-ordinate my whole schedule: Here's a guy playing here that I wanta see, another guy the next night over here, another over there, and so on." Fergy watches up to half a dozen televised games a week, taping those he can't watch live, and professes to know at least something about every "upper-level amateur or pro" playing in North America or in Europe. He acknowledges with a grin that judging hockey players bears uncanny similarities to judging horses. "You're looking for strength, speed, balance, desire – one of the big differences is that, when I see a good horse I can often buy it. Good hockey players aren't for sale."

He makes as many as four trips to Europe a year, to scout tournaments and league play, and, by his own admission, derives as much pleasure from his side trips to the great tracks of Europe as from his hours in the arenas of Prague and Stockholm and Helsinki. "My ideal day," he enthuses, "is seeing the horses in the afternoon and a hockey game at night. And I guess you might throw in a good meal with a good bottle of wine. I love good wine; I go looking for it."

As befits a man of the track, Fergy also loves a good cigar, a hand-rolled Honduran cigar to be precise. He smoked his first cigar as a junior in Saskatchewan, and now smokes three or four a day, imported for him by a Detroit tobacco shop. "Because of the grandchildren, I'm not allowed to smoke indoors any more," he says solemnly (this explains the rain-swollen cigar butt by the curb in front of the condo).

"He can at least *read* about cigars indoors," says Joan, producing the latest issue of his subscription to *Cigar Connoisseur*, a perfect-bound glossy magazine with a slew of up-market advertisers and the panache of a journal of high fashion.

"He smokes continuously when he plays golf," says Joan. "I think that's why he likes playing so much."

More than ever these days, Joan is an integral part of Fergy's professional life. Today, in fact, she is somewhat weary, having accompanied him to a game the previous night, in Toledo, Ohio – a trip on which she did most of the driving so as to allow John to concentrate on paperwork and scouting reports. "If I'm along, it gives him a chance to doze off," she smiles. "He gets up early, and he likes a twenty-minute snooze during the day, so he can keep functioning."

Tonight, she will be with him at a game in Sarnia and tomorrow night at the arena in Windsor. And the next night in Chatham or London or Saginaw. In early 1994, she accompanied him to the Olympics in Lillehammer, Norway. "He thinks if he doesn't take me I'll have nothing to do," she whispers, so as not to be overheard by Fergy, who is assessing scouting reports in the next room. "I have lots to do. But I don't like to see him go off on his own. Last week, he came though a terrible snowstorm on the way back from Barrie in the middle of the night."

While his name is proposed frequently as a potential general manager for one NHL team or another, John has no immediate desire to be anything other than what he is. At least for now. "I've always been one for challenges," he says, "and I guess if the right one came along I might still be tempted to consider it." Even as he speaks, he is interrupted by a phone call from Sweden, from an official of the International Hockey League, who wonders if he'd be interested in investing in one of the league's proposed European entries, and perhaps playing a role in its development.

"It sounds intriguing," he says on hanging up the phone. "But who needs the stress? I had fifteen years of it in New York and Winnipeg. I'm not saying there's not *some* stress in what I do now, but it's nothing compared to being responsible for a whole franchise. Besides, Joan's the most important part of my decisions now. If I got back in the fast lane, it'd be hard on her, and I wouldn't get to see my children and grandchildren. They're very important to me."

The "children," all four of whom are married, range in age from late twenties to mid-thirties. "The three girls all married guys named Paul," says Fergy. "Our oldest daughter, Chris, and her husband are in Vancouver; they have three children – Chris is into horses like Joan and me. Kathy and her husband and son are in Louisville (I have two reasons to go to Kentucky now). Our son, John, and his wife are in Boston, where John's in law school at Suffolk University. And Joanne, our youngest, works at Scotia–McLeod in Toronto and does choreography. She choreographed the Toronto production of *Oliver Twist*. It was just great."

Despite their current career stability and the high esteem in which John is held at both the track and the rink, Joan and John have seen enough of the vicissitudes of hockey and horse racing to know that nothing about the future can be taken for granted. "Sometimes I can't believe we've come through the *past* as well as we have," says Joan. "It took me years to realize that I'd married a riverboat gambler. We certainly didn't have much financial security for a long time. I guess, in some ways, we still don't. Mind you, there are always things and people to complain about if you want to look for them. I think our salvation has been that we've always understood how lucky we've been. It's hard to believe at times that the young people in hockey can be so callous about their good fortune. Of course, *our* attitude was influenced by growing up while the war was on; it made us grateful for what we had. Anybody who's enjoyed their interests as much as we have, and been able to make a living at them, *has* to be grateful!"

"It's been an adventure," says Fergy. "And we're still having fun at it. I know I'm not ready to retire. My contract with Ottawa's good till '97. Maybe after that I'll wind it down a bit.

"Then again," he shrugs, "maybe I won't."

# IN THE WILDS OF NEW JERSEY

BY THE TIME REG LEACH headed west to play for the Montana Magic, a Central Hockey League franchise in Billings, Montana, in the autumn of 1983, his playing career had lapsed into a stifling and irreversible aimlessness. He was thirty-two years old, not exactly a fossil, but of an age when any pro hockey player who has suffered heavy injuries or has not taken particularly good care of himself is likely to be in decline.

Reg's hockey career had been almost miraculously free of injuries; he had last been laid up at the age of sixteen, with a separated shoulder. But to say that he had not taken care of himself is a truth of such gasping proportions that it can barely be addressed without a significant stretch of the imagination. He had been binge drinking since the age of twelve, for example, and acknowledges having been hungover for at least half of his nine hundred big-league games. "On average, I probably played at about seventy-five per cent of my capacity," he says. "Sometimes less, sometimes more."

One is left to guess what a player of Reg's talent might have accomplished had he not consumed up to a dozen bottles of beer the night before virtually every game he played as a pro.

Even amidst his alcoholic blackouts and sweats, he scored more than four hundred NHL goals and had his name inscribed on the Stanley Cup in 1975. The following year, he led the league in goal-scoring, was an all-star right winger, and played for his country in the Canada Cup tournament. He won the Conn Smythe Trophy as the outstanding performer of the 1976 playoffs. The postseason achievements for which he was honoured that year included a remarkable nineteen goals (in sixteen games) and a record five-goal game on May 6 against the Boston Bruins. The *Philadelphia Inquirer* used the words "stunning," "pulsating," and "electrifying" to describe the five-goal performance. *The Hockey News* wrote, "Philadelphia hockey fans were treated to the greatest single-game scoring exhibition put on by a National Hockey Leaguer in the last 33 years as Reg Leach singlehandedly blasted the Boston Bruins out of the Stanley Cup playdowns."

Readers of the aforementioned rave could hardly have been aware of the unintended irony of the writer's choice of verbs. For the Boston Bruins were by no means the only "blasted" party at the Philadelphia Spectrum that day. The star of the show, Reggie himself, had consumed so much alcohol the previous night that, at 10 o'clock the morning of the game, as the team gathered to prepare for its 1 p.m. faceoff (the Sunday game was to be shown on national television), he was lying in the basement of his suburban home in a state of alcoholic unconsciousness.

When his whereabouts were discovered a couple of Flyer teammates were dispatched to the Leach residence where they coaxed their felled comrade through a cold shower and poured a quart or more of galvanizing coffee down his throat. Within half an hour, he was alert enough to realize that his best chance of making it through the afternoon was, as he puts it, "to have a drink or two."

With a couple of fresh Budweisers awash in his system, he and his teammates headed for the Spectrum. There, however, Fred Shero, the team's coach – himself a drinker of considerable reputation – pronounced his leading scorer unfit to play. "I was still stone drunk!" exclaims Reg. "Except by this time I was starting to feel really loose, actually pretty good, and I said to Clarky [team captain Bobby Clarke], 'I think I can go,' and he went to Freddie, and Freddie said, 'Suit him up, then.' So I got my stuff on, and the last thing I remember telling Clarky before the game was, 'Just get me the puck. I'll put it in.'"

And that is what Clarke did. And what Reg did. And by the end of the afternoon the Bruins were gone from the playoffs, and the Riverton Rifle was co-holder of a historic record that has yet to be broken.

The lessons of that long-ago afternoon are ambiguous at best. As Reg himself notes, "Some of the guys probably weren't all that happy about my showing up plastered for a playoff game. But there wasn't much they could say when I went out and scored five goals." In fact, a number of them helped Reg celebrate the occasion by accompanying him to a favourite team oasis after the game and continuing the party they had begun the night before.

In all, Reg's party lasted twenty-two years – from the time he was twelve to the time he was thirty-four. It swallowed up some twenty thousand bottles of beer and took in towns as small as Riverton and Flin Flon, Manitoba, and just about every notable city in North America. "In the end, there weren't many places where I didn't know the bars," says Reg.

But by the time he got to Billings, Montana, the lessons of his profligacy were far more apparent than they had been on that heroic afternoon in Philadelphia. His agent, Frank

Millen, had been busy all summer trying to get him a last-ditch gig in the NHL. Reg had spent the previous year as a member of the Detroit Red Wings, with whom he had signed a one-season contract worth $145,000. Under the severe eye of coach Nick Polano, he had tried to curtail his drinking. But he had argued with Polano over other matters, had fallen out of favour, and now no other NHL team was willing to take a chance on him. "I knew the booze would eventually catch up with me," he says. "What surprises me, looking back, is that I lasted as long as I did."

Whatever the condition of Reg's baggage, the owners and coaches of the Montana Magic were more than happy to have him on their team. For one thing, they were a new franchise in need of a marquee player. For another, the team was half-owned by an oil-rich Aboriginal band from Hobema, Alberta – the same band fictionalized and made famous by Canadian writer W.P. Kinsella. "They were determined to have some Native blood in their line-up," says Reg, whose mother is Ojibwa and whose late father was Métis.

While, to date, he had shown little interest or pride in his Native roots, he was happy now to accept the cultural accountability of his new role (he was happy just to have a job). But he was no more inclined to devote the best of his energies to hockey than he had ever been. He continued to party with Dionysian abandon, drinking nightly, deeply, and, by this time, at significant risk to his health. Whereas the previous year he had taken his family with him to Detroit, he was now missing the moderating presence of his wife, his thirteen-year-old son and eight-year-old daughter, whom he had left at home in the Philadelphia suburb of Cherry Hill, New Jersey. "It was the beginning of the end of my marriage," he allows. But almost before he can complete the thought, he is laughing. "What are the first two things to go on a hockey player?" he grins, pausing for effect before answering, "His legs and his wife! Which is pretty much the way it happened with me."

On the ice, the man who seven years earlier had scored sixty-one goals during a single NHL season had to content himself with a season total of twenty-one, against players who, five years earlier, would not have been deemed worthy to appear on the same ice as the one-time scoring champ.

"To make matters worse," says Reg, "the band council in Hobema stiffed me on my contract." When he had arrived in Billings in the autumn, a group he calls "the big shots of the tribe" had travelled to Montana and had worked out an agreement with him whereby his salary of approximately $90,000 would be split in two, half to be paid by team management in instalments throughout the year, half to be paid directly by the tribe at the end of the season. The band council, he was told, would draw up a contract to cover its part of the bargain. "But they never did!" says Reg. And in the spring of 1984, when he attempted to collect his money, the council informed him that because there was no signed contract he should not expect to be paid. "I gave them a few phone calls at the time," he says, "and they promised to have another look at the matter, but they never called back, and I never went after them legally. I couldn't really prove anything. I trusted them and they screwed me. They still owe me $45,000."

What made the shafting doubly painful for Reg was that, over the years, he had made a number of visits to Hobema, at the band's request, to speak to students, attend banquets, and endorse a variety of Native causes. "I haven't been back since," he says, "and of course they don't call, although, once in a while, I still see the boss, Larry Mine, at Native functions. When we end up in the same room he just hides, I guess out of guilt."

In the end, the lessons of Billings and Hobema were no

less ambiguous than those of the five-goal binge in 1976. Even today, eleven years later, the Billings fiasco poses an unsolvable moral conundrum for Reg, who would still be happy to see his money, or even a portion of it, but prefers to tiptoe around the issue so as not to be seen to raise his hand against the Native community, or to cast even the slightest shadow over it. "These days, I do a fair bit of promotion for Native causes and sports," he says. "The last thing I want is to create a situation that reflects badly on Natives, which is exactly what would happen if I took the matter to court. Everybody'd say, 'Oh, look, these Indians are robbing their own people.' I have no argument with the band out there; it's just a few guys who for some reason decided not to keep their word."

Within days of the end of the hockey season that year, Reg returned to Cherry Hill, where his drinking continued unabated. "I guess in a sense it got worse, because I started drinking liquor," he says, "I'd always been strictly a beer drinker. On the hard stuff, I could get hammered in half an hour instead of an hour and a half." He had saved little or no money from his hockey days and in the monthly grope to make a living, he turned to selling cars. "That lasted two months," he says. "I couldn't stand being inside all the time, and I just hated all the lying you were expected to do to the customers." He took courses to become an insurance salesman like his fellow Flyers Orest Kindrachuk and Rick MacLeish. But he was no happier selling term and investment policies than he'd been selling automotive fantasies. And no better at it either. "The only thing that made insurance preferable to cars," he says solemnly, "was that it was easier to drink on the job. After a few months I was doing more partying than selling. I'd go for days without even making an appointment."

By this time, Reg had begun to experience alcoholic blackouts, the result of blown synapses and brain cells that, in their journey to the bottom of the bottle, carried with them all recollection of hours of bar-hopping and socializing.

By mid-1985, he had taken a bachelor apartment in Cherry Hill, and he and his wife of sixteen years had initiated divorce proceedings. "I gave up everything I had," he says with no apparent bitterness. "The house in Cherry Hill, our cottage up in Canada, whatever was worth anything." The liquidation included the sale of a summer ice-cream parlour that the Leaches had opened in Arnes, Manitoba, near the family summer cottage just a few miles from Reg's home town of Riverton. "The only thing I kept," Reg says, "was my NHL pension, which kicks in next year when I turn forty-five. . . . At the time all I wanted was to get out of the marriage and get on with my life."

What Reg did next would not jibe with most people's ideas about getting on with life. "I decided to take a year off and do nothing," he says. "As long as I was drinking, there didn't seem to be much I could do anyway."

At this point, his self-destructive slide might have seemed headed toward flat-out disaster, if not tragedy. His story, however, is not one of ruin but of redemption. And of remarkable self-renewal. As he has demonstrated throughout his forty-five years on the planet, he has extraordinary physical and psychological powers when he commits himself to using them (the five-goal game in Philadelphia is, in itself, a microcosmic paradigm of will over wobble). Nevertheless, in 1985, few would have bet on his chances for long-term salvation. "I'd always just thought of myself as a guy who did a lot of partying," he says, "but I can see now that I had a serious problem. I wasn't well at all."

By the time I met Reg in the summer of 1994, he was in robust health, and the signs of it were as obvious as the signs of his sickness had been in 1985. During the years since his recovery from alcoholism he had built a successful business that now grosses nearly half a million dollars (U.S.) a year; had gained a measure of domestic contentment that he had not known in years; and had become a respected spokesman against drugs and alcohol in the Native community. "Most guys play sober and drink after they retire," he told me at the time. "I played drunk and sobered up afterwards."

That redemptive sobering began not with the sort of moral or mystical revelation one might expect would trigger such a dramatic turnaround but with a fierce bout of vomiting on a long weekend in August during the summer of 1985. "I'd been drinking pretty heavily the night before," he explains, "and for the first time in my life, I woke up sick – *really* sick. So I went to see a doctor friend of mine. He sat me down, gave me a shot, and said: 'Reg, you're going to have to quit drinking. If you don't you're going to be in very deep trouble. Your liver's still okay, but it won't be for long; you're right on the edge.' This was a Sunday. On Tuesday, I checked into the rehab centre in Marysville, New Jersey."

During the next thirty-two days, Reg was obliged to confront aspects of his inner and outer life that, by his own admission, he had never before considered. "I got a whole new view of my past, from childhood right through to the present," he says. "And a lot of what I saw I didn't like."

More importantly, he got a new view of his (alcohol-free) future. He says, "I still wasn't sure what I wanted to do with my life, but I've always known that if I put my mind to something, give it all my energy and focus, I'm going to be able to do it. The trick was to find something I'd like."

To understand what Reggie did, and why, it helps to know that during his teenage summers in Riverton, and during summers early in his NHL career, he had been an all-but-constant presence at the Northernaire Golf Club near the tiny settlement of Arnes, Manitoba, a few miles south of Riverton (his daughter, Brandie, who attends college in New Jersey, now works summers in the Northernaire clubhouse). The place is owned by the Luprypa family, a Riverton clan that had befriended Reg as a youngster and given him part-time work in their general store. By his mid-teens, Reg had become a skilled golfer, as well as something of an expert at seeding and cutting grass, laying sod, tending shrubs and trees – in effect, doing whatever landscaping was required on the breezy, rural links.

During the mid-seventies, he applied the skills he had developed at Arnes to beautifying the large suburban lot that surrounded his home in Cherry Hill. "One day, after I'd come out of rehab," he recalls, "I was talking to a former neighbour, who said, 'Why don't you go into landscaping, Reg? You're good at it. Look what you did at the house!'"

Reg glimpsed a future in the advice, and by the following spring had founded a bare-bones company named Reggie Leach's Sports Lawn Service. Head office was Reg's bachelor apartment in Cherry Hill, and by the time he had canvassed his ex-neighbours and sporting associates, he had corralled fifteen clients, all of whom he knew personally.

As the weather warmed up he started making house calls. Fifteen dollars bought a client a weekly mow and snip. A few dollars more bought anything from gardening to patio work to tree-pruning. At the time, the company assets totalled two Lawnboys, a Weed Whacker, and a tiny Mitsubishi truck that Reg had obtained in a trade for his car. Asked recently whether it was humbling to cut grass for people who had once cheered his exploits as a sports hero, Reg responded without hesitation that it "wasn't nearly as humbling as being an out-of-work alcoholic."

By the following spring he had ninety customers, the price of a visit had risen somewhat, and his weekly gross often totalled more than two thousand dollars. "The problem with having so many clients," he says, "was that I was racing around all the time and finding it harder and harder to collect my money. I didn't have a clue who a lot of the people were – they were friends of friends, and when I'd go to the door and tell them they owed, say, eighty bucks, they wouldn't wanta pay."

On a fateful day in 1988, Reg was introduced to a pair of natty strangers at a Philadelphia golf tournament. As it turned out, they were senior executives with Interstate Realty Management, a multimillion-dollar corporation that controls hundreds of low-cost housing projects all over the eastern U.S. "Because these properties are full of people on welfare," says Reg, "the government pays Interstate hundreds of thousands of dollars a year to keep the grounds around them landscaped and tidy." Interstate, in turn, spends the money to hire independent landscapers who do the grass-cutting and tend to the shrubbery and fences. "So these fellas asked me if I'd like to do some work for them," says Reg, whose response was so unequivocal that the pair immediately assigned him landscaping duties on the grounds around their main office and at the enormous Salisbury housing project in the nearby city of Camden, New Jersey.

"By the next year, I had five Interstate properties," says Reg. "Then nine, then eighteen, now twenty-six." Many of the properties are multi-unit tenements that cover a city block or more, and include dozens of acres of lawn. They range in location from southwest New Jersey and Philadelphia to as far north as the outskirts of New York City. To take care of them, Reg employs a foreman and ten crew members. He owns six trucks with trailers, five or six sit-down mowers, earth-moving equipment and truckloads of smaller implements. "If I were to put all my mowers side by side," he says, "I could cut a swath forty feet wide across a field."

But that day on the golf course, he could not have known the dimensions of the job he was about to take on – that it would eventually place him, for instance, in some of the most dangerous and degenerate ghettos in North America, places where, by his own estimation, "your life isn't worth much at the best of times and isn't worth any-thing after dark." (One day in the slums of central Philly, he had to leap for cover to avoid being picked off in the cross-fire of a gun fight.)

On the second day of my visit with the former Flyers star, he took me to visit the Salisbury housing project on the south side of Camden. It was an experience for which nothing I had seen to that point in my life could possibly have prepared me . . . except perhaps the previous evening's conversation, a dinner-hour primer on the staggering abuses and injustices of the ghetto, and on the poverty, defiance, and dissipation (and the seemingly irrepressible good humour) of Reg's own remarkable boyhood and youth.

Today, Reg lives with his fiancée, Debbie Copper, and her thirteen-year-old son, Brandon, in a antique shiplap house on a rural sideroad in the township of Sewell, New Jersey, some twenty miles southwest of Philadelphia. For anyone who does not know the area, it is not an easy place to find. When my wife, Betty, and I travelled to Sewell to meet Debbie and Reg in August 1994, I was so hopelessly con-fused in my attempts to locate their home I was forced to call from a house less than a mile away and have them come and fetch us. It was explained to me later that even people who have spent their lives in central New Jersey suffer flop-sweats at having to find their way through the insufferable tangle of poorly marked highways, sideroads, and freeways that dissect the countryside into a zillion inaccessible fragments – and on which the traffic seems always to be moving about thirty miles an hour above the (rarely) posted speed limit. The area's countless towns and villages, once a day's ride by stagecoach from Philadelphia and Camden, are now bedroom communities for the affluent bondservants of the Philadelphia skyscrapers. By and large, these are places that once had boundaries and identities, but they have spread during the past half-century to form an amorphous semi-rural sub-city, a vast municipal protozoan, that gloms onto the east bank of the Delaware River, providing both an escape dream and an alter ego for the city of Philadelphia. "Most of the people who live in these places can find their way comfortably onto the nearest freeway and into Philly, or out to Atlantic City," I was told by a gregarious Amoco attendant near Glassboro, "but ask them to get from Jefferson to Glassboro or Sewell to Runnymede, and they'll look at you like, don't be ridiculous, I'm not an explorer." A map of the area, photocopied for me by Reg, reminded me of the winter windows of my boyhood, covered in an infinite network of delicate frost tracings. Except that frost tracings generally show signs of a pattern. The roads in New Jersey show none.

But if the cartography is uncertain, the hospitality at Debbie and Reg's is not. Debbie, who has known Reg for four years but who moved to Sewell from northern Delaware just two years ago, is chatty, outgoing, and has a happy capability for making her guests feel instantly comfortable and relaxed. She has a motherly smile, an easy laugh, and a striking pile of long blond hair. Part of her considerable facial charm resides in the slight leftward deviation that the bridge of her nose takes as it descends in an otherwise flawless line from her brow to her upper lip.

Reg is equally friendly but, in the tradition of Ojibwa society, is somewhat less forthright in extending himself conversationally. He speaks when he has something to say. And yet there is nothing awkward about the silences that occasionally occur in his presence, sitting, say, in a restaurant or car, or even in his own living room. He is such a gentle and unassuming man, so intuitive and good-humoured in his communication with the world, that when the silences occur they seem less like holes that need filling than like breathing spaces, natural punctuation, in a dialogue that is unfolding at some rhythmically predetermined pace and will recommence when the time is right.

Reg is part of the last generation of helmetless hockey players, but, considering that he has suffered countless nicks and cuts between the chin and hairline, his face is remarkably free of visible scars. He has hair the colour of ravens' feathers and warm dark eyes, the lids and corners of which crinkle softly when he smiles. At first glance, he does not seem to be a particularly big man. Compared to most hockey players, he is decidedly narrow through the hips and thighs; and his hands are lean and graceful. But he has the strength of a blacksmith in his forearms, shoulders, and rather sturdy torso. His weight these days is about ten pounds above his playing weight of 205.

Mention Reggie around anyone who knows him and they'll tell you pretty much the same thing: that he's one of the most decent, genuine, and generous men on the planet. "He'd give you his last dollar if you needed it," says Debbie. "He's always giving away money and buying things for everybody. Beautiful gifts. Last Christmas, he bought me a Ford Explorer, but he bought it a little early, so that when Christmas came, he figured I'd better have some Christmas presents, so he went out and bought more. I said, 'Reg, please!' He'll just give, give, give. I think some of it goes back to his boyhood, when they had so little.

There were certainly times when there wasn't much food in the house."

The difficulty with Reg's generosity, as Debbie sees it, is that people are inclined to take advantage of him. "He's *such* a soft touch," she says. "Guys he hasn't seen for twenty years will phone up out of the blue and ask if he can lend them five thousand dollars. They think that because he was a pro hockey player he's some kind of financial institution. He always tries to help out, and when he does, of course, so many of the people are right back asking for more." Debbie pauses, smiles selfconsciously, and says, "I've kinda tried to protect him from some of that. I mean, Reg is famous for giving it all away, and now he's at an age where he has to think about his own future. You can't just keep making unrepayable loans."

Debbie acknowledges that it's a little more difficult to stand in the way of those who come asking for favours rather than money. "They say, 'Oh, Reg, you're in the land-scaping business, can you design some little thing for my backyard?' And of course they expect it for nothing. Reg'll get a shipment of shrubs or chrysanthemums, any number of things for the job sites, and people will come over and say, 'Do you mind if I just take this little bush or these flowers for my mom; it's her birthday?' And Reg'll say, 'Sure, go ahead, take what you need.' It doesn't seem to occur to them that he's paid a lot of money for these things and needs them himself. I mean, he likes to help people out, and that's great. It's just when people want so much that it's hard."

Reg and Debbie first crossed paths in 1990, in Wilmington, Delaware, at a Flyers' alumni charity game. Debbie had gone to the game with a girlfriend because her girlfriend's boss, the one-time NHL goaltender Roger Crozier, was playing that night for the Flyers' alumni. "They had a buffet after the game," says Reg. "Funny thing is, I usually don't go to the meals after these games because of the socializing. I try to avoid places where people are drinking. But I was so hungry that night, I decided to swing by the hotel for a bite."

Debbie had not intended to be at the post-game party, either. "But then we got invited," she says, "and I happened to get seated at a table beside Reg. The room was pretty loud, and Reg was so sweet and quiet, I thought, this guy must really be from Canada. It was funny, because I'd always had the impression that hockey players were guys with no teeth and no brains, and here was this guy being so sensitive and nice. We didn't really say all that much, but during the months after that I kept running into a fella who works for Reg, and I'd say, 'Tell Reg that Debbie from Delaware says hi.' Then my girlfriend and I got invited to attend another alumni game in Philly. Reg played, and we saw one another afterwards, and one thing led to another, and we started going out."

Debbie, a former legal secretary, now handles the Sports Lawn accounting and helps Reg in whatever ways she can with the clerical aspects of the business. The two plan to marry during the autumn of 1995. In the meantime, they have decorated the communal house in Sewell in a way that pretty much represents their respective tastes in furnishings and bric-a-brac. The ground floor combines Debbie's preferences for bucolic antiques and contemporary rustic charm with Reg's giant television and a varied display of remembrances from his hockey career. A tiny antique highchair used by Debbie's grandmother stands in the dining room among other piney throwbacks to the beginnings of the century. A trophy case at the far end of the living room is chock-a-block with family photos, hockey medals, and commemorative silverware, while the walls are crowded with Reg's extensive collection of "limited edition" framed prints of Emmett Kelly, the original sad-faced clown.

The windowless cellar below is by no means a typical office (it is by no means a typical cellar) but it is Reg's domain, the low-level wheelhouse from which he pilots the ever-expanding affairs of Sports Lawn Service. Its walls are mortar and stone, and its appurtenances include a photocopier, a fax machine, and an elaborate computer that has never worked. At the leisure end of the office, a comfortably battered chesterfield faces an equally world-weary television. It is from this rather eccentric sub-station that Reg co-ordinates the ordering of shrubs, flowers, fencing, mulch, and sod; figures costs, labour, square footage, invoicing and equipment needs; sets staff schedules and deployment routes – everything required to contain the human and botanical forces that threaten constantly to make chaos of his twenty-six job sites. "What surprises people," he says, "is that I never write anything down; I keep it all in my head – thirty, forty, fifty things that I have to remember to do on a given day."

The house is surrounded by old trees, newish gardens, and, out back, perhaps an acre of rolled gravel that makes a parking lot both for employees and for company trucks and machinery.

On our first evening in Sewell we drove with Debbie and Reg through monsoon rains to a first-rate rural roadhouse called The Library. Rows of old books lined the walls of its various nooks and ramifications, and its menu included beef filets that could be ordered custom-cut off the loin to any size the customer might want. In the habit of the pro hockey player whose years in the game were fuelled by outlandish infusions of protein, Reg began his meal with an appetizer of mussels and followed with a strenuous filet mignon that in mass equalled five stacked hockey pucks and, in leaner times, might well have been called upon to feed the entire table. As he ate, he told us first about the ghetto into which he planned to take me the following day . . . and then about his boyhood. There is about Reg's early years a kind of woolly implausibility, a truth stranger than fiction, that suggests the wild plotting and texture of a John Irving novel: sometimes funny, sometimes outrageous, sometimes tragic. Sometimes triumphal. As he recounts the details of those years, it quickly becomes clear that he remembers every setting and circumstance, apparently every soul, that made him what he is today.

Reg was born in 1950 in Riverton, Manitoba, a town of some six hundred people on the low-lying borderland between the prairies to the south and the boreal forests of northern Manitoba. If you stood atop the town's lone grain elevator and looked east across a couple of kilometres of marshland and willow, you'd see Lake Winnipeg, a shallow body of water roughly the size of Lake Ontario. To the west you'd see the thin-soiled hardscrabble of the Manitoba Interlake ("You don't so much farm the Interlake as play it as it lays," Winnipeg writer Ted Allan once wrote.) The town is a low-built flat-lying place, in which the wind – off the lake or off the prairie – almost never stops blowing. Its gravel streets are dotted with smallish frame houses surrounded by large gardens in summer and even larger snowbanks in winter. A ways south of town, on Highway 9, stands a conspicuous plywood sign bearing a freshly painted likeness of a black-haired young man in the sweater of the Philadelphia Flyers. Accompanying the image are the words "Riverton. Where the Rifle scored his first 500. Reggie Leach."

By the time Reg was born, his father, a hard-drinking itinerant, had left Riverton for work in the northern mines. His mother, barely more than a child herself, departed for Edmonton shortly after his birth, leaving Reg with his paternal grandparents, who adopted and raised him with twelve children of their own in a wood-heated house on William Avenue. Reg's grandfather was physically disabled and was incapable of holding a job, although Reg no longer recalls the nature of his disability. Throughout Reg's childhood, the family lumped along on welfare payments, and on whatever bits of income his grandmother could generate. He says, "I remember her bringing in the town's minor-hockey sweaters and repairing them by hand and washing them up."

Reg maintains gamely that he was largely unaware of the poverty and that it did not particularly affect him. "I guess I just thought it was normal for a whole bunch of people to be crowded into one house, drinking in the afternoon," he says. Being the youngest, he was, for the first fifteen years of his life, the last stop in an endless cascade of hand-me-down clothes. At times, his second- or third-hand shoes pinched his feet so badly that, even today, he occasionally suffers intense cramping in his toes.

"Things weren't all bad," says Reg. "We had good times, too. It's just that there was so much to deal with and overcome . . . One of my stronger memories of childhood was when my older brother wrapped a car around a tree – killed himself." A second brother, an alcoholic, froze to death, drunk, in a Riverton snowbank, and a sister died of asphyxiation in the front seat of a car. "Another sister," says Reg, "died in a mental hospital in Portage la Prairie."

By his own assessment, Reg was "no good at all" in school. "By the time I got to grade eight," he says, "it was either high school or hockey, and I chose hockey." It was a choice that must have been applauded by the staff of the local high school. For Reg's years at elementary school had been distinguished by mischief-making of a sort that outflanked even the thorniest peccadillos of Bart Simpson and the Little Rascals. "In grade four or five," he says, "my two best buddies and I had a contest to see who could get the strap the most times, and I won; I got it fifty-six times. I used to pull my hand out just as the strap was coming down, and the principal would hit himself."

"I remember one time," says Reg, "a buddy and I got shut in the cloakroom for acting up. By the time they let us out at noon hour, we'd eaten every lunch in there – fifteen or twenty of them."

For two weeks every summer, Reg attended catechism school, in preparation for service as an altar boy at the local Catholic church. However, he admits to having spent most of his time kneeling outside the church door "as a punishment for goofing around."

It seems extraordinary in retrospect that, until Reg was nearly eleven years old, no one thought to harness his energy, or at least diffuse it, by putting a pair of skates on him and introducing him to the sport of hockey, which was played by virtually every male kid in Riverton. But it was not until the autumn of 1960 that he was given a pair of battered blades and his first hockey stick. Immediately, the game became not just a focus for the rampant energy that was threatening to consume him but a welcome respite from the poverty at home and from his continuing failures at school. He took to it with such passion that by the spring of 1961 he was the most accomplished young player in Riverton, if not in central Manitoba. "Every chance I got," he says, "I'd sneak into the arena and skate – with whoever happened to be on the ice. When I couldn't get in, I'd skate outdoors, for hours a day: on ponds, on the river, anywhere I could find ice. I even built a rink behind the house. It wasn't big enough to skate on, but I could use it to shoot pucks against the little shack my mom kept out there. Shoot, shoot, shoot, every spare minute, morning, noon, and night. After a few months, I'd knocked all the siding apart."

To maximize his ice time at the arena, Reg joined Riverton's predominantly female figure-skating club, which monopolized the ice on Wednesday evenings and Saturday mornings. He stayed with the club for four years – "I had the little picks and all," he says – and credits the experience with giving him the balance and speed that would eventually distinguish his skating in the NHL.

In warmer weather, the boys of Riverton played street hockey. "We'd divide the town into four segments," says Reg. "Each had its team. We'd have a schedule, playoffs, fights, everything."

Shortly after his introduction to hockey, Reg was introduced to what quickly became the other great influence on his young life: alcohol. "I guess I kinda blame my [adoptive] parents," he says. "I wouldn't say they gave me my first drink – they weren't really drinkers – but they were aware of my drinking, and, by the time I was twelve or thirteen, they'd always allow me to have a beer or two, homemade wine, whatever my older brothers and sisters were drinking. I mean, it was my fault, too, but I was a kid; I didn't know any better. I thought it was normal for kids to drink at home. I see now that if my parents had given me a little advice instead of just watching me drink, things would probably have been a lot different for me. When I go to speak to Native groups I always stress the role of the parents in helping the kids along." Reg recalls occasions on which he and his best friends pooled their winnings from skating races at the local winter carnival and gave the cash to "a local drunk" who would in turn buy the youngsters twelve-packs of beer.

Booze or not, Reg was sufficiently skilled at hockey by the age of thirteen that he was able to play regularly for the Riverton senior men's team, in a league that was about as close as sport can get to legalized criminality. "Oh, it was rough," laughs Reg, who was perhaps spared the worst of that roughness because of his great manoeuvrability and speed. "I weighed 185 pounds at that point," he says. "But I didn't have the strength of the men, so I had to be sharp – mind you, I had to be tough, too, or I couldn't have played at that level."

Along with his introduction to high-level hockey came a grisly introduction to the realities of racial discrimination. "I'd been exposed to it in low-key ways pretty much since I was a kid," he says, "but when I'd get on a hockey rink, where there was something at stake, it seemed to get a lot worse." In senior hockey, and then Junior A, Reg grew accustomed, and eventually inured, to taunts such as "dirty Indian," "smelly Indian," and "drunken Indian."

"As much as possible I tried not to let it get me down," he says. "At the time, I was one of the best players in western Canada, and I'd say to these guys who'd give me lip, 'Look, fella, I've got the puck; you've gotta chase me.' They'd call me something, and I'd just go down and score a goal. Take that, white man!"

In the winter of 1963, during a senior game in Winnipeg, Reg was spotted by a Detroit Red Wings talent scout, who the following autumn enticed him to attend the training camp of the club's junior affiliate in Weyburn, Saskatchewan. "I was the last guy cut from the team," says Reg, "so they sent me to their farm team in Lashburn, Saskatchewan." The fourteen-year-old prodigy endured two months of intense homesickness in the dreary farm community before pulling up stakes, boarding the bus, and returning to Riverton. "At that point," he says, "I wasn't sure I'd get another chance, or whether I even deserved one."

The most stabilizing influence on Reg during his years in Riverton's minor-hockey program had been his coach, the late Siggi Johnson, a descendent of one of thousands of Icelandic immigrants who settled the Manitoba Interlake during the nineteenth century. "My dad spent a lot of time with Reg at the arena," says Siggi's daughter Sigrid Palsson, who is now Riverton's librarian. "He really thought the world of Reg. He was very proud of him, and concerned, too, that perhaps he wasn't getting the direction he needed."

As a way of encouraging Reg during the weeks after his return from Lashburn, Siggi bought him his first pair of CCM Tack skates. "Till then," says Reg, "I'd never even had skates that fit me right. . . . Siggi told me that the town bought them for me, but I've always figured he bought them himself. I know he couldn't afford them, either."

At the same time, Siggi gave Reg the most important motivational lecture he has ever received. "Basically," says Reg, "he asked me whether I wanted to be a bum for the rest of my life, or whether I was prepared to get out of Riverton and do something with my talent – make a name for myself."

The following August, an opportunity arose to join another Detroit affiliate, the Flin Flon Bombers. With fifteen dollars in his pocket and Siggi Johnson's words smouldering in his skull, Reg boarded a bus that took him first to Winnipeg, then north to Flin Flon, Manitoba, where, after fifteen hours on the highways, he disembarked at the local bus depot at 6 a.m. "There was no one there to meet me," he says, "so I just sat in the bus-station restaurant and waited for the coach, who was supposed to be there." Eventually, the restaurant owners, Mary and Jack Reid, asked Reg if he needed assistance. "I told them who I was," he explains, "and even though they had nothing to do with hockey, they told me I could stay at their place for a few days, until I got settled."

By Reg's estimation, meeting the Reids was "one of the best things" that ever happened to him, and he ended up staying three years in their home. During the weeks that preceded training camp, he also struck up a friendship with the home-town hockey hero, a sixteen-year-old diabetic named Bobby Clarke, who would dramatically influence the rest of Reg's career. "We were close right away," says Reg. "We even bought our first car together, a '55 Chevy that cost us eighty-five dollars. We drove it all over the countryside." The pair particularly enjoyed trips across the provincial border to Creighton, Saskatchewan, where the drinking age was eighteen, instead of twenty-one, as it was in Manitoba.

Clarke was a classic alpha centreman, a team leader and an extraordinary playmaker, who set up nearly every one of Reg's several hundred goals as a Bomber and would eventually set up hundreds more as a Philadelphia Flyer.

Away from the rink, Reg worked mornings as a steward for the Hudson Bay Mining and Smelting Company, which operated the Bombers as a winter diversion for the town's residents, most of whom lived in Flin Flon because of the mine. "The tougher the hockey, the better they liked it," said Reg. "In fact, our guys were so rough, some teams wouldn't even make the trip up to Flin Flon to play us." Fist fights and brawls were commonplace in games involving the Bombers, and coach Pat Ginnell was practically sadistic when it came to keeping his team in pitbull trim. "One time we were on a three-week, twelve-game road trip," recalls Reg. "It was just go, go, go, on the bus, all over western Canada. We'd won eleven in a row and were ahead, 6–2, during the second period of the twelfth game in Saskatoon. But we were so exhausted from all the travel, we ended up losing it, 7–6. After the game, we bused straight through to Flin Flon, seven hours, got in at about 6 a.m. But before we got off the bus, Ginnell ordered us into the arena, made us put our wet equipment back on, then worked us like dogs for an hour. I'll tell ya, we never blew another lead like that."

Despite his continued drinking, Reg quickly became one of the league's best players and a top NHL prospect. During his second-last year with the Bombers, at the age of eighteen, he scored eighty-seven goals, and during each of his last two seasons won the Western Canada League scoring title.

But his transition into the National Hockey League was by no means a flawless progression. The Boston Bruins, who drafted him in 1970, had won the Stanley Cup the previous year and had an all but impenetrable line-up that included the likes of Phil Esposito, Bobby Orr, Ken Hodge, Derek Sanderson, and Johnny Bucyk. As a result, Reg played more than half of his initial pro season with a minor-league team in Oklahoma City, just blocks from the now-tragic site of the Alfred P. Murrah Federal Building. After polishing the bench for most of his second season in Boston, Reg was traded to the Oakland Seals, a club whose collective ambition was so desultory that he was unable to persuade himself even to get properly fit to play.

Meanwhile, in Philadelphia, Bobby Clarke, the captain of the Flyers, had been quietly agitating to have team management bring his one-time linemate to Philly.

When the deed was accomplished in a three-for-one trade on May 24, 1974, Clarke announced to the press that, "even in a bad year," Reggie Leach could be expected to score forty-five goals for the Flyers.

But by Christmas of his first season with the team, he had scored just five, and sceptics questioned the wisdom of the previous spring's trade. In the new year, however, Reg reeled off forty-one goals in some forty-five games, and ended the season as the team's leading goal-scorer. He added ten goals in the playoffs, helping the Flyers win their second straight Stanley Cup.

The following year, he led all NHL scorers, logging sixty-one goals during the regular season, nineteen more in the playoffs. The team's general manager, Keith Allen, dubbed his star winger "the Riverton Rifle," a fitting moniker for a man whose shot seemed indeed to possess the speed and accuracy of a bullet. "One of my advantages," explains Reg, "was that I could get the puck away extremely quickly. I didn't take a full wind-up, just about three-quarters of the way back. I'd get the puck from Clarky, take a couple of strides, and let 'er go. Always the slapper. I could shoot about 115 miles an hour – the same speed as Bobby Hull. In those days I could stand at the top of the slot and put nine out of ten pucks into an imaginary six-inch square in either of the top corners of the net." Every day after practice, he took two hundred slapshots and, at times, would intentionally ding as many as ten shots in a row off the goal post or crossbar, from thirty feet away. "When I'd shoot, it was as if my eyes were out on the blade of my stick," he says. "I'd make allowance for the differ-ence in perspective between the stick and my actual vision. In other words, if my eyes could see a two-inch opening, my stick could probably see four inches, and that was enough to put the puck through. I used to tell the guys to imagine their eyes out there on the blades of their sticks; a lot of them had never considered it."

Reg is neither long-legged nor notably strong-legged, but he was nonetheless a deceptively fast skater, a smooth skater, who, like a figure in an Alex Colville painting, seemed at times almost to float above the ice. "I imagine there were a few guys in the league who might have been a little faster than I was," he says. "But proba-bly nobody at that time who was faster and had quite my feel for the puck."

While the combined skill and brawn of the Flyers of the mid-seventies made them largely unbeatable on the ice (they won Stanley Cups in 1974 and '75), the team's col-lective proclivity for after-hours dissipation may well have stubbed their chances of becoming a longer-standing force at the top of the NHL. "Pretty much the whole team was into partying and drinking," confides Reg. "It just seemed to be part of what we did. There was beer on the bus, on the airplanes, in the dressing room. It was always available to us. On the road, we often seemed to have nothing to do *but* drink. Freddie Shero's rule was that if the players came into a bar where he was drinking, we could say hello and stay for one drink, then we had to go – that was his bar for the night. And if he wandered into a bar where the guys were drinking, same thing, one drink; that was *our* bar for the night. We did have a curfew of eleven o'clock, but the guys never really bothered with it. Once in a while, management would do a room check, but they'd always warn us in advance, and we'd all be in our rooms like choirboys at eleven. But we'd leave again around midnight, and we'd drink till three or so.

"If I'd had a particularly bad time the night before a game, I might say to [defenceman] Ed Van Impe, 'Could you watch my side a little closer tonight? I'm not feeling too good.' And, similarly, he'd say to me, 'Reg, I was out a little too late last night – could you make sure to come back?' We worked together that way."

At the time, Reg thought of his drinking – rationalized it – as a means of coping with the intense pressures of life in the game. "It wasn't till later," he says, "that I realized I was using the pressure as an excuse for doing what I was probably going to do anyway – or was addicted to doing. But there was never anyone around to give us any advice about that sort of thing. From time to time, some of the guys would encourage me to cut back, but they didn't have a clue about the nature of addiction, and it was pretty hard to convince me to rein it in when I could score sixty-one goals on the sauce."

Reg played nine seasons with the Flyers, making at

most $145,000 a year. He feels, in retrospect, that he was considerably underpaid, given what he accomplished. "Guys who weren't doing any more than I was were making as much as $250,000 a year with other teams," he says. "What you've gotta understand is that, with the Flyers, no one could make more than Clarky. And that was right – he was our best player." But Clarke, according to Reg, was on an extremely long-term contract that amortized his salary at an artificially low annual rate. "When his numbers were used as a yearly ceiling for other players," says Reg, "it kept their pay lower than it should have. Don't get me wrong; I have no argument with Clarky – it wasn't his fault."

Reg's disgruntlement toward the Flyers' management by no means extended to his coach, the late Fred Shero, whom he remembers not only as a talented hockey coach but as "an intelligent, honest man," a man unafraid to give his players the news, in whatever form it took. "He'd some-times give Clarky and Bill Barber the day off," says Reg, "and I'd be out there working, and he'd come up to me and look me right in the eye and tell me that all players weren't created equal; some needed more work than others. He'd leave little sayings and quotations on my locker, always trying to teach me something, get me thinking about things. One day during the year I scored all those goals in the playoffs, he wrote on the board, 'No man is an island.' He was referring to me – suggesting, I guess, that if we were going to keep on winning I'd need some support from the rest of the team."

But the Flyers did not keep on winning. They lost the finals that year to Montreal, in a four-game sweep, and over the next half-decade would mount just one more serious challenge for the Stanley Cup. By 1981, they were little more than a ghost of their once-fearsome selves.

Reg's years with the team ended in 1982, in a way that

was neither as happy nor as dignified as he might have wished. In March of that year, general manager Bob McCammon had fired coach Pat Quinn and his assistant, and had taken over at the bench. "I had a chat with him," says Reg. "I told him that, in spite of the changes that were going on in the organization, I'd like to finish the year with the team, and he said that was fine."

Two nights later, without consultation, Reg was scratched from the line-up before a game in Hartford, and was scratched again the following night in Philadelphia. "The next thing I knew," Reg says, "they told me they were releasing me. They were going to pay me until the end of the year, but they didn't want me around the rink."

Reg has always believed the key to his dismissal was that he had scored twenty-nine goals so far that year and that a contract he had negotiated the previous autumn called not only for a substantial bonus if he reached thirty goals, but for a year's extension on his contract if he achieved a total of fifty goals and assists. "I sat home for the rest of the season, collecting my paycheques," he says, "and when the team got knocked out of the first round of the playoffs, I was the happiest guy in Philly. At that point I had absolutely no use for them. The owner Ed Snider was a good man in many ways, but hockey players are no more than cattle to the owners. There's no loyalty. You can give everything to an organization for years, and they'll still dump on you and toss you out the door without giving it a thought. I mean, I realize now that I wasn't exactly the greatest guy in the world to have on the team. You're not much good to them when you're drunk half the time. Anyway, I had nothing to do with the Flyers for years after I left."

And the Flyers had nothing to do with Reg . . . until one afternoon in the late autumn of 1991. At that point, a representative of the team's front office phoned to congratulate the disposable star on his election to the Flyers' Hall of Fame, and to notify him that he would be inducted with flying colours into the Broad Street shrine on the night of Thursday, February 13, 1992.

Camden, New Jersey, sits on the east bank of the Delaware River, and, these days, is less a city unto itself than a kind of back door to the city of Philadelphia which towers above it on the west bank of the Delaware. Settled in 1681, it is, among other things, the home of Rutgers University, Campbell Soups (founded in 1869), and Del Monte canned goods. It is a port and shipping centre for the farms and orchards of central New Jersey, and was the last home of the great American poet Walt Whitman, who lived in the city from 1884 until his death in 1892. It was in Camden that Whitman produced the final version of his life-long opus, *Leaves of Grass*.

The Salisbury housing project on Camden's south side lies in the shadow of the gargantuan Walt Whitman Bridge, the main link between southwest New Jersey and the city of Philadelphia. The project was Reg's first assignment in reclamation landscaping and tends to typify the sort of places in which he works.

And so we toured Salisbury and the surrounding ghetto, street by street, in a company pick-up, on a sweltering August afternoon. The area is infested, quite literally, with rats, cockroaches, and termites – and, more visibly, with block after block of alarmingly degenerate tenements, three- or four-room flats, their windows smashed, their doors busted, their porches rotted or burned. The assumption evoked by such places is that nobody could possibly live in them (who could survive the winter without heat, windows, or doors?). But people do live in them – not just the walking dead of the drug and alcohol wars, but, in some cases, whole families, generations of families, who simply have no place else to go. At one time, the buildings made solid fronts along the streets, but these days they are interspersed with empty lots, sometimes two or three in succession, where the buildings have seemingly been vaporized out of existence and where the remaining patches of hard-packed dirt support a potentially lethal debris of hypodermic needles and broken glass, as well as the more benign trash – the chunks of concrete and scrap steel, the tires and cans and endless piles of plastic and paper – that accumulate anywhere there is a space that can be turned into a makeshift dump.

"This is a main street, so you're not likely to get hurt here during the day," says Reg, as we motor along Eighth Street, past brick walls dense with hateful graffiti, past men collapsed in doorways with their bottles, past junkies, crackheads, and grim-faced prostitutes, on the beat in their platform shoes at 3 in the afternoon. "But you get off onto some of these side streets, and, even in broad daylight, you can get yourself into big trouble." Seconds later, we turn down precisely such a street – an alleyway *posing* as a street – and almost immediately are among conclaves of contemptuous young men in outrageous haircuts and clothing, and among the filth-ridden carcasses of twenty-year-old roadboats that sit along the curbs, some so thoroughly ravaged it is impossible to tell that they ever had paint, windows, or tires. There is no grass, no trees, no greenery, either on the boulevards or in the yards; and garbage of every description lies strewn across the dusty clay. Bored black faces stare balefully from the buildings, while the emaciated forms of other unfortunates lie in doors or on steps, even on outdoor couches, apparently in drug-induced or alcoholic stupefaction.

Such ghettos are frequently depicted as war zones or battle zones. But the depiction is inaccurate, in that it suggests a kind of closure on the attendant horror and desperation, a sense that this is where the war goes on, confined, self-limiting, destructive to itself but little more than a sound bite or news item to those of us who live safely on the outside. But to get up close to such places, even for an hour or two, creates an impression by no means of limits or definition but of a boundlessly degenerate no-man's land, a (barely) demilitarized zone, between affluent North America and some enormous social lesion that is unlikely to stop festering just because it has expanded to the boundaries of south Camden, or central Philly, or Newark.

Reg has been working in these areas for eight years and avers that their economies are based almost entirely on drugs, alcohol, and on any variety of minor or major crime, from petty theft and prostitution to extortion, armed robbery, and murder. And of course on welfare payments, which are inclined to dovetail with everything else. "Every second guy down here has a gun," he says. "Even the kids have guns."

In the context of south Camden, the Salisbury project, which houses approximately a thousand people, is a relatively stable habitat. Its two-storey row-houses, block after block of them, have functional windows and doors, have working appliances and facades free of graffiti. Because of Reg and his crews, the project has landscaping – not just lawns, fences, and shrubbery but *cut* lawns and *trimmed* shrubbery.

"But don't get it wrong just because it looks good," says Reg. "A lot of the people who live here are either users or dealers, and most of them have guns. When you cut grass in here, you're constantly cutting around beer bottles, crack piles, needles, whatever." He points out a late-model white Cadillac and beige Mercedes-Benz parked among a half-dozen rusted-out beaters. "Dealers," he says. "I tell the guys when they come in here, 'Always be polite, always agree with everything anybody says.' If you argue, some of these guys'll just shoot ya."

Every second week, Reg sends a crew of eight men into Salisbury. "Four of them cut," he says, "the rest do trimming and Weed Whacking. They're in at seven in the morning, out by one; I often go with them; I get the easy job, riding around on a big mower."

On the rare occasion that the crews are called upon to plant gardens at Salisbury or other sites, the flowers are frequently torn up within hours, by teenagers or older addicts who sell them to buy crack. "Even stuff that can't be sold," says Reg, "gets ripped up just for the sake of it. When I order shrubs for these places I always get barberries, or something with heavy thorns, so they'll at least stand a chance. Even chain-link fence gets ripped right out! I have to use wrought iron."

Reg admits to discouragement at seeing the repeated wreckage of what he and his crews have painstakingly created. His frustration, however, is tempered by empathy for the people who would seem to be frustrating him most. "I know what they're going through," he says. "What bugs me is that so many of them don't care; they don't wanna do anything to help themselves out. Some of them, mind you, are great people. I even know drug dealers who are good people; they're just trapped."

Perhaps because of his own disadvantaged boyhood, Reg shows a particular affinity for the children of the ghetto. "I certainly can't say I blame a lot of them for dealing drugs," he says. "They understand that's where the money is. They're ten or twelve, they're making $500 a week! What hope do they have otherwise? Who's gonna convince them to go to high school, so that they can make six or seven bucks an hour when they graduate? That's no way out. The worst thing is, most of them don't live to see eighteen."

Many of the inhabitants of the ghettos in which Reg works know him as a professional athlete, which he believes gives him "a bit of an advantage" in his dealings with them. "I know it helps me get the kids on my side," he says. "I can sit down and talk to them. I let them help us with the work if they want; buy 'em a Coke or a candy bar, or something. Once in a while, I'll offer a bit of advice, but you can't really do too much counselling; it's too crazy down here. You make a false move, put somebody off, and they'll whip the gun out."

If Reg has an additional advantage in the ghetto, it is, of course, that he, too, has known poverty, addiction, and discrimination. "These people are a lot like Canadian Indians," he observes, "except these guys are trapped in ghettos, while the Indians are trapped on reserves – or sometimes in ghettos of their own. There's a lot of similarity in the disadvantages and hopelessness." Reg feels that what he can best show them from experience is that their curse "is not necessarily permanent," and that there are ways in which they can help themselves. "They can't all be pro athletes, obviously – maybe none of them can," he says. "But they can quit drugs and drinking, and if they do that, you never know what else they might be able to do for themselves."

Ghetto relations notwithstanding, Reg attributes his business success to hard work (he frequently rises at 5 a.m. and does not finish his day until suppertime), to efficiency (he manages his time and maintains his equipment almost religiously), and to his "easygoing" personality. "I don't let too much bother me anymore," he says. "I guess it's partly an A.A. philosophy: get through the day; there'll be another one tomorrow."

He is somewhat more sanguine about his ambitions for Sports Lawn Services. "My goal," he says, "is to get the business to a point where I can leave it alone, let it run itself. I wanta get to where I'm grossing $700,000 a year – that's the plan. I'm getting there fast. You've gotta remember, this is an expensive business. Hundreds of thousands of dollars go into wages and equipment and materials. I hope to take on more properties this year. My aim is to be able to travel more with Debbie and Brandon, go south in winter, north in summer."

Reg also wants to spend more time working for the betterment of Canadian Natives – "especially the kids," he says. "I know what it was like for me, and I hate seeing the same mistakes repeated." He admits to feeling guilt that he has not been more involved with Native causes, or been a better model for children and young adults. "When I was playing," he says, "I'd often get held up as an example of a Native guy who was making it out there in the world. But of course I *wasn't* a good example. When I'd visit a reserve, I'd know the kids were drinking, but I wouldn't say anything about it – what could I say? I've got some ground to make up. I only wish the various bands would use me more than they do."

As it is, Reg makes anywhere from five to ten trips a year to speak to Canadian Native groups, largely in Saskatchewan, Manitoba, and Ontario. "The exposure to the culture has been good for me," he says. "When I was playing I really didn't have much interest in it. Native pride wasn't big back then. In fact, if you were an Indian you did your best to cover it up. So, I'm learning."

Reg's message is not complicated: "I tell them what happened to me, then I tell them what I did about it, and then I tell them what I think about it. I often get told about this Indian or that Indian who had all this talent and could've been this or that. 'That's great,' I say, 'but there are all sorts of couldabeens. And why didn't they make it? Because they drank too much.'"

During the summer of 1994, Reg conducted a week-long

Native hockey school in Gimli, Manitoba, just a few kilometres from his home town. "Sixty-two kids," he says. "We taught hockey, we talked about drugs and alcohol, we kept 'em busy." Reg's son Jamie, who has played for four NHL teams, and is now with the Buffalo Sabres, assisted with the school. "One thing I'd like to do somewhere down the line," says Reg, "is get a Native *men's* tournament going in central Manitoba. Mid-winter. Promote Native hockey. For the number of good Native players out there, there are very few in the NHL. Somewhere along the way, we're losing them."

At the moment, Reg is committed to an assortment of public-service ventures in the Philadelphia area. The Flyers' alumni organization, of which he is a member, supports some forty charities through benefit sporting events, and Reg personally hosts a charity golf tournament that raises $15,000 a year for the Easter Seals campaign.

He seldom plays hockey these days, largely because of a serious shoulder injury he incurred during the spring of 1994. "I'd gone to Brandon's skating class to demonstrate a few things," he explains, "and I got horsing around, skating backwards, and I fell over a kid. Three hours of surgery. I'll never be able to lift my arm over my head again. No more slap shots. . . . I still like to get the skates on when I can, though."

One thing Reg does not do is watch the game, either on television or live. "We didn't go to a single game at the Spectrum this year," says Debbie. "Last year we went once. And, ya know, even after all these years, as soon as we got in there, you could hear the people whispering, 'There's Reg Leach, there's Reg Leach.' We can go to the most remote restaurant in Maryland, and people will go by and say, 'Hi, Reg!' At first, I thought, boy, this guy has a lot of friends. I used to wonder why he never introduced me to people he'd be talking to, and I got kinda upset at him one day. I said, 'Why don't you introduce me to your friends?' And he said, 'Because I don't know who they are.' They often tell him they met him somewhere, and he tells them he remembers. But he doesn't. He just doesn't want to seem rude."

On our second evening in Sewell, Debbie served a heaping meal of fried chicken, after which Betty and I and our year-old daughter, Georgia, got into the car and headed north on the New Jersey Turnpike. As we said our good-byes, Reg allowed that, at some point in the future, he'd be quite happy to return to Canada full-time to get involved in Native causes, athletic and otherwise. "I'd sell the business here," he says.

"Back to Manitoba?" I asked.

"Probably around Riverton somewhere. If you're going home," he mused, "you might as well go home."

The exchange reminded me of something he had said earlier in the day as we drove through the back streets of Camden. "I look back," he'd told me, "and it seems as if I've been saving up lessons in life for forty-five years – mostly on how not to live it. . . . Now that I'm doing a little better at it, I guess I've reached a point where I figure I've got something to tell people."

Something they're not likely to hear from anyone anywhere else.

# A SIMPLE MAN AT HEART

WHEN EIGHT-YEAR-OLD Kurtis Cournoyer asks his dad for a bedtime story, he knows pretty much what to expect. "Yvan sits down beside him," says Evelyn Cournoyer, "and, without exception, the first words out of Yvan's mouth are, 'Once upon a time, there was a little boy who had a dream.' . . . And Kurtis and I say to ourselves, *Oh, no, not the Dream again!*"

The little boy, according to the tale, lived in a small town in rural Quebec and wanted nothing more in life than to play hockey for the Montreal Canadiens.

Because he was smaller than most boys his age, he was prepared to work extremely hard to make his dream come true. And every day, all winter, he spent every possible moment either on the town rink or on the tiny sheet of ice in his backyard.

In summer, he fired hundreds of shots a day against the wall of his parents' garage.

Eventually, he moved with his family to Montreal, where, as a teenager, he continued to pour every ounce of his energy into improving his hockey skills.

And, sure enough, one day when he was nineteen years

old, his hard work bore fruit, and he was summoned by the great coach Toe Blake to suit up with *Les Glorieux*, the Canadiens, the titans of French Canada.

He could not have been prouder as he pulled on the Canadiens sweater for his first game. And he could not have been more excited as he lined up for his first shift, beside two of the heroes of his boyhood, Henri Richard and Jean Béliveau.

And he could not have been more daunted as he glanced across the faceoff circle at perhaps the greatest of all hockey players, Gordie Howe.

The little Dreamer scored his first NHL goal that night, and the following season had his name inscribed on the glistening flanks of the Stanley Cup.

"That's where the story always ends," laughs Evelyn, "with the boy winning the Stanley Cup. Then it's lights out."

Were it not for Kurtis's sleep requirements, Yvan could easily extend the triumphal little *roman à clef* into the wee hours of the morning. He certainly has a storyteller's capital in his nearly five hundred big-time goals; his four all-star team selections; not *one* Stanley Cup but ten. He could add heroic subplots from the most remarkable hockey series ever, between the Canadians and Soviets, in 1972, or from the 1973 playoffs when he led all combatants with fifteen goals and won the Conn Smythe Trophy as that year's premier playoff performer.

If he decided to darken the narrative, or take it into the shadows of the campfire, he could introduce his numerous debilitating injuries: to knees, back, head, shoulder, Achilles tendon, ankle; or his thirteen trips to the operating room; or the intense psychological pressures of life in the National Hockey League.

Or he could bring in the goblins he encountered in the early autumn of 1979 when it struck him with the finality of a death sentence that the resonant dream of his boyhood was over. "I'd missed most of the previous season with a back injury," he explains, "but I'd come to training camp in September and had scored a few goals, and I thought I was going to be okay. If everything went well, I hoped to play another couple of years."

But when he awoke the morning after a pre-season game against Philadelphia, he was unable to walk, let alone skate, "and I knew that was it," he says.

The intervening years have brought Yvan enviable domestic and professional success. But any discussion of the eighteen months that followed his retirement from the Canadiens still brings a perceptible strain to his normally beatific face.

"It took me five years to accept that I was really retired!" he exclaims. "You play hockey all winter from the time you're five years old; you have the excitement, the camaraderie, the schedule to follow, and then, boom, it's over, and there's a very large hole in your life. In order to fill it, you do this, you do that, you go to work, probably at a job you don't understand, and every time you see a game, you have to convince yourself again that you're no longer a part of what's happening on the ice. Although deep down you still believe you are. You still think maybe you could play."

"Even now, looking at pictures from back then, I can see how drawn he was with the stress," says his wife, Evelyn. "We've been together eighteen years, and in all that time, it's the only rough period he's had."

Evelyn submits that part of Yvan's post-retirement agony was his lack of any choice concerning the termination of his career. "If he'd been able to say to himself, okay, I'll play this season, or the next one, and that'll be it, he'd have had at least *some* sense of control, as well as the time to prepare himself mentally."

What made the separation even harder for him was his extraordinary emotional attachment to the Canadiens' franchise, to its personnel and players, and even to its historic building. "You've got to remember," he says, "that I played my entire career, from bantam to the end, in Montreal, and that from the time I started with the Junior Canadiens, at seventeen, I played at the Forum."

Not surprisingly, his evocations of those years are liberally sprinkled with the vocabulary of blood connection. Toe Blake, he says, was "like a father," his teammates "like brothers," the whole organization *"une grande famille."* To the players, the Forum was known affectionately as *"la maison."* "It wasn't my second home," says Yvan, "it was my first."

In the months that followed his abrupt departure from the game, he and Evelyn cast about futilely for a manageable approach to the future. As a distraction and a means of staying fit, they took up skiing, one of the few sports Yvan could handle with a bad back and reconstructed knees.

"One day," brightens Evelyn, "Yvan hit on the idea of a brasserie. He and I had always enjoyed restaurants, and with his popularity – well?"

A short time later, as they drove along Thirty-second Avenue in Lachine, a working-class suburb in west Montreal, where Yvan had lived as a boy, Yvan noticed a large open lot near the busy intersection of highways 13 and 20, not far from Dorval Airport. "It was a perfect spot for a restaurant," he says, and within days he was negotiating its purchase from Canadian National Railways. Within weeks, he was dickering with architects over plans for the capacious restaurant and bar that would eventually stand on the site. "Yvan always thinks big – no half measures," says Evelyn. Indeed, Brasserie 12 – so named for Yvan's sweater number – was to be a six-hundred-seat show place, a monument not just to eating and drinking but to the life and accomplishments of its famous founder. (Coincidentally, it would stand directly across the street from *La Bibliothèque Municipale Saul Bellow*, a monument to Lachine's other widely celebrated son, who was born in the town in 1915 and won the Nobel Prize for Literature in 1976.) Moreover, the brasserie was to be a model of proprietary accountability. "I didn't just want to own it, I wanted to run it," declares Yvan, "to be there, to meet the people, sign autographs – if they were coming to my brasserie, they weren't going to go away disappointed."

So concerned was Yvan about his personal role in the development of the place that, before construction began, he took the unusual step of naming himself official project contractor, defying local building ordinances to a degree that cost him thousands of dollars in fines. But the price of his misdemeanours was insignificant compared to the value and satisfaction he got from unfettered management of everything from the pouring of the concrete foundations to the erection of the walls and the installation of the plumbing and wiring.

The fascination with trades and with manual productivity was by no means new for the novice restaurateur. As a teenager in Lachine, he had spent countless hours in his father's machine shop on Remembrance Street and had taken four years of machine-shop training at technical school. "If I hadn't been a hockey player," he says, "I'd have been a machinist like my dad." In fact, he once wedded his passions for hockey and for machining by cutting a dozen solid steel pucks on the lathe in his father's shop. "They weighed two or three pounds each," he smiles. "I'd go downstairs at home and shoot them at the basement wall, to build up my strength." When the foundations of the house began disintegrating from the pounding, he was ordered by his parents to move outside, where he fired his pucks into bales of hay against the family garage.

When Brasserie 12 opened to the public in late 1981, the food was as good as promised – the house specialty was what Evelyn refers to as "top-quality roast beef" – and a veritable *rapides* of beer flowed out through the taps, across the bar, and down the patrons' throats. In no time, the place was one of Molson Brewery's largest accounts in the province. And for the next dozen years, Yvan and Evelyn poured as much energy and time into the ambitious watering hole as Yvan had ever poured into hockey. The two routinely showed up three hours before the restaurant's 11 a.m. opening time to receive deliveries of meat and vegetables, to work with the chef, and generally to prepare for the day. "Yvan was always up to his elbows in something," says Evelyn. "He'd help in the kitchen or deal with the suppliers or staff. At noon hour, of course, he'd be behind the taps, right there in the middle of things, where the people could see him."

More importantly, he was positioned where the brasserie's thousands of patrons could *approach* him, *greet* him, make the (albeit fleeting) acquaintance of the five-foot-seven-inch bullet who was at one time the fastest man on skates. Hour after hour, day after day, Yvan smiled his wide, unassuming smile for the customers' cameras, and dispensed autographs on four-by-eight-inch postcards bearing effulgent likenesses of himself, plus the logos of the brasserie and of its preferred intoxicant, Molson Export Ale. "Yvan is really very shy," says Evelyn. "He's not one to initiate any sort of social interaction, so, the set-up was perfect – he'd just be there, and the customers would come up to him, or he'd walk among the tables and people would stop him as he passed. If, say, a ball team or a hockey team was coming in late, they'd phone ahead, and Yvan would wait and meet them. In the beginning, we were both there all the time, twelve hours a day, easy. Kurt spent the first few years of his life there! He'd be under the tables, or, when he got a little older, helping stack glasses or doing other little jobs."

Evelyn makes it clear that she and Yvan did not merely *serve* their customers but entertained them, provided a sybaritic parade of Christmas parties, Hallowe'en parties, "Western" parties, lobster parties, oyster parties. She produces a stack of corroborative photos, showing revellers in various states of merriment, wearing cowboy outfits, goblin suits, softball uniforms, invariably snuggled up to her and Yvan – or just to Yvan – and, for the most part, to one or more pitchers of freshly tapped suds. "We knew these people!" she enthuses. "That's what made it fun! The place would be packed to the doors every Thursday, Friday, Saturday night. If you were a non-smoker, forget it."

Fast-forward a decade to a Sunday afternoon in late June 1994, a day on which most of Quebec is celebrating the first long weekend of the summer. But the celebrations have by no means penetrated Brasserie 12, which, although open, is as silent as the Pharaoh's tomb. In a corner of the glass-enclosed *terrasse*, three rather wide-angled men, the only occupants of the cavernous establishment, are loading up noiselessly on omelettes and Texas-style fries. They are sharing a pitcher of draft beer which, for all the pleasure it is giving them, might just as well be vinegar.

More than a year has passed since Yvan and Evelyn relinquished ownership of their once-cherished brasserie. And yet even in his absence, Yvan's spirit pervades the place in much the way a vapour extends to every nook and niche of its container. It's in the panoply of Habs' memorabilia on the walls; in the framed photos and ubiquitous numeral 12 that appears on the menu and placemats and outdoor signs; it's in the phone number: 637-12-12.

Perhaps most poignantly, it resides in the memories of

the customers – a significantly reduced crowd these days – for whom the place will never be anything less than the house that Yvan built. "I ate a lot of meals in there over the years," says Lachine resident Guy Sabourin. "I never knew Yvan well, but I used to like to see him behind the bar. It was nice to go in there and see him."

"He still comes in once in a while," says a brasserie waitress. "But not very much any more."

On a morning in late August, Evelyn Cournoyer sits in the living room of her and Yvan's home on the northern out-skirts of Montreal, speaking circumspectly about their departure from the restaurant trade, which had apparently supported them well for nearly a dozen years. While she is reluctant to say much, she makes it clear that their move was influenced both by economics and demographics. "A lot of things changed between 1981 when we opened and 1993 when we sold," she says. "Certainly the recession made things harder for us. I mean, it was hard everywhere, but Lachine, in particular, tends to be industrial, and during the late eighties and early nineties a lot of local fac-tories and warehouses went out of business. There just wasn't as much money around, or as many people."

In addition, by 1990 customers had a far broader choice of local bars and restaurants in which to spend their money than they had had a decade earlier. Barbecue St. Hubert, the corporate chicken shack that has become Quebec's pre-eminent chain of restaurants, capitalized directly on the locus of activity created by the brasserie by putting up a large outlet immediately next door.

"People were also drinking less by the early nineties," observes one brasserie bartender. "And the laws against drinking and driving had gotten stricter. Today's average drinker has two or three beers and says, 'That's enough.'

Whereas in the old days a table of guys would come in and plough through five or six pitchers!" He points unenthusiastically at the self-operated breathalyzer machine, the "alcotest," that stands just outside the brasserie's washrooms. "Until recently," he says, "you didn't see many of those."

In addition to the economic and sociological pressures that were impinging on their operation, Evelyn and Yvan had quite simply grown tired of the quotidian demands of food ordering and menu preparation and staff scheduling; the endless cash-outs, the payroll and accounting responsibilities, not to mention the necessity of being on the premises day in, day out, month after month, year after year. "You don't notice your weariness as much when things are going well," says Evelyn, "but with the recession we had to work harder and harder, and of course we weren't getting the same rewards."

During the couple's last year at the brasserie, they found themselves attempting daily miracles both in the kitchen and on the balance sheet. "We were determined not to compromise our standards," says Evelyn. "We always used the best meat and vegetables, for example. But at the same time, we were cutting our prices to the point where we were putting out daily specials, full-course meals, for under three dollars. . . . The long and short of it is, we'd given all we could to the restaurant business. We miss the customers and staff – we had a lot of friends at the brasserie – but we were ready to do something else."

Part of the "something else" that followed the sale of the brasserie was a move from urban Laval to the semi-developed farmlands around Blainville, a saturnine village off Route 640, some twenty-five kilometres north of Montreal. The elegant grey-brick home into which the Cournoyers moved is part of an upscale subdivision built by Yvan's friend Mario Grilli, a Montreal developer for whom Yvan was doing publicity work when he first laid eyes on the place. "Yvan called me and said, 'You've gotta come see this house,' and as soon as I saw it I knew we were destined to live here," says Evelyn, who was attracted not only by the structure but by its seductive view across field and forest to the distant skyscrapers of downtown Montreal. In the months since taking possession, she and Yvan have turned the surrounding acreage into an arboretum of conifers and hardwoods scattered with birdbaths and feeders that attract a summer population of finches, warblers, and hummingbirds.

Inside, despite its rather lean decor and lines, the place invites both relaxation and play. Indeed, just to the left of the front door, where a visitor might expect to see a dining or sitting room, stands a full-sized billiard table, surrounded by choice remnants of Yvan's career in hockey. Draped casually on a chair are three hockey sweaters of different vintages and repair. The oldest, Yvan's first as a Canadien, is of knitted wool, decidedly faded, and suggests an era far dimmer to the memory than the early sixties, when it was worn. By comparison, the newest of the three sweaters, Yvan's last as a Hab, seems, in its shapeless dimensions and bright, uninspired acrylics, to embody some zipless season inhospitable both to comfort and to the spirit of the man who wore it. The two sweaters are fitting symbolic parentheses to a career that began in a parochial six-team league whose teams travelled by train (and whose players began their careers at $10,000 a season), and ended in a financially free-wheeling twenty-one-team league that spanned four time zones and included teams in sub-tropical climates.

But it is the third of the three sweaters, a yellowed and tattered relic, that most stirs the imagination and curiosity – partly because it was worn by Yvan in the epochal

Soviet–Canada series of 1972, but more so because of its comically crude hand-customization. Six inches, at least, have been snipped off the bottom, and the resulting edge bound with awkward hand-applied stitches. The sleeves have been likewise chopped and hemmed, while the neck has been expanded by two or three inches, by way of a hand-ripped vent through the neckline and down the front of the sweater. The impression, understandably, is that the garment – neck excluded – was initially too big for Yvan (in his red uniform, the short but sturdy Montreal captain was once compared to a mailbox). And yet looking at it now, it is difficult to see how even the smallest of NHL players could have compressed himself into such a tiny piece of apparel. "I don't think he could get into it today, even *without* shoulder pads," jokes Evelyn.

Which isn't to say that Yvan, at fifty-one, is in anything less than top-notch shape. While not exactly thin, he is certainly trim and muscular, and, although his blondy-grey hair has pretty much retreated from the foredeck of his scalp, his face is that of a slightly prankish cherub and is all but free of wrinkles.

Yvan was born in 1943 in Drummondville, Quebec, a town of some forty thousand inhabitants, a hundred kilometres east of Montreal. Like many boys from provincial Quebec, he served mass at the local parish church. He allows, in fact, that he knew his catechism better than his school lessons, which he detested. "I was always happy to be in church," he grins, "because when I was there it meant I wasn't in school."

But more than any place on earth, he loved the local outdoor rink, which he shovelled for small pay, and where he embraced organized hockey with such fanaticism that, as a peewee, he played goal because he couldn't bear the thought of coming off the ice, as forwards and defencemen occasionally had to do.

His father worked in a machine shop in Montreal and saw his wife and children only on weekends. "Then when I was thirteen," says Yvan, "he bought the shop, and we moved into Lachine."

There in west Montreal, Yvan's hockey career began in earnest, although not without encumbrances. At the time, he explains, Lachine was "quite English," and the first hockey team he joined was exclusively anglophone. Unable to speak anything but French, he was forced to use hand gestures to make himself understood to his coaches and teammates. "I was shy anyway," he says, "and I'd get so nervous about not speaking the language that I'd probably have quit and gone home if I hadn't loved hockey so much."

In order to improve his English, Yvan eventually signed on with the Lachine Lakers, an English football team, whose season overlapped with the hockey season. "I played linebacker and ran back kicks," he says. By late winter, however, he was so exhausted by the efforts of autumn that he could barely finish his hockey schedule.

If the pro scouts were concerned about his apparent lack of stamina, Yvan was not. "By this time," he says, "nothing was going to stop me. From the time I was fourteen, I had a very strong belief that I was good enough to make it in pro hockey."

The Montreal Canadiens, who owned Yvan's professional rights, had much the same feeling and, throughout Yvan's teenage years, watched the young prodigy with possessive anticipation. When he was seventeen, they assigned him to the Montreal Junior Canadiens, a team for which he scored a remarkable fifty-four goals during his final year of junior eligibility. But it was not just his scoring that impressed the Montreal management; it was his astonishing speed. "From the time I was a kid," he acknowledges, "I was always the fastest guy on the ice."

But speed and offensive skills were initially not enough

to earn him a regular shift with the Canadiens after joining the club full-time in 1964. Wary of what he perceived as a weakness in Yvan's defensive game, and concerned by his lack of stature, coach Toe Blake used him almost exclusively on power plays. Not one to brood, Yvan did what he had always done: applied himself to the chore at hand, becoming in the process so proficient in his specialized role that, during the 1966–67 season, playing at best part-time, he scored twenty-five goals, no fewer than twenty of them when the team had a manpower advantage. "This was at a time," he notes, "when twenty goals was still a very respectable season in the NHL."

Yvan's emergence as an all-round star coincided roughly with Blake's retirement in 1968 when Blake's successor, Claude Ruel, decided that his speed and savvy were far too valuable to leave cooling on the bench. What's more, he had proven that he was perfectly capable of handling the prodigious physical battering that pro hockey inflicts even on a player as elusive as Yvan.

Off the ice, Yvan's life was moving at a pace to rival his speed at the rink. Shortly after joining the Canadiens, he married his teenage sweetheart – "my first girlfriend," he confides – and by 1974 was the father of three children.

"Looking back," he says, "I know I made a mistake getting married too young. But at the time I was naive. I didn't know. I just stuck with it."

From the point of view of some players on the team, Yvan was something of an enigma. "He was a *private* person," says teammate Gump Worsley, whose observations are echoed by fellow Hab John Ferguson. "He didn't say much, didn't socialize much – I never felt I knew him very well. Except on the ice. I knew him as a player."

"I was *shy*, not private," insists Yvan. "Even after five years with the Canadiens, I still wasn't confident enough to express myself comfortably in English."

If he needed a cross-cultural coming out, he got one in 1972 when he was chosen to represent Canada against the best hockey players from the Soviet Union, many of whom, it turned out, were also among the best in the world. Many saw the series as a kind of ideological dust-up between the individualized gamesmanship of the West and the bloodless functionality of state-controlled sport. But initially it was governed less by ideology than by conditioning. The Canadians significantly underestimated the strength and skill of the Soviets and, after a summer of inactivity, spent much of the first four games – the Canadian leg of the series – struggling to catch their breath. But by the time they reached Moscow, their endurance was at game level, and ideology had indeed become a factor. It was never more significant than in the fabled final game, when the Canadians played on the fiercest of competitive instincts against the daunting but inflexible mechanics of the Soviet "system." In the clinching moments, none other than Yvan Cournoyer, who minutes earlier had scored the game-tying goal, made a play no Soviet of that era would have dreamed of, let alone perpetrated, placing a Westernized instinct for chance above any measure of form and, in the process, deciding the outcome of the series.

"Let me tell you what happened," says Yvan, whose detailed recollections of the play might suggest that it had been enacted that morning, not twenty-three years before. "The puck was in the Russian zone, and my left winger and centreman both went off the ice. I went to go off, but in the middle of the ice I suddenly changed my mind; I thought, I'm going to give it one last try, and I went back on my wing. The Russian defenceman must have thought I'd gone to the bench, because he threw the puck blindly around the boards to clear the zone. And there I was," says an animated Yvan, whose boyhood compulsion for staying on the ice beyond his time was not only alive but was about to spark the most heralded play in the history of Canadian hockey. "I intercepted the puck, and saw that Phil and Paul [Esposito and Henderson] had come from the bench. I tried to give it to Paul, but it shot ahead of him and went into the corner. Phil picked it up. Paul fell, got up, came in front of the net. Out came the puck, and he put it in!" Yvan's face broadens in a smile. "And it all went back to my changing my mind about going off. If I hadn't stayed on, there wouldn't have been a goal, because there wouldn't have been anybody to intercept the puck."

Appropriately enough, Yvan figures prominently (albeit seen from the back) in Frank Lennon's famous photograph of the celebration that followed the goal – a shot often referred to as a photo "of Paul Henderson."

That Yvan is seldom, if ever, identified as a figure in the famous depiction hardly seems to register with him. "When I see it," he shrugs, "I know what I did. I don't have to read my name or see my face. I had a good series, but I give Paul all the credit for scoring. He scored winning goals in each of the last three games."

Yvan's success in Moscow carried over into that year's NHL season, bringing him his sixth Stanley Cup and the Conn Smythe Trophy for a remarkable playoff performance that featured fifteen goals and ten assists in seventeen games.

In 1975, he succeeded Henri Richard as captain of the Canadiens. But his successes with the team were not reflected in his private life, where his marriage was sinking slowly into emotional receivership. "Then it was over," he says, "and I was back on my own."

Yvan's emotional life, however, would soon take a dramatic about-turn. "One day in, I guess, 1977," he says, "I was passing through Dorval Airport with the team – we were going to a game in Chicago – and I noticed a very pretty young woman in an Air Canada uniform." The two exchanged glances and Yvan subsequently left a note with the young woman's co-workers, asking if she would meet him for a drink upon his return the following Monday.

"We met," says Evelyn, "and what can I say? – it was love at first sight. I always say it was his eyes that caught my attention; he says it was my smile that caught his."

Physical attractions notwithstanding, the pair's personalities have been ideal complements through eighteen years of courtship, marriage, and business. Where he is taciturn, she chats; where he is retiring, she is social, drawing him out, encouraging him to expand his range of self-expression – "but in a good way," stresses Yvan. "Evelyn is very sincere, very loving, very considerate."

"Yvan is certainly more outgoing than he was," smiles Evelyn. "It used to be, he'd hardly even smile for a photo."

Evelyn has given Yvan a refined command of English, and he has taught her French. "When we met, we could hardly speak the other's language," she says. "Now Yvan speaks English so much, I have to encourage him and Kurtis to keep up their French."

One thing that has not changed for the couple is their obvious sensual compatibility. When they speak of one another their voices take on a perceptibly elevated charge, and each of them remembers vividly the intense chemistry that united them when they met nearly two decades ago. "Evelyn is beautiful," Yvan says unselfconsciously. "It still gives me a thrill," says Evelyn, "when we pass one another and he gives me that special little look that he gave me that day in the airport."

On a morning in late June, Yvan sits ten rows up in the Montreal Forum, watching the Chicago Cheetahs, a professional roller-hockey team, during their game-day work-out. He is nattily attired in a white shirt, navy blue dress slacks, and tasselled loafers. His black socks are of the sheerest silk. The Stanley Cup ring on his left hand and the Hall of Fame ring on his right are each as big as King Solomon's seal and resplendent with commemorative diamonds.

In quiet, confident English, he describes how, in late 1993, he made a business move that brought him not only into the brave new world of roller hockey, where he is coach and manager of the Montreal Roadrunners, but happily back to *la maison*, the home he had known for sixteen years as a junior and professional hockey player.

"I first saw roller hockey in 1992," he says. "And one of the first things I noticed about it was that the players were having such a good time, and so were the fans; they just loved it, and this impressed me. In a lot of sports, the players and fans just don't seem to enjoy themselves much any more."

Six months later, the owners of the Montreal franchise approached Yvan about running the team that they were about to found. "I thought about it for three or four months," says Yvan, "and, based on what I'd seen of the league and the game, I decided to take a chance and go with it."

The job, for Yvan, means an intense commitment of time between early May, when the team begins coming together, and the Labour Day weekend, by which point the league's twenty-four-game schedule and playoff tournament are over. "The other eight months are much less demanding," says Yvan. "Some promotion, some meetings, player signings, some planning for the future."

An hour earlier, Yvan himself had been out on the Forum floor, in a T-shirt and in-line skates, leading the Roadrunners through their game-day observances, dispensing a morsel of advice here, encouragement there, as his players coasted soundlessly around on the tiny plastic wheels that have replaced the blades on which they learned their hockey. Yvan has modelled the Roadrunners after the firewagon teams for which he played; indeed, they are named after the speedy desert bird that provided his own nickname during his years as an NHL dervish.

"The whole thing has just been terrific for him," says Evelyn. "And for me too. We're always talking about it, discussing the coaching, thinking about promotions. Yvan's a competitive sort of person, and it's really exciting for him to have that challenge back in his life."

At 7 p.m., as the Cheetahs and Roadrunners take to the Forum floor, Evelyn is seated ten rows up, directly behind the Montreal bench. She is a slim, attractive woman, with long blond hair and an exuberant smile. And when she goes to Roadrunners' games, she puts every ounce of her ample enthusiasm for life not only into support for the team but into a kind of psychic endorsement of her husband's efforts behind the bench.

Behind the bench, Yvan is no longer the easygoing conversationalist of the morning hours but a preoccupied strategist, pacing impulsively, working his gum, blowing the odd bubble. Periodically he leans over the backs of the players on the bench to shout directions and encouragements onto the floor.

"When you play for the Canadiens, you develop a real fear of losing," says Jocelyn Guevremont, who played for several NHL teams and has since worked at developing roller hockey in Quebec. "Yvan brings that to the Roadrunners. He's very fiery behind the bench, very intense."

On this night, he is particularly intense, as the Cheetahs, a bigger, more aggressive team than the Roadrunners, take early control, pretty much having their way with the home side. In the stands, Evelyn sits with her hands clenched, chewing her gum and wincing as the Chicago lead mounts to 3–1, then 4–1.

But when the Roadrunners come to life toward the end of the first period, so does she, cheering and clapping as they score a second and a third goal. When they tie the score early in the second period, she throws her fists in the air and whoops.

The noise of the crowd and the thumping interjections of amplified music at every stoppage of play seem exaggerated in a game that possesses almost no aural component of its own, none of the familiar *shussh* and *skritch* of ice skating. By comparison to ice hockey, even the visual content of the game seems reduced, in that there are no blade marks or snow flurries – the sinuous grooves and tracings that are the familiar leavings of the ice skater.

As the teams depart for their dressing rooms between periods, teenage cheerleaders pour onto the floor, performing a kind of rolling musical ride. Rock music rattles through the Forum and above the floor a remote-controlled dirigible floats out, emblazoned with advertisements for "Multi-feu, Foyers & Poeles," and for "Chenoy's Deli, 1936, charcuterie & grilladerie."

Roller hockey, it hardly needs saying, is at best a distant cousin to the version of the sport on which Yvan made his mark as a player. But that is not to belittle it. Because there is no way to stop quickly on roller blades, the game is an ongoing exercise in loops and long turns, balletic perpetual motion. The skating is somewhat more deliberate than in ice hockey, but inasmuch as there are only four skaters per side, and no bluelines to restrict play, there is plenty of open space, allowing for a stylistic anarchy unknown to the more traditional game. Play features extraordinarily long passes and (mostly) unobstructed free-wheeling for the better players. It is a sport that favours speed and manoeuvrability, but not size, and at which Yvan in his salad days would have excelled. In fact, it is easy to see why he and numerous other ice-hockey stars – Mark

Messier, Bernie Federko, Ralph Backstrom, Garry Unger, Doug Wilson, Rick Kehoe, Dennis Maruk, Terry Harper, Tiger Williams, among others – have been attracted to it as owners, managers, or coaches.

It is equally easy to see why it is reported (albeit by its own touts) to be the fastest-growing sport in North America. For beyond its aesthetics and openness, and its apparent appeal to investors, it carries none of the hoary old cultural baggage, evinces none of the traditional partisanship, that burdens the hopes and expectations of NHL fans, not to mention the players' and coaches' hopes for themselves. It is actually possible to go to a game and enjoy it no matter who wins, a feat seemingly unachievable for the average NHL fan.

What's more, the game is manifestly less ponderous about its image than are more established sports. Aimed largely at families, and particularly at children and teenagers, it is replete with brightly costumed mascots and cheerleaders. The players in their high-tech skates and gear look like road warriors, and the souped-up team names – Sacramento River Rats, Florida Hammerheads, St. Louis Vipers – would not be out of place among the preposterous plastic "action figures" that infest contemporary toystore shelves and have an undeniable lock on the imaginations of six- and seven-year-old boys. Those same names, it might be pointed out, are all but interchangeable with those of the post-punk grunge bands that pretty much define the poetics of late-twentieth-century teenagers. All of which is far from coincidental; the marketing is shrewd, although transparent enough that it maintains a kind of pleasingly funky innocence. Games in some cities are accompanied by barbecues, rock concerts, and displays of indoor fireworks.

The sport, in brief, is more "fun" than ice hockey. Yet establishing it in Montreal has been what Yvan refers to as "a major challenge," requiring "a lot of patience and a lot of hard work." The press in particular has been resistant.

"The good news," says Evelyn, "is that the kids are really into it – you see Roadrunners T-shirts all over Montreal. And people are coming out of the Forum saying, 'Wow, that was great!'"

The game's latter stages are a triumph of style over brawn, and the Roadrunners surge ahead, finishing with a 10–5 victory. Yvan's arms remain resolutely crossed during the game's final seconds, but for the first time in the evening his face is relaxed.

At the post-game press scrum, he is buoyant. But his facial muscles are beginning to droop with weariness, and his eyes, which are the colour of Aqua Velva, are showing the strain of the day. He has been up since 5:30 in the morning, and has not only practised and coached the team, but has done a brisk work-out of his own in the Forum training room, has visited his eighty-one-year-old mother in a Montreal nursing home, and, among other things, has conducted a three-hour interview with a persistent journalist.

"Which is not an unusual day for Yvan," declares Evelyn, "at least in length. He just never stops. If he's not involved with the team, or on some other business, he's gardening or cutting grass, or he's doing something with Kurtis, or working with his tools around the house."

Occasionally, he takes a little time off. In fact, if Yvan and Evelyn's years together could be captured in a metaphor, it might well be found in the magnificent retreat they have built for themselves in the Laurentian Mountains, a ninety-minute drive north of Montreal. Although they refer to the place modestly as "the chalet," it is in fact a prepossessing vacation home that features an expansive interior of cedar and pine, soaring vertical spaces, and a vast stone fireplace. Yvan has done much of the work on the place himself, inside and out. "He's got a shed full of tools and equipment up there you wouldn't believe," says Evelyn. "Every sort of implement you can imagine, some of them made years ago by his dad in the machine shop. He just loves working with his hands." She disappears into the recesses of the house in Blainville, reappearing presently with a photo album gorged with pictures of the cherished mountain residence, and of Yvan at work: here on a ladder tending to the eaves, here chopping wood, sawing lumber, mixing cement, yukking it up with Evelyn and friends. Here are the two of them placing stones in an extensive outdoor retaining wall. "Eventually, we'll retire there," she says. "As it is, we go up year-round – for Thanksgiving, for Christmas, for skiing. In winter, we build a bobsled run down the hill beside the house, right out onto the lake."

Back home, Yvan exercises his love of manual chores in a myriad of ways that includes ironing, dish-washing, and household repairs. He recently installed hardwood trim on the kitchen counter and built a wine cellar in the basement to house the wine he has begun to make and bottle. He acknowledges having something close to a fetish for hand tools and admits to "going crazy" in the tool departments of stores. "I'm a simple man at heart," he says. "I like a project." He does not like reading – and says so with the certainty of a man who knows and accepts himself and is not about to explain or apologize. "I watch TV instead," he says. "I could watch CNN all day."

"He doesn't even read about himself!" laughs Evelyn. "On the rare occasion that he does pick up a book, he turns to the last page first – I guess from all those years of picking up newspapers and turning to the sports pages at the back."

These days, when he checks the sports pages and local television stations, it is in the hope of finding mention of the Roadrunners. Coverage is improving. On the night of the game with the Cheetahs, he arrived home to a thirty-second item on the team's victory. The next day's newspaper carried a game photo accompanied by eight column-inches of print.

For the few days that followed the game, Yvan was happy to forget the daunting task of establishing the Roadrunners in a city where the yardstick for sporting obsession is, and will perhaps always be, the Montreal Canadiens. The following morning, first thing, he was up and away with Evelyn and Kurtis for a weekend at the Laurentian chalet. "Unfortunately, since roller hockey started, we haven't been able to spend as much time up there as we'd like," laments Evelyn.

But to imply that roller hockey is the only restriction on Yvan and the family's time in the mountains would be far from accurate. Like so many former Canadiens, Yvan is a part-time public-relations representative for Molson Brewery, attending golf and hockey tournaments on the brewery's behalf and playing exhibition softball on their team of former Canadiens. He also does public relations work for a variety of local and national businesses. For several years, he and Evelyn have operated an agency through which Yvan can be hired as a promotional front man by any company or endeavour that might need fronting and that the couple deems worthy of their services. "And he's an inventor!" smiles Evelyn, who explains that a one-piece suit of hockey underwear designed by Yvan was marketed briefly by Winnwell sporting goods, who paid Yvan a royalty on every set of longjohns they sold.

Yvan himself has not played hockey for many years – at least not in public. "My knees are too bad," he says. "People expect you to play like they remember you in your prime, and I can't. And I don't want to disappoint anybody." He admits to a fondness for good food, but whatever calories he adds he sheds just as quickly on the fitness equipment in the basement at home, where he works out for an hour or more a day, mostly on the treadmill. "He's too shy to work out in public or at a club," confides Evelyn.

He is not so shy, however, that he is reticent to express an opinion, or reluctant to speak out if he feels an injustice has been perpetrated. He is scornful, for instance, of the NHL's all-but-criminal insensitivity in failing to provide an adequate pension plan for the players of his era. "You'd think they'd have been bright enough to establish a decent plan," he says, "but they weren't. And we're paying for it now. I get the pension, but you can't go far on eight or nine thousand a year. Some of the guys'll have to work till they drop."

Yvan will not. "I've done well," he admits. "I had good contracts in hockey; I've had great jobs since. I've fulfilled my dreams. If you can get up in the morning and look forward to going to work, and don't just see it as so many hours on the job, you can't complain. I can't complain."

Nor can Yvan complain about his place in Quebec's cultural pantheon, where he enjoys an almost iconic status. His relationship with his public is uncomplicated. They are adoring; he is appreciative – and singularly unassuming about his fame and accomplishments. "I just don't see myself as special," he says. "Hockey was my profession, my job. A great job, yes, but still a job. When you need a plumber, send for this guy, a carpenter this guy.

"When you need a hockey player, send for Yvan. He'll try to get the job done."

# 6 RANDY GREGG

## ON HIS OWN TERMS

IN LATE 1982, SHORTLY after Randy Gregg began his NHL career with the Edmonton Oilers, a reporter for the Montreal *Gazette* flew to Pittsburgh where the Oilers were about the play the Penguins, and approached Randy in the lobby of the Hilton Hotel. He wanted an interview. It was not uncommon for reporters to follow the Oilers around in those days. They were still a season away from winning their first Stanley Cup, but clearly they were the decade's coming attraction, and their line-up included the personable mega-star, Wayne Gretzky, who, the previous season, had scored a preposterous ninety-two goals.

At the time, Randy had completed medical school and half of a two-year internship, but apart from his distinction as the first medical doctor to play NHL hockey he had yet to establish even a modest reputation in the league. "So, I was kind of surprised," he explains, "when this guy just ignored Gretzky and Messier and Kurri and came up to me asking if we could talk."

They could, and did, and Randy recalls feeling "extremely uneasy" when the reporter asked immediately how it felt to sit in his room reading medical books while

Yvan Cournoyer joined the Canadiens for the 1963–64 season. He is seen here in his official team photo from that year.

Yvan on a mission against Eddie Giacomin, Harry Howell, and Arnie Brown of the Rangers.

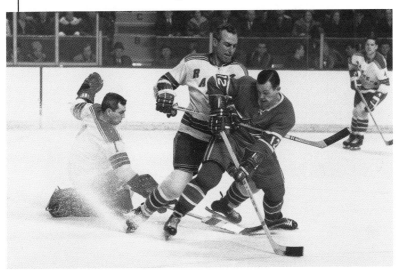

During fourteen
years with the
Canadiens,
Yvan played on
ten Stanley
Cup winners.

Yvan and Evelyn.

Yvan and Kurt on Lac
Labelle, in front of
the family chalet, 1994.

Randy Gregg on tour with the University of Alberta Golden Bears in Japan, 1979.

Randy as a playing coach with the Kokudo Bunnies in Japan, 1981.

Randy, Kathy, and
the family bring
home the Cup,
May 1990.

Dr. Gregg.

Randy played his final
NHL season, 1991–92,
with the Vancouver
Canucks.

Johnny Bower with the Rangers, pictured on a 1955 hockey card.

John as a Maple Leaf, during the glorious sixties.

John and Nancy with their daughter Barb's children, Kelly and Dale.

John at his favourite pastime.

John playing Santa Claus at a Maple Leaf Gardens Christmas party, shortly before his retirement.

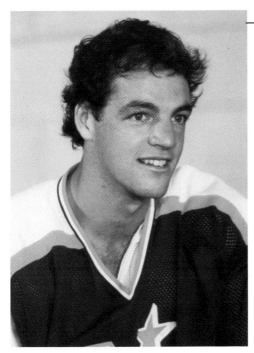

Bobby Smith began his
pro career with the
Minnesota North Stars
in 1979.

Bob scored the Stanley Cup-winning goal for the
Montreal Canadiens in 1986.

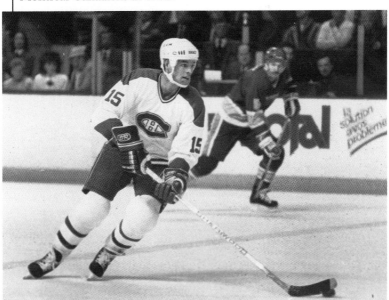

Bob and Beth, with Ryan (left), Daniel, and Megan, in Florida.

Daniel Smith, in goal on the neighbourhood pond in Eden Prairie, Minnesota.

Bob and Ryan, heading for the pond.

the rest of the players were sitting in their rooms reading comic books. "I knew something was up," he says, "but I wanted the truth told, so I said, 'Well, first of all, I'm not in my room reading medical books, and they're not in theirs reading comics. And, secondly, I have more respect for these guys and their dedication than I do for many of the doctors I've worked with.'"

The resulting profile appeared a few days later in the *Gazette* and was reprinted shortly afterwards in *The Hockey News*, where Randy saw it. "I was just furious, just outraged," he says. "The thing ended with a quote, supposedly my words, quotation marks and all: 'While they're in their rooms reading comic books, I'm in my room reading medical books, but on the whole they're pretty good guys.' I saw this reporter six months later, and I'm not really an aggressive person, but even that long after the fact I was still so furious that I picked him up by the shirt collar and, well, you know, went through the customary ritual threats: if you ever do that to me again, and so on, and so forth."

Randy Gregg is not a particularly religious man, and is certainly not a pious man. And yet there is something distinctly apostolic in his personality – most notably in his eminent regard for the truth. He has no apparent fear of it, and does not like to see it violated, either in word or spirit.

If he has a concern about telling it, at least for public consumption, it is, to paraphrase musician Paul Simon, "that his meaning will be lost or misconstrued" – or downright ignored, as it was during the interview in Pittsburgh.

He is perhaps equally concerned that his *motives* will be misinterpreted. He is quite happy to speak his mind about Peter Pocklington, for example – and to speak it rather critically – but at the same time is determined that he not be seen as some frosted agent of moral indignation (which he is certainly not) or as someone with an axe to grind (which, again, he is not). After spending a twelve-hour day with him in July 1994, I came to the conclusion that he is simply a person for whom the truth, even in its harsher measures, is more liberating, useful, and instructive – and infinitely more interesting – than its opposite or its denial.

In this, he is a journalist's dream . . . and a conciliator's nightmare. For part of his commitment to the truth and its attendant freedoms is a powerful resistance to compromise. "Randy can be extremely stubborn," smiles his wife, Kathy. "If he believes in something, there's very little point in trying to change his mind. He's not likely to back down."

The claim was amply demonstrated in 1985 in the aftermath of a nationally televised NHL game between the Oilers and Chicago Blackhawks. "At a certain point in the game," says Randy, "we were killing a double penalty, five on three, and Gretz got the puck and wheeled up ice over centre. And suddenly I noticed the whole neutral slot open up, and, even knowing that I had no business leaving my defence post and going in there, I jumped forward, and he put a pass right on my stick, and miraculously there I was with nobody between me and the net. I skated in, managed to fake the goaltender and was about to put the puck in when I was just *seized* by some notion that I was in the wrong place at the wrong time, and I tightened up and shot wide."

In commenting on the blown opportunity, between periods, broadcaster Don Cherry declared "With hands like those, I'd never let the guy perform surgery on me!"

"It didn't bother me too much really," says Randy, "but it bothered some people a lot." Among the offended were the Oilers' Peter Pocklington and Glen Sather, who wrote a letter to *Hockey Night in Canada*, demanding an apology from Cherry. "The result," says Randy, "was that about two weeks later, in Pittsburgh, we were having our pre-game meal, and who should walk into the room but Cherry, joking away, not really talking to anyone in partic-ular, but mouthing off about how we had to understand that he liked to make his broadcasts fun, that he didn't really mean what he said, no big deal, and so on. And he got to me, and he put out his hand, apparently to apologize, but I just kept eating my meal; I wouldn't even look at him. If I'd believed he was sincere in his apology, I would have accepted it, but of course he wasn't. And, besides that, I'd been thinking about how the things people like Cherry say in the name of entertainment can significantly affect the attitudes of children and coaches and parents. In many ways, I think a clown is important; that's why I take my kids to the circus. But when a hockey clown publicly belit-tles dedicated professional players because they're European or wear facemasks or don't fight – or says things such as 'I like so-and-so because he sticks people' – you have to wonder what a twelve-year-old thinks when he hears it, or a parent who'd like to see his or her child in the NHL. When it comes to this, we can't keep laughing at our clowns. A lot of damage is being done. So I didn't shake his hand. I find it hard to make concessions to people who stand for things I don't believe in."

It hardly needs saying that the hockey establishment is crowded with people who stand for things that Randy Gregg doesn't believe in: owners, managers, coaches, media toadies, pitchmen. And over the years he has made a point of challenging their attitudes, occasionally attempting to change them, but more often simply flushing them into the open, whether directly or by simple contrast with his own rather forthright attitudes. His initial contract negotiations with the Oilers were a note-worthy example of his methods – in fact were not so much a negotiation as an exercise in moral extortion. "At the time I had no intention of playing more than a couple of years," he says. "They wanted me to play four, minimally, but I thought that would be far too long to stay out of medicine. Really all I wanted was a chance to test myself against the best in the world. Anyway, I went to see [general manager] Glen Sather one day, and he made me a contract offer: $50,000 to sign and, I think, $120,000 for the first year, increasing to 125, 135, 145, and 150, over the next five years. I realized of course that I was in a pretty unusual situation; with medicine to fall back on, money wasn't my main concern, and I only wanted a brief pro career. On top of that, I was an unrestricted free agent; I could go to any team that wanted me, and I knew there were others that did. So, I could afford to think that I was going to do things a little differently – that in one way or another Sather and I were going to establish an association that wasn't just a function of some bloodless business contract." Randy pauses, collects his thoughts, and says that, for years, he has been "really bothered" by the relationship between management and players, in particular by the process of establishing contracts. He says, "It's basically a one-way street; if they want to send you to the minors, they do; if they want to trade you, they do; if they want to pay you so much money, that's what they pay you. And I wanted Sather to understand that, this time, he couldn't do that. So, I simply said, 'Thanks for the offer, but it's not quite what I had in mind,' and I got up and walked out. As a player, I had no real right to be acting so presumptuously; I was never going to be one of the stars of the team. But I felt I had a right as a human being. And I was determined they were going to acknowledge that right. I said, 'Look, I don't even *want* any signing bonus. If I'm not good enough to be here, we can just tear up the contract; I'll quit. But if you people think I'm good enough to be part of this team, you're going to have to see things at least partly from my perspective.' It was all a risk, of course, because I really did want to play in my home town."

As Randy walked through the door, Sather called him back, and upped the salary offer. "We talked a little further, but still didn't seem to be connecting," says Randy. "So I walked out again, thinking, 'This is probably it.'"

Again Sather called him back. "Very very gradually," says Randy, "we established not just a contract but an understanding, part of which was that if, at any time, the Oilers decided to send me to the minors or trade me to another team, I'd simply quit and go back into medicine."

More important, Randy established himself as a human presence, not a mere mercenary, in an organization that he would eventually realize was as mercenary as any in sport. By no means incidentally, he also placed himself on what was then the best hockey team in the world.

If the personality of Dr. Randall John Gregg could be reduced to a descriptive cameo, the miniature profile would almost certainly include the fact that he has had the same home phone number all his life. "Isn't that amazing!" laughs his wife, Kathy, who explains that, for her, this seemingly trifling detail has always epitomized Randy's unimpeachable constancy and reliability. "He was born and raised in the same house," she says, "never moved out and ended up buying it from his parents while he was at university. I moved in when we got married, had two of the four kids there, and when we moved out a few years ago we stayed close enough that we kept the same phone number." Not surprisingly, the Greggs also kept ownership of the house they left behind, which had been built by Randy's dad in 1945 and which they now rent to friends.

Asked for a more expansive tour of Randy's character, Kathy submits that he is generous, patient, and "extraordinarily popular with kids" in the family's Edmonton neighbourhood.

He is also almost pathologically modest. "He's never wanted to be the centre of attention," says Kathy, "although it's pretty hard not to be when you're six-foot-four, have red hair, and have played on five Stanley Cup-winning hockey teams." Randy expresses recurring disparagement of his talents as a player (the self-deprecation is exaggerated by the radiant praise he lavishes on almost everyone he ever played with), and exudes genuine incredulity that he made it as far as he did in the hockey world.

His modesty is complemented by an ironic sense of humour and remarkable self-possession. "I never fought in hockey," he says, "because I couldn't stand the thought of anybody, particularly my kids, seeing me lose it, seeing me that far out of control. . . . My attitude toward fighting was, If you win you've got sore hands; if you lose you've got a sore face!"

Despite his reserve, Randy is ambitious in business and possesses the work habits of a bee in June. Besides running the sports medicine clinic that he co-owns in Edmonton (he takes home as much as three hours of paperwork a night), he is the co-founder and president of a community-based athletic charity called Funteam, and owns both a sports art gallery and a family investment company named for his favourite James Clavell novel, *Taipan*. During the mid-eighties, he founded a company that imported and sold the first four thousand pairs of Rollerblades in Canada.

On average, he spends a couple of hours a day with his children, who, along with other family members, are far and away the paramount people in his life.

Randy was born in Edmonton in 1956, in the same hospital where he would one day intern as a doctor. He is the youngest of six children, whose father worked as a train engineer, supplementing his income by operating a tiny industrial supply business out of the back of the family station wagon. "When I was little," says Randy, "our idea of an exciting time was to unload the hoses and fittings, and so on, jump in the station wagon and head to the lake for the weekend."

As a high school and university student, Randy helped his dad with the business. By this time, however, it had taken over the basement of the family home, from where it eventually moved into a warehouse (it is now run by Randy's brother Gary, and employs some eighty people).

"But in the early days," recalls Randy, "it was just my dad, doing the two jobs, and us kids having to keep quiet in the house while he was sleeping, so he could keep going when he was awake. I remember wondering at times why we had to live that way, but overall it was a good experience to be able to see his dedication at close range and to see its effects."

Randy entered the science program at the University of Alberta at the age of sixteen, with the hope that he would one day follow his brother Ron into the field of medicine. At the time he was playing midget hockey, and it never occurred to him to try out for the university team. "I didn't even consider myself a particularly good player," he says. "I loved it, but I was just having fun – in midget and then juvenile." During the summer he played what he describes as "fairly high-level baseball."

A few days after he'd been accepted into medical school, in 1975, Randy's brother approached him with the stern admonition that the time had come to forget about sports, get down to business, and make something of himself. "I said, 'Well sure, Ron. Absolutely. That's what I intend to do.'"

But during the first days of medical school that

September, Randy, in a rare reversal of form, reneged on his promise, responding to a deeper urge to test himself at try-outs for the U. of A. Golden Bears, who were at that time the champions of Canadian university hockey. "I knew it would be impossible to do medicine and hockey, too," he says. "But I also knew that I'd be cut from the team long before it made any difference or before my brother found out."

What he discovered at the earliest practices was that a number of the team's prominent defencemen from the previous season had graduated and that the coaching staff was pleased indeed to have a mobile, 210-pound blueliner in camp. "In a nutshell," says Randy, "two or three practices became ten, then twenty, then we had exhibition games, and – well, four years of university hockey later," he laughs.

His methods for coping with his studies in the face of daily practices, weekly games, and regular road trips were as cool as an Alberta stream – and, for Randy, somewhat uncharacteristic. "I never really worried about doing all that well," he says. "It was important to know the information, and of course you had to pass; but I was by no means at the top of my class. What I wanted, really, was the degree of knowledge that would enable me to be a good physician, not just a good test writer."

His coolness under academic stress was such that, smack in the middle of final exams during his last year of medicine, he accepted an invitation from the New York Rangers to fly to New York with his brother Gary to see a playoff game between the Rangers and the Islanders. "It was just great," he says. "They put us up in the Waldorf-Astoria, even got us tickets to Yankee Stadium, basically laid it all on. I probably should have passed it up to study, but I really didn't want to – I did manage to spend some time with the books on the airplane. My salvation at school was always that I kept up as we went along. I worked hard at night and I worked hard on weekends."

And he worked hard at the rink. Twice during his years with the Golden Bears, he took a Clydesdale's role in helping the team to Canadian university championships. During his final season, he was named Canadian Intercollegiate Player of the Year. As with so many of his awards and achievements, however, he tends to minimize the degree to which the award was deserved. "There were much better players around," he shrugs, "but I think they wanted to say: we appreciate that to play this level of hockey and to go to medical school is a little different, maybe something of an accomplishment."

One night during the CIAU finals in Moncton, New Brunswick, during his final year, Randy was approached in a restaurant by a personable man in a clerical collar. "He introduced himself as Father David Bauer," says Randy. "I knew his reputation as the founder of the national hockey program during the sixties – otherwise not that much. But, you know, during about three minutes of conversation with the guy, he made an impression on me that has really never worn off – I was extremely intrigued by him."

As it turned out, Father Bauer was in the process of putting together a hockey team that would represent Canada at the 1980 Olympics in Lake Placid, New York. "He'd already identified some players that he felt might work out in the program," says Randy, "and I was lucky enough to be one of them."

One evening that summer, as Randy bided his time in Edmonton, playing amateur baseball and waiting for the try-out camp that Father Bauer was to hold in that city, he got a phone call. "This guy introduced himself as an NHL agent and asked if I had a minute to talk," he says. "I thought, yeah, sure, somebody's joking with me. But it did sound like long distance, so I thought I should at least be polite."

The agent, no joker, informed Randy that the New York Rangers were willing to offer him a $50,000 signing bonus and a two-year contract at a salary of $100,000 a year if he would join the team. "I guess it should have been an internal crisis for me," says Randy. "But I tend to be pretty single-minded, and at that point my ambition was to be part of the Olympic program. Besides, down the line, I figured the hundred thousand wouldn't be as important, looking back, as going to Lake Placid – if I could make the team. So I thanked him for the offer, and that was that."

Randy calls the Lake Placid Olympics in 1980 the most enjoyable experience of his life. "The guys played the entire year for four thousand dollars," he says, "and we spent most of our training time living in Atco trailers, in eight-by-ten-foot cells, near the present site of the Saddledome in Calgary. But I wouldn't trade any of it for anything else I could have been doing. We travelled to Europe, to Japan; we were incredibly close, and we had the benefit of working under a terrific coach, Clare Drake, and under Father Bauer, the team's general manager."

As an example of the unassuming strength and integrity that he so admired in David Bauer, Randy tells the story of how in the autumn of 1979, he and four teammates planned a late night joyride to a Hallowe'en party in Edmonton, at the house Randy owned and was then renting to a group of young women. "Dave Hindmarsh and I had gone together and bought a three-hundred-dollar car, a real rattletrap," he says, "and we figured we could make the trip and be back in time for practice in the morning."

The car made it safely to Edmonton and back, the partiers had some fun, and a month later Randy found out that Father Bauer had been in the next room, listening, as the fivesome had planned the junket. "Not that he was eavesdropping," says Randy, "he could just hear – the walls in the trailers were like paper. He knew there could be a serious accident, especially with an old car; he knew that we could be injured or even killed, and that the whole Olympic effort could be jeopardized. And yet he told me later that he didn't feel he could walk in there and tell us not to do it. He believed in free will, in learning by experience. Not that I learned anything from making the trip, but I did learn from his attitude toward it. And I've never forgotten the lesson. Father Bauer's emphasis was on character development, the whole person, not just athletics. When we travelled, he'd encourage us to go to museums, art galleries, to interact with the people around us. There was very little emphasis on winning for its own sake. Which of course just made you want to win all the more for the guy."

In the end, the team did not win for Father Bauer. They won several games early in the Olympic tournament, then lost a heartbreaking game to Finland, when a 180-foot shot slipped between the Canadian goaltender's legs. But they were still in a position to make the medal playoff if they could somehow defeat the seemingly invincible Soviet team, whose roster included a number of the world's finest players. Randy says, "I remember during the second period intercepting a pass and thinking I'd just dump the puck into their end. But as I came across the blueline, I changed my mind and took the hardest wrist shot I could. It hit Tretiak's glove and snuck in over the goal line. I thought, this'll never happen again. It made the score 3–1 for us. Then they scored right at the end of the second, and I remember looking around the dressing room between periods; it was kind of a Kodak moment. These guys were like brothers; we'd spent six months together, we'd given so much to this and knew one another so well, and we could just feel that the Big Red Machine was starting to come to life. And indeed they came back and beat us, 5–3."

The scene in the dressing room following the game was one of emotional exhaustion and turmoil. Randy says, "I can still see Glenn Anderson sitting in the corner crying his eyes out, just losing it, because the whole thing had been so intense. I showered and got dressed, feeling pretty fragile myself. I took three steps out the door, and there in my face was this NHL agent who'd called me the previous summer. Inside, I just snapped. I mean, he'd told me he'd be calling after the Olympics, and I'd said that was fine. But this was ridiculous, and I told him in terms that I'm afraid weren't very polite that he should leave and leave now, that the Olympic experience was not yet over for me."

Indeed it was not. One of the girls who rented Randy's house in Edmonton had alerted him to be on the look-out for her friend Kathy Vogt, a speed skater from Winnipeg, who would be representing Canada at Lake Placid. Likewise, the friend had told Kathy to look for a tall, red-haired hockey player. "I certainly wasn't going to the Olympics to meet women," says Randy, "but just before the games started, there was a reception for the Canadian athletes at what was called Canada House. As usual, the hockey players got there and lined the walls, then the skiers came in, then the speed skaters, and I noticed a very attractive young woman in braids, and it occurred to me it might be Kathy; I thought, boy, I should make the acquaintance, but I was just too shy to walk up and introduce myself."

Kathy felt no such diffidence. A few nights later at the Olympic Village disco, she recognized, approached, and greeted Randy. She says, "At first, we just kinda chatted, nothing much, but a few nights after that we went to a movie, and by the end of the evening I felt, this is the guy I want to marry."

Randy was felled by the same potent virus. "I knew pretty much from the beginning," he says, "that I wanted to make a future with Kathy."

For the next few years, the pair's courting was conducted across half the globe. At the time, Kathy was spending her winters training with the Canadian speed-skating team in Inzell, Germany, returning to Winnipeg to study during the summer. Six months after the games, Randy went to Tokyo, Japan, for two years, to play hockey for the Kokudo Bunnies, a team owned by Yoshiaki Tsutsumi, owner of the Prince Hotel chain and president of the Japanese Ice Hockey Federation. During summers, he interned at the Royal Alexandra Hospital in Edmonton.

He was in Japan, in part, because, shortly before Lake Placid, the players on the Olympic team had been visited by Judge Willard Estey and Alan Eagleson, who were on the board of Hockey Canada and who told the players that if they'd commit to four more years as amateurs, and to playing in the next Olympics, the national program would continue. "For me, the decision wasn't hard at all," says Randy. "I was completely sold on Hockey Canada, happy to commit to it."

Two weeks after the games, Estey, Eagleson, and company betrayed the faithful and wiped out the program they had vowed to perpetuate. "I guess the sixth-place finish wasn't as impressive as what they'd hoped for," says Randy. "But I wasn't about to change direction; I'd loved the Olympics so much, I wanted to keep my amateur status, just in case. So when I got a chance to play in Japan, I jumped at it. I'd been there twice for tournaments – once with the Golden Bears, once with the Olympic team – and I'd loved it. Technically, I played as an amateur and earned my living as an assistant manager at one of Mr. Tsutsumi's hotels. Both years, when the season ended, I jumped on a plane in Tokyo and was interning in Edmonton a couple of days later."

One afternoon during his second year with Kokudo, Randy got a fateful phone call from Glen Sather, who wanted to let him know that the Oilers, who had courted him earlier, were still interested in signing him if at any time he should decide to turn pro. Since the Olympics, he had also had offers from the New York Rangers and Calgary Flames. "Being Canadian," he says, "I knew what big-league hockey meant. I was twenty-four years old by this time and figured it was probably my last chance to see where I stacked up against the best. I was ready to give it a try." The choice of a uniform was easy. "I'd never wanted to live in New York," he says, "and my family were passionate Oiler fans; they'd have disowned me if I'd signed with Calgary." So, even though the Flames had offered considerably more money than the Oilers, Randy returned from Japan and signed with the home-town team. His intention was to play for two years – then get back to medicine.

He was barely off the plane when he was propelled into service during the 1982 playoffs. "We were playing Los Angeles, at home," he says. "My parents were there, my family, all my friends. When I skated out for my first shift, I remember thinking, What am I *doing* here? Surely, I don't belong!"

Despite his doubts, Randy had a solid first year, and during his second season helped the franchise to its first Stanley Cup. A few weeks later, Randy and Kathy were married in Winnipeg. Part of the service was conducted by the Reverend David Bauer, part by Kathy's father, Roy, an economics professor at the University of Winnipeg and an ordained Mennonite minister.

That same summer, Glen Sather asked Randy to try out

for Team Canada, which was about to come together for the 1984 Canada Cup tournament. "I told him 'Absolutely not!'" says Randy. "'The Canada Cup is for stars; you don't need someone like me.' Glen said, 'No, no, we want a rounded team: goal-scorers, checkers, defensive defence-man – that's how we won the Cup.'"

Half-convinced, Randy went to camp in Montreal and made the team along with fellow Oiler Charlie Huddy, amidst controversy over the exclusion of all-star players such as Scott Stevens. "I sat out the first game against Germany," says Randy, "and I'll never forget looking into the stands at the Forum and seeing a sign: HUDDY PLUS GREGG EQUALS SATHER – as if to say, 'What the heck are *these* guys doing here?' And I agreed! It ended up that I played a few games, and we won the Canada Cup. But I knew my place wasn't in the limelight. I was a support player, getting the puck to the forwards, clearing the net area, playing my position. I've often said I was a fifty-goal scorer in the NHL, but that it took me nine years to get the fifty."

I met Kathy and Randy and their four children in July 1994 during their yearly summer vacation at Kathy's parents' cottage at Belair, on Lake Winnipeg, in central Manitoba. As it happened, my visit coincided with the annual reunion of Kathy's closest friends from her years as a competitive speed skater. Four of her former teammates came with their husbands and children, so that the day became a kind of private festival of games, swimming, trampolining, reminiscence, and horseplay – and expansive meals around the barbecue. During the mid-afternoon, Kathy brought out a colourfully decorated *piñata* she had made, and the kids whaled away at it until it showered them with candy. Early in the evening, the whole gathering, twenty-five in all, trooped down the road to the local ice-cream stand for cones the size of five-pin balls.

Randy takes profound pleasure in his children (in fact, in everybody's children) and maintains a gentle equanimity toward them, whatever their moods or antics. His good-humoured equipoise is a talent that he undoubtedly carries to his work and that, over the years, must significantly have impressed not only his teammates and coaches but his medical colleagues and patients. He and I drifted in and out of the day's activities and socializing, managing (against the odds) to claim five or six hours of conversation on an elongated swing chair that was situated on the edge of a bluff, looking out over Lake Winnipeg. The wind was high, the sun strong, and, above the silvery expanse of water that spread out beyond us, pelicans and terns performed an unending aerobatic ballet, a significant complement to the dream-like quality of the day. By late afternoon, we were both wearing unhealthy-looking sunburns on our faces and legs.

When we settled to the swing chair and tape recorder after lunch, Randy began an unexpectedly candid appraisal of his years with the Edmonton Oilers – an assessment that was, by turns, wistful, appreciative, and scathing. If his honesty is heartening to a journalist, so too is his thoroughness. He describes his career in much the way he played it: with an unswerving commitment to order and detail. During the course of the afternoon, he occasionally cut me off in mid-question, because a previous question had not yet been answered to his satisfaction. He'd say, "Let me just back up a moment and finish what I wanted to say . . ."

He made it amply clear that he felt deeply privileged to have played on the same team as the likes of Gretzky, Messier, Coffey, Lowe, and Anderson, and to have had his name engraved five times on the Stanley Cup. He said, "I have nothing but the deepest respect for the talents and dedication of these guys."

He made it just as clear that, after three or four years with the team, he developed an equally potent *lack* of respect for the team's ownership and management – and that his attitude was shared by the majority, if not all, of his teammates. "We kept on winning into the late eighties," he says, "but it was largely because of the incredible closeness among the players and the leadership and talent of guys like Messier and Gretzky. Essentially we were playing for one another and for the fans, not for the organization."

In Randy's view, the divorce between players and management was effected about equally by the attitudes of Glen Sather and Peter Pocklington. "Glen's great ability to bring a team together," he says, "is first of all that he understands talent and the value of particular players; he knows what the puzzle should look like, and is prepared, say, to go to Japan for a defenceman, or to trade for a tough third-line centre. Beyond that, his success is largely in motivating by intimidation, essentially by bullying. And in the early days, this was fine; the guys accepted it, and it probably helped us win the first couple of Cups. But later on, as the team developed professionally and we matured as individuals, it got really old and tiresome, and began to create this irreversible disenchantment."

Randy recalls two particular flashpoints, "significant indicators" that the coach's methods were no longer working. "The first," he says, "was during the '86 playoffs, the year Calgary beat us out after our second Cup. We were down 3–2 in games, going into Calgary for game six, and the day before the big game, we were in the dressing room, and Glen walked in, and instead of venting his anger on a relatively passive guy like Mike Krushelnyski, as he usually did, he looked at Mark Messier and said, 'What's the matter with you, Mark? You're not playing with any heart!' Now, you have to understand that this was not the sort of thing you said to Mark Messier, who was pretty much the embodiment of the team's heart and soul. Glen thought he could get away with it in the name of motivation. But as soon as we heard the word 'heart,' we knew he'd made a mistake. And sure enough Mark jumped up – he was livid; he could hardly speak; his face was just contorted with anger. And he started advancing on Glen, stammering, 'How *dare* you question my blankety-blank heart! How *dare* you!' And Glen of course is backing up by this time, afraid that Mark's going to tear his throat out. And then Mark starts in, 'If you ever question my blankety-blank heart again, if you *ever* do that again, I'll *never* wear this blankety-blank uniform again!' And Glen's still backing up, pleading, 'Calm down, Mark! Calm down! I'm not questioning your heart.' And Mark keeps jumping back in, 'If you *ever* question my heart again . . .' And Glen's saying, 'Mark, I'd *never* question your heart . . .'

"Sometime later, as if he hadn't learned anything, Glen pulled the same stunt on Wayne, who was another guy you just didn't trifle with in that way! I mean, Wayne was our spiritual leader; he was such a gentleman and a caring person. And one day Sather came in and told him, in front of everyone, that he wasn't working, he wasn't playing well, that it looked like he couldn't care less. I guess he figured he could motivate Wayne by challenging him in front of everyone, and motivate the rest of us, because we'd figure, if he thinks Wayne's playing badly, what must he think about me? But, in effect, the ripple that went through the team was not one of motivation but of plain disgust at Glen's tactics. We were grown men; we weren't into being humiliated."

At times, Randy explains, Sather's humiliations were little more than meaningless ritual. "One of my teammates," he says, "played eleven years, two as captain – really nice fella, committed to the team. He was making $125,000, which is a lot of money, but well below the NHL average. And he went in to Sather to negotiate his contract in, I guess, 1986. He said, 'I'd like to play one more year, help the young guys, work in the press box if necessary, but I'm way below the average salary, and I thought it might be possible to play for $130,000, a five-thousand-dollar raise.' And Glen looked him in the face and said, 'Let's make it twenty-five-hundred and flip a coin for it.' And the guy said, 'Forget it.' And he walked out and played his final year at the old salary and never set foot in the Northlands Coliseum again.

"Of course a chill goes right through the team when they hear that a good friend has been treated like that. Certainly it's not the money itself that means anything to guys like Sather and Pocklington. In '86, I retired for a bit, because the team seemed to be coming apart, and six weeks later when the team wasn't doing so well, Sather asked me to come back, and I re-signed for $30,000 more to play sixty games than I'd have made if I'd played eighty. Which more than anything else made me realize that money's just a negotiating tool for these guys! When you're making eight, ten, twelve million a year, as these guys were reported to be at the time, a few thousand dollars one way or the other – or even a hundred thousand – is little more than a minor detail."

Randy takes particular umbrage at Pocklington's frequent claim that, even at the height of the Oilers' success, he was losing money: "Any prudent businessman can tell you that if you want a team or organization to appear to be losing money, you can make the books show losses. But people who know the NHL say he'd have had no trouble making between eight and twelve million a year through the mid-eighties. Most people think he's pulled about

$120 million out of the Edmonton economy. And what really hurts is that, for all this taking during those years, he and the organization have put so little back in!"

Randy describes how, when he joined the Oilers, he offered to buy and donate a pair of season tickets for the use of children in wheelchairs. "There wasn't much wheelchair space at the Coliseum, so, if these kids were going to be accommodated, more would have to be arranged, some ramps constructed, and so on. Glen was pretty open to the idea; he has a sense of decency. But, in all, it would have cost the team three or four thousand dollars. And, for that reason, it never happened, and the offer of the tickets went begging. The attitude always seemed to be, why should I give back when I can just keep taking?

"Later in my years with the team, we formed a players' group that went and spoke to kids. We did it on condition of complete anonymity, no media, no cameras. When you went out on a visit organized by management, it always had to be shown – or why do it? I thought if I could contribute something to the young fellas on the team – guys like Bill Ranford and Adam Graves – it was to demonstrate that you could give to the community for no reason other than giving. And the young guys loved these outings. They'd come back asking when we could go again! Anyway, we had a long road trip, didn't play very well, and the day after we got back our promotions guy came in and said, 'Fellas, I know you're tired, but we've got two events coming up: our annual trip to the hospitals and the advertisers' dinner.' The dinner's an event at which the players go and sit with the people who advertise in the rink, the program, whatever. I'd been talking up the hospital visit with the younger guys, because I know how much these things mean to the disabled kids; they talk about it forever. So, our promotions guy said, 'Since you're worn out, and we've got a bit of a conflict, we're only going to do one of these events – it's the advertisers' dinner on Wednesday night.' And as soon as he said it, I could see our younger guys looking at me, as if to say, how can this happen? How can we make a priority of taking and taking and taking, when giving is so easy? So two weeks later we organized by ourselves, and a fair number of the players went out to hospitals independent of the team.

"Really, there are more examples than I can count as to why my respect for the organization isn't greater. Little things. Daily things. Bonus cheques would be delivered two hours before the absolute deadline for them. Fake diamonds would get put into the Stanley Cup rings of the training staff, who, for the players, are very important people. In fact, when Wayne found out this had happened the first year, he had all the rings fitted with diamonds, at his own expense."

Randy recalls with a grin that, in the days when Pocklington owned the infamous Gainer's meatpacking plant, he would occasionally burst into the dressing room between the second and third periods of games in which the Oilers were playing the Calgary Flames – "games in which we were down a goal or two" – and offer each of the players a box of beef if they could come back and win. "And in fact the guys enjoyed the little challenge," says Randy. "But after a while, like so many other things that went on, it got kind of grating, this assumption that, even as grown men at the top of our profession, we could only hit peak performance for a few kilos of frozen meat. What was funny about it, though, was that when we did win our beef, it often wouldn't show up – for weeks! This was at a time when Wendy's restaurants had a commercial in which an old lady would walk into a competitor's restaurant and demand, 'Where's the beef?' So, when Pocklington came in to give a speech or something, Kevin McClelland, who didn't like him, would be at the back of the room; and from somewhere in the shadows we'd hear his low voice, *'Where's the beef?'* It'd just crack us up."

On other occasions, Pocklington himself cracked the team up. Unintentionally. "Every year, before the playoffs, he'd come into the dressing room to try to get the players going," says Randy. "And he'd always tell us the same story: about how when he was younger he'd gone to Egypt and had visited the site of a cathedral that was being built. He'd tell us how he'd gone up to this worker, and had said, 'What are *you* doing?' And the guy had replied, 'I'm a stone cutter.' And he'd gone to a second worker and asked what *he* was doing, and the guy had given him the same answer, 'I'm a stone cutter.' He asked a few more guys, and then he got to a man who had a slightly different look in his eye and said, 'What are *you* doing?' And the guy had looked at him and replied, 'I'm a cathedral builder.' The gist of it was that if we were going to get anywhere we had to be more than hockey players; we had to be visionaries, cathedral builders. And the first couple of times he told the story, it was kinda nice. But by the third or fourth year, it had worn a bit thin.

"This particular year – 1987, I guess – we hadn't been playing very well, and when he finished the story this time, he said, 'Fellas, I've been lying awake at night, I'm so frustrated I can't sleep.' He said, 'All of you are like sons to me, like family. I believe in you, I *feel* for you, I care about each one of you.' He looked at Mark Messier, who was sitting next to me, and he said, 'You know, Mark, we need you to be our team leader.' Then he said to me, 'Randy, we need you to provide strength on defence.' Charlie Huddy was next, and he said, 'Charlie, we need your experience and determination.' Next to Charlie was a guy named Doug Halward, who had come in a trade from Detroit a few months back. And Pocklington looked at him and obviously didn't have a clue who he was. So he didn't speak to

him, went across the room to Kevin Lowe and told him we
needed *him* for some special reason. Craig Simpson was
next, in a stall that had somebody else's name on it; he'd
been with us a year by this time. And Peter stammered,
'And, uh . . . our friend from another team; we need what
you can give us.' Well, by this time, half the players had
their heads between their legs to keep from howling out
loud. Here was the big inspirational speech reduced to a
total farce, because truly we meant nothing more to Peter
than his next chunk of revenue. I mean, I don't care if
somebody wants to make money, but at least be honest
about it. So, finally he gets all around the room to Chris
Joseph, who'd just been called up from the minors; he was
in Mark Lamb's stall. Peter glances at the name plate above
the stall and says, 'And Mark, we really need you working
hard.' And by this time he's back to Doug Halward. He
says, 'And *Dale*, we need your effort, too.'"

Randy pauses momentarily and says, "I think in life you
don't have to be everything to everyone. But the most
important thing is, you have to be honest. And when intuitive people like hockey players get the feeling someone's
not being honest with them, they lose their respect awfully
fast. I mean, nobody was asking Peter to know us all by
name – it was no offence not to. But *just don't tell us we're
like sons*, when really our relationship is nothing more
than business, and the players' main function from his
point of view was to earn him millions of dollars a year!"

Today, more than five years after Sather and Pocklington's dismantling of the Oiler juggernaut – a process
that, from public perspective, began with the sale of
Wayne Gretzky to the Los Angeles Kings in 1988 – Randy
still views the wreckage with manifest regret: "For me, it
was very disturbing, both as a player and an Edmontonian,
to see it happen the way it did," he says. "The players
were reduced so transparently to commodities. And the

management was just contemptuous of the community and the support it had given to that great team. For me personally, it was also *really* unpleasant to watch the cynicism settle on the players; finally, it was just every man for himself – if I can get more money over here, I'll take it."

Randy notes, with traces of regret, that he has not been back to the Northlands Coliseum since his playing days, and that he is unlikely to return. He says, "I'm happy to support an organization that is concerned with putting something back into my community. I take my kids to see the University of Alberta Golden Bears play their games. But I think many people would agree that, with the Oilers, the taking still seems to eclipse the giving. And I'd say the same thing if Pocklington were standing right here in front of me. The government has spent millions of dollars of tax money to support professional hockey in Edmonton, and I just don't think it's important that the city or province guarantee a private individual's success. Organizations like the women's shelter need help a lot more than Peter Pocklington does."


Randy's first "retirement" in 1986 lasted just six weeks. But after his third Stanley Cup, in 1987, with the mortar beginning to loosen in the Oiler stronghold, he decided to leave hockey for good. He applied for admittance to the residency program in orthopedic surgery at University Hospital in Edmonton, and by early summer had been accepted. "They notified me on a Monday," he says, "and on Wednesday, Juan Antonio Samaranch, the president of the International Olympic Committee, announced that former professional athletes would be allowed to compete in the 1988 games."

Hoping to recapture the well-remembered highs of 1980, Randy withdrew from the residency program and turned his sights on the Calgary Olympics. "Kathy had never wanted me to play more than a couple of years," he says. "When I told her about my decision, we were right out here on Highway 59, on the way to Belair, and we actually had to pull the car over for a discussion. Her thinking was, enough is enough – let's get on with life."

"Actually, I didn't mind him going back to the Olympics," says Kathy. "It was *pro* hockey I was tired of – being in the limelight, all the expectations off the ice. I'm sure Randy's told you that the Oilers really didn't treat their players all that well. And they were always trying to keep the players' families out of the way. It was as if we were lepers, or something. It was a drag."

Kathy is a warm, straightforward woman with attractively angular features and a rake of chestnut-coloured bangs that fall low on her forehead. She says, "The positive side of Randy's decision was that we moved down to Calgary for the year, where a new speed-skating oval had been built for the Olympics. I got really involved, working with the skaters."

For Randy, alas, love was not as lovely the second time around. The coach of the team was Dave King, who would go on to coach the Calgary Flames; and initially Randy was highly enthused about playing for him: "In fact, I said to Kathy after we met him, 'I absolutely have to play for this man.'"

Over the next couple of months, however, Randy's attitude changed dramatically. "It turned out the organization was focused almost exclusively on winning, with absolutely no interest in the sort of character development we'd seen under Father Bauer," he says. "I'd given up a couple of hundred thousand to do this, but more importantly, the young guys were cheated out of what could have been a great Olympic experience. We came in fourth, which I think had something to do with Dave's coaching.

He's a terrific hockey man, a great technical coach, but he doesn't have much understanding of personal relationships. As far as I'm concerned, the Olympic program shouldn't be a feeder for the NHL, and, indirectly, that's what it had become."

When the Olympics were over, Glen Sather invited Randy to rejoin the Oilers, and, despite Kathy's reservations, he did, and was with them for their fourth Stanley Cup.

That summer, both the team and the city of Edmonton – indeed large parts of the hockey world – were staggered by the news that Wayne Gretzky had been sold by Peter Pocklington to the Los Angeles Kings. "Knowing Peter, we more or less understood what was going on," says Randy, "but there was still a part of us that just couldn't fathom how anybody could have gotten rid of Wayne after all he'd done for the sport and the city." At the time it happened, Randy was on a fundraising mission in Saskatchewan. "A buddy and I were driving from Saskatoon to Regina," he recalls, "and I just kept looking at him, shaking my head in silent disbelief – how could it happen? *How could it happen?* Glenn Anderson used to say 'the moment Gretz is gone we're outa here.' And it turned out he was dead right. Not much time passed before we were all gone."

Even without Gretzky, Randy and the Oilers won a fifth Stanley Cup in the spring of 1990. In the meantime, the Gregg family had blossomed, and now included four children: Jamie, Ryan, Jessica, and Sarah. Randy laments the difficulties of playing pro hockey and trying simultaneously to be an attentive father. "Certainly, over the years, I felt very fortunate to have somebody as strong and dedicated as Kathy to take charge when I wasn't around," he says. "People used to say to me, 'Boy, those road trips must be tough.' And I'd tell 'em, 'You wanta see something tough, go to my house when I'm outa town.' I remember playoff games when I'd hardly had any sleep because of the kids, and I'd be exhausted. Other guys were in the same boat, but of course the fans don't see this side of it. To most of them, we're not so much human beings as some sort of warriors – no soft spots."

As much as possible, Kathy and Randy attempted to keep their children insulated from the undue attention that can accrue to the children of pro athletes. Randy says, "We wanted them to grow up as kids, not just the offspring of some hockey player." According to Kathy, the children knew their dad worked at a rink, but didn't know whether he was "the janitor, the ice cleaner, or what."

"We used to play hockey in the basement," says Randy, "and one day when Jamie, the oldest, was four or five, he picked up his stick and said, 'I wanta be Mark Messier,' and this was interesting to me, because I wasn't even aware that he knew who Mark was. And my little guy, Ryan, said, 'I wanta be Jeff Beukeboom.' He liked the name. Then they turned to me and said, 'Dad, who do you wanta be?' I thought, we must be doing a pretty good job."


The spiritual affinities that unite Father David Bauer and Randy Gregg were never more in evidence than in early 1990, when Randy and a group of Edmonton associates undertook an extraordinary athletic venture that for hundreds of children and adults would change the meaning of sport. Under Randy's leadership, the group founded a non-profit, private organization called Funteam. The purpose of the organization, in broad terms, was to provide a nurturing neighbourhood alternative to the frequently over-zealous (sometimes misguided) municipal children's athletic programs – to take the emphasis off winning and put it back on enjoyment with its attendant social and psychological benefits. "I'd heard about too many situations," says Randy, "in which a kid played a good game of hockey, but his team lost, and he ended up throwing his stick, or some such thing, and saying he hated it. And the fact is he didn't hate it. He probably had fun. But somehow society has taught him that the only satisfactory result is winning. And of course it's not! Sport is about developing self-esteem, skills, co-ordination, an ability to work with others. It's also about learning to win, but if we can teach the kids that it's just as important to learn to *lose* without sacrificing enjoyment or self-esteem, we're way ahead. This is the message that Funteam tries to project."

The organization was (and is) acutely aware that in today's madly competitive sporting environment, an increasing number of children seldom get an opportunity even to play. Some, as Randy explains, are too small, others not well-enough co-ordinated, others too shy. "Some are too poor!" he says. "Hockey in particular is expensive. It's *these* kids that most need the boost in self-esteem and that Funteam has been most committed to helping."

Randy stresses the importance of parental involvement in the program. "So many moms and dads go to the arena or ball diamond or soccer field and completely lose their perspective on the game, on their children, even on other parents," he says, noting that it is not uncommon to have fights break out among parents – male or female – at atom or peewee hockey games. "We felt if we could get parents out on the ice," he says, "they'd understand their kids better and understand themselves better."

The means to accomplishing all this were, by the standards of organized sport, revolutionary. "It was all very grass-roots," says Randy. "First of all, we did a lot of fundraising, speaking to groups about our intentions, going out into the communities, explaining who we were. Then we had to get people to join – parents, families, whoever. Twenty dollars buys a lifetime membership. There's very little ongoing administration. We send members a manual which basically encourages them to get together and form semi-organized soccer or shinny games, whatever they want, on their neighbourhood fields or outdoor community rinks. By holding our games outdoors we keep the costs down. And of course we encourage the parents to take part. You get six or seven adults on a rink, and they can teach the kids a lot more, both about hockey and about living, than a single coach ever could."

It is stark evidence of the need for such an organization that Funteam now has two thousand members in Alberta. Its board, of which Randy is president, holds fundraising golf tournaments throughout the province during the summer.

As a testimony to Funteam's successes, Randy tells the story of a nine-year-old Native boy with cerebral palsy, who had never been able to play on a regular hockey team, although he had several times tried. "With his condition he'd always had to play either in his boots or on bob-skates," says Randy. "So, he got into Funteam, where this sort of thing doesn't matter so much, and, you know, the other kids have just been terrific in supporting him. He's a goalie, and even the five- or six-year-olds will often shoot the puck into his pads when they're on a breakaway, so he can make a save. And when he does, everybody cheers. I went to see him play, and, I'll tell ya, of all the games I've been in, none was more important to me than that game of shinny with that nine-year-old kid in goal. He just felt so good about himself. These are kids who often aren't getting a lot of support from society, and in our own small way we're able to provide them with a bit of what they're missing. When I see the results, it just makes me want to work harder on this project."

During the summer and autumn of 1990, when Randy was putting every available hour into organizing Funteam, the Oilers decided he was expendable and left him unprotected in the league's annual equalization draft. "Sather told me he'd faxed every team telling them not to bother drafting me, because I wouldn't report," says Randy, "but Vancouver drafted me anyway and offered me an enormous amount of money compared to what Edmonton had been paying me."

The Canucks were interested in the thirty-five-year-old rearguard partly as a player but more so as a model for their young defencemen. "And I was interested," he says. "But I'd already committed myself to getting Funteam going, and I knew that if I left Edmonton at that point it just wouldn't happen. So I turned them down."

By the next summer, however, with Funteam well established, Randy signed with the Canucks. It would be his last year in pro hockey, and, to judge by the record book, it could hardly have been especially fulfilling: twenty-one games, one goal, four assists. "The truth is," says Randy, "it was one of the most rewarding years of my career. I was supposed to be there to help the young guys, and I ended up learning five times as much as I taught. And it was almost exclusively because of Pat Quinn [the Canucks' general manager and, at that time, coach]. He's such a great guy, an amazing man; I developed so much respect for him." Randy praises Quinn as introspective, disciplined, and committed to his players: "It's a real rarity in hockey to find a guy who can be a friend to the players, as Pat is, without losing their respect. Even after all my years in hockey, he showed me things about dignity and relations within the game that I'd never seen before."

During his season as a Canuck, Randy flew home every couple of weeks to be with his family in Edmonton. He also spent numerous hours observing proceedings at a sports medicine clinic in Vancouver. "For the first time," he says, "I realized that I'd seriously begun my transition out of hockey."

Randy also realized that, at heart, he was an Edmontonian and that, if there'd ever been any question about it, he wanted to make his permanent home in the city of his birth.

In April 1992, he retired from hockey for the fourth and final time. He returned to Edmonton and immediately entered a one-year program to complete his internship, which, at that point, had been stalled for exactly a decade. He also teamed up with Dr. Bob Steadward, a professor of anatomy at the University of Alberta, and began laying plans for the impressive new sports medicine clinic that the pair now runs in central Edmonton.

The clinic opened in June 1993, in six thousand square feet of leased space, and, typical of Randy's involvements, it is founded on progressive principles and demands a giant's helping of his time and energy. "What we wanted," he enthuses, "was an integrated clinic that would provide the highest level of care to people with sports injuries. We thought, when we diagnose something, let's see the treatment through to conclusion, not send the patients somewhere else as a lot of clinics do."

The resulting facility is a space-age conclave of physicians (three full-time, one part-time), physiotherapists, athletic therapists, nutritionists, orthotists, and exercise physiologists. In keeping with Randy's democratic philosophies, the clinic gives equal attention to high-level pros and to sandlot shortstops or tennis-playing grandmas. "As pro hockey players," Randy says, "we always had five or six doctors waiting in line to see us if we got hurt. But let's say a high school kid gets an injury of some sort, or the sedentary housewife who enjoys a little curling. Often, they can't even find a doctor who will take them seriously, let alone provide any long-term care. So they may have to give up an activity that's important to their psychological well-being. We treat those people. And if they happen to be kids, I try to give them some help not just with their injuries but with their attitudes toward sport."

A typical work day for Randy begins with an 8-o'clock rising and breakfast with his children. By 9, he is at the clinic, where he sees patients steadily until 5 p.m. "I see between fifteen and twenty a day, not nearly as many as, say, a family doctor," he says. "It takes four minutes to see a sore throat. A torn knee ligament takes thirty minutes. And so it should. Some doctors say they couldn't afford to work in sports medicine."

For Randy, however, there is no such financial pressure. Inasmuch as the security of his medical background allowed him to approach hockey in his own way, so have the monetary rewards of hockey given him freedom to create a medical career on his own terms. "It's great to be able to do something because you want to, not because you have to," he says.

If there is a trace of self-satisfaction in the remark it should not be taken at face value. There is little doubt that Randy is doing what he wants to do. But despite his freedom from financial and career pressures, the evidence would suggest that in most of his working and charitable endeavours, he is, more than most mortals, compelled by some irrepressible inner imperative and does indeed "have to" do what he does. When I present the notion to Kathy, she ponders for a moment and says, "He's certainly driven toward accomplishment; he has a very strong work ethic." His compulsion to work is well exemplified by his labours at the clinic, a facility set up in such a way that he can take more free time than can the average physician, without serious consequences to the clinic's operation. "But I don't really take a lot of that time," he says somewhat selfconsciously. "I'm there a lot. Too much for Kathy's liking, I'm afraid. Then I'll often put in several hours of work at home after the kids are in bed."

But his work at the clinic – indeed the breadth of his "work ethic" – is only part of the story. The greater part of his compulsion – the part that drives Funteam and plans hospital visits and resists the insidious corruptions of NHL hockey – is clearly a matter of accountability. Despite Randy's good fortune, he has evolved a remarkable capability to see not just his own rather rarefied domain but the whole human battlefield. And on that sprawling plain, he is a tireless advocate both of social and occupational justice and of individual worth.

At a certain point in our discussion of the insensitivities of pro hockey, he said: "In, I guess, 1986, when the collective-bargaining agreement was signed between the NHL and the Players' Association, Alan Eagleson said, 'Okay, fellas, if you play four hundred NHL games, you'll get a cheque for $250,000 when you're fifty-five.' And I thought, well, that's okay, but if you've played four hundred games you probably don't need the money. What about the guy who only plays two hundred games? Or one hundred? Or the guy who wrecks his knee after three months in the league and never makes it back? Or who never makes it at all? Thousands of players spend their whole careers in the minor leagues. What do they get? If we're truly interested in the players and their well-being, let's support the ones who need it most."

Such socialistic ideas are far more seditious in the venal world of pro hockey than throughout the rest of society. But they are the sort of thoughts that, apparently, Randy cannot stop having.

"I have very simple expectations of myself," he said at another point in the afternoon. "If I'd never played a game in the NHL, I think I'd feel just as fulfilled in life as I do now. Sometimes players come up to me and say, 'I was a junior player, but I never made it to the NHL.' And I like to tell them, 'Look, there are a lot of people like you who've done other things and have been much more happy and fulfilled than a lot of guys who did make the NHL.' I mean, the NHL is a great goal to achieve but it's only one of thousands that are out there. We've got to make the kids see that success in one narrow field isn't necessarily important – in fact that the very idea of success can get exaggerated, and that people can be successful in all sorts of ways, in all sorts of pursuits. I think as adults we should be telling them that *we'll* be happy with what *they're* happy with."

Occasionally, Randy's thoughts would seem to veer from his larger philosophies – or at least extend them in unexpected directions. He says, "Many people say that the awful thing about the NHL is that the players are just pieces of meat, and at the end they just throw you out. I think differently. Now, more than ever, an intuitive player goes into it knowing where he stands, and as long as he knows it going in, the owners can make their money, and the player can have his career. A player gets in trouble when he starts believing the owners have a personal interest in him. We should never call the NHL sport; it's business. And if you realize this, you can come out saying, 'It was a pretty good experience. It could have been better, but it was pretty darn good anyway.'"

Randy turned a two-year experiment in the big time into a ten-year career. However, he is not likely to amplify his medical career to quite the same degree. "Medicine's a great challenge," he says, "but eventually I'll probably want other challenges. I'm sure I'll do other things."

"In addition to medicine or instead of medicine?" he is asked.

"I'm not sure right now," he smiles.

And does he have anything particular in mind?

"Nothing in particular," he says, creating a distinct impression that he may indeed have something in mind.

Late in the afternoon, I asked Kathy what, in her view,

it was important that I say about her husband in writing his profile. "Oh, gosh," she said, "there are so many things you could say. It's hard to know where to begin."

"Where would you begin?" I asked.

"I guess I'd just begin with what an exceptional human being he is. I'm biased of course. I know that's not very specific."

Nor is it so much a beginning as a thematic undercurrent to almost anything that might get said about Randy Gregg.

And as good a parting thought as any other.

# JOHNNY BOWER

## IN THE MANTLE OF METHUSELAH

ON A DRIZZLY DAY IN mid-August 1942, some five thousand Canadian soldiers set out secretly by boat from the south coast of England, crossed the English Channel, and clambered onto the Normandy shore at the port of Dieppe. They were part of a six-thousand-man mission, whose purpose was to regain the port from the Germans, to destroy the surrounding installations and, in broad terms, to test the strength of the German defences.

The results of the ill-omened test were conclusive. Nearly thirty-four hundred soldiers lost their lives or were seriously wounded. Some two thousand were taken prisoner.

"I'd been all set to go," says Johnny Bower, who at the time was an eighteen-year-old infantryman with the Prince Albert Volunteers stationed in Horsham, England, "but a day or two before the raid, nine fellas in my company, including myself, got so sick with a respiratory infection, they had to take us off the boat and put us in hospital – we could hardly breathe. I guess if I'd gone, I probably would have lost my life. Most of my friends did."

Instead, John returned to Canada and resumed a more

personal war in which the bullets were round rubber pro-
jectiles and the guns were made of kiln-dried ash.

The risks of this secondary engagement were by no
means as insidious or deadly as the risks on the battlefields
of Europe. But they were nonetheless real for a young man
whose job it was to stand barefaced (and relatively lightly
padded) in a four-by-seven-foot shooting gallery and to concentrate not on ducking the unfriendly fire that regularly
came his way but on throwing himself in front of it.

"When I look back now," says John, "I think I must
have been crazy, but there was a time when I was so intent
on stopping everything that came at me I guess I would
have put my head in the way of a puck if I'd had to. In fact,
I remember once when I was with the Leafs – we were
playing the Bruins, and I somehow got tied up – my hands
were behind me or something. A shot was coming, and I
realized it was my face or nothing. So, I dived across and
just managed to get my forehead in front of it, deflected it
past the goal post. It was a wrist shot, not that hard. If it'd
been a slap shot, it probably would have killed me."

Other shots and collisions nearly did kill the Hall of
Fame goaltender: "The Rocket took half my ear off one
night. Dickie Moore sliced up my palate something awful.
I'm fortunate I never lost an eye. I had dozens of cuts either
just above or just below the eye – never got hit directly on
the eyeball."

Like most of his maskless peers, John believed that the
trick to dispelling any breaches of self-confidence that
might have followed a puck in the face, lost teeth, or a
broken finger, was to return immediately to action once
stitches, splints, or "freezing" had been applied. "In the
early days," he says, "we'd only dress one goalie; we only
*had* one goalie – your second-stringer was playing in
another league somewhere. In practice, we had what we
called a practice goalie – usually an amateur who got paid

to practice – and for road games, you'd have a junior goalie in the stands, for absolute emergencies. So if you didn't want a junior in net, you *had* to play hurt; you weren't much good to a team if you couldn't. They'd give you a needle, and away you'd go. I've played with broken bones, all sorts of cuts and bruises. I've played with my face so swollen I could hardly see out of one eye."

"I've seen him unconscious on the ice from being hit on the head, and then playing again twenty minutes later," says Nancy Bower, John's wife of forty-six years. "One night in Chicago, he got an *awful* hamstring injury; the whole thing just seemed to blow up on him – his leg was twice its normal size – and there he was, dragging the leg around, trying to keep playing on it. He couldn't of course. He was a week in the hospital just getting the swelling down. He's still got an ugly scar from the time he almost got his jaw cut off. Fortunately, he was a good fast healer."

During the years after the war, the treatments afforded injured players in the American Hockey League, where John spent his first thirteen years as a pro, were, at times, barely more advanced than the barbarous medical practices of the Middle Ages. Team trainers, whose surgical skills had evolved out of their responsibilities for darning hockey socks and sewing up shoulder pads, were occasionally called upon to do emergency suturing on eyelids, ears, and nostrils. Grubby, ill-lit dressing rooms, some of them inhabited by rats, doubled as operating theatres. "When John was with Cleveland during the early fifties," says Nancy, "he got hit so hard in a game in Pittsburgh, he lost nine teeth at once. They took him off, used a flashlight so they could see inside his mouth to stitch it and to clear out what they could find of the teeth, then they froze him up and sent him back on the ice."

After the game, without further treatment, John took the team bus back to Cleveland and, still under local anaesthetic, drove from the arena to the Bowers' home in Euclid Beach. By morning, he was delirious, from shock and from loss of blood. "He'd begun to hemorrhage during the night," says Nancy, who, more than forty years later, still manifests anger and anguish over the incident. "We were in the middle of a snowstorm in Cleveland, but, being from the prairies, I knew how to drive in winter, and I managed to get him to the car and to the nearest hospital." There, the attending doctor prescribed immediate surgery. "John's lips had been so terribly stitched," Nancy says, "that if they'd healed the way they were, his mouth wouldn't have worked properly. Beyond all this, it turned out I'd taken him to the wrong hospital, not the one where the team doctors worked. So he had to go by ambulance to a second hospital. And all this time, he was moaning and mixed up and of course in severe pain."

Eventually, surgeons opened and re-stitched John's wounds, removing impurities and bits of teeth. "The guy in Pittsburgh had done the quickest job he could, with no regard for the consequences, simply so the game wouldn't get held up," says Nancy. "I was so upset, I called Jim Hendy, the manager of the team, and went at him with both barrels. It was the only time in my life that I ever bawled out one of John's coaches or managers – although there were certainly other times when I felt like it."

Understandably, Nancy is quick to praise the protective qualities of contemporary goaltending equipment, and surmises that, had John had access to such space-age armour, his life as a goaltender would have been significantly less painful than it was. "He hardly had any padding at all from his abdomen to the top of his head!" she exclaims, noting that, throughout John's playing days, he would regularly come home with what she refers to as "these horrible black bruises" on his chest and shoulders.

John's belly pad, which is now in the Hockey Hall of

Fame in Toronto, was, indeed, not the sort of safeguard one might wish against pucks sailing in at nearly 200 kilometres an hour (the average Canadian uses nearly as much protection to stop wind and cold on a January day.) The surprisingly feeble appurtenance was custom-manufactured by Leaf trainer Tommy Naylor shortly after John came to the Leafs in 1958, and consists of nothing more than a circle of black cowhide, roughly the size of a dinner plate, appliquéd onto a pallet of off-white felt about the diameter and thickness of a medium pizza. "One of the problems with it," says John, "was that it didn't come up very far onto my collarbones – oh, I took some awful shots up around there. Mind you, when the pad was new, it was pretty good on my stomach and chest. It wasn't until it was about five years old and started to soften up that I really began to feel the shots. You had to know how to move with the puck not to get hurt. Of course, when guys like Hull and Geoffrion and Howe shot the puck, it didn't matter how you moved; you felt it."

John's vulnerability would have been checked somewhat by decent shoulder protection, but he refused to wear anything more substantial across his clavicle and upper arms than a pair of flimsy arm protectors, quilted cotton sleeves, joined across the neck and shoulders with an insubstantial laced yoke. "There was so little to them," he says dismissively, "that every couple of years they'd rot out from the sweat and so on, and fall apart. When I got hurt, Tommy Naylor would stitch a little extra padding into them to cover the tender spot. But not too much. See, I couldn't stand anything tight on my body, anything at all that restricted my freedom of movement. I wouldn't have been happy wearing the bulky equipment they wear today."

John reports that, during his years with the Maple Leafs, he regularly dreamed about pucks being fired at him by the likes of Howe, Hull, and Rocket Richard. "They weren't pleasant dreams," he laughs. "I imagine I did some twitching in my sleep." Awake, he was less inclined to ponder the slings and arrows of his somewhat outrageous fortune. "I was always *aware* that I could get seriously hurt," he says. "You have to be to stay sharp. But I never allowed myself to start worrying about it. If I had, I'd have been finished."

Beyond the damage inflicted on his anatomy by the game, John suffered for his profession in ways entirely unknown to his fans, or perhaps even to his teammates or coaches. Much of his discomfort hearkened directly to his war years when, as a trainee in Vernon, B.C., he spent an inordinate number of hours trudging through rain and swamps and sleeping in sub-zero quarters. "Along the way," he says, "I got such severe arthritis in my hands, I used to think I'd never be able to hold a goal stick again."

By 1944, the condition had become so acute that John was discharged from the army and sent home. He could still hold a goal stick but, at times over the next twenty-five years, he experienced considerable difficulty letting go of one. "When I was with the Leafs," he says, "I'd finish a game, and my stick hand would be locked right up like a claw. Some nights, it was so stiff and sore, it'd take me an hour just to get it open and working." When his arthritis was at its worst, John was barely able to perform even the simplest chores, such as washing his face or tying his shoes. "I always had to be careful when I shook hands," he says, "particularly with hockey players, who tend to have pretty firm handshakes. Sometimes I had to warn them to take it easy. With some guys, I wouldn't shake at all."


In July 1994, I arranged to meet John in the new arena at Teen Ranch, a Christian sports camp in the Caledon Hills north of Toronto, where, for a week, he was instructing young goaltenders. I had last seen him during the spring of

1988, when I interviewed him for a brief magazine story I had been asked to write about his love of the outdoors. At the time, he was still scouting for the Maple Leafs, and we met and chatted at Maple Leaf Gardens, in the primordial little coffee shop that, until recently, operated just inside the Carlton Street doors, selling the plainest of fare to players, Gardens employees, and whoever else happened by in need of nourishment or a bump of caffeine. The place was part of Conn Smythe's original Gardens design (1931), and as John and I sat there kibitzing, another original, an aged Gardens maintenance man, tottered in, put his hand on John's shoulder, and growled at me, "Ya writing about this guy?"

"I am," I said.

"Well, you tell the people he was the most courageous bloody goalie ever to strap on a pair'a pads! He wasn't afraid'a nothin'!"

Six years later, as I crossed the parking lot at Teen Ranch, I passed what I assumed was the most courageous bloody goalie's vehicle, a notably unpretentious Suburban 1500, the back windows of which had been pasted with photocopied flyers for the Johnny Bower Goalie School, which takes place annually, in August, at the Glen Abbey Arena in Oakville.

Inside the rink, the man who "wasn't afraid'a nothin" was out on the ice ministering not to the young commandos one might expect to find in such a situation, but to two twelve-year-old girls who, in their goaltending bulkies, bore a passing resemblance to a pair of salt and pepper shakers.

As I watched John work that morning, it quickly became apparent that he is a natural teacher, happily, patiently committed to imparting his Hall of Fame skills even to a couple of twelve-year-olds. He tutored them with infinite good humour, cajoling, encouraging, occasionally gathering them into a conclave to explain a fine point of skating technique, or to diagram a manoeuvre, then taking to the crease himself, demonstrating how to play the angles, control rebounds, clear the puck – how to hold the post or move across the net with maximum efficiency. Even the smallest signs of progress in his charges evoked his smiling endorsement, a pat on the back, or a tap on the pads. He carried a regular hockey stick and, unlike the youngsters, wore not the trappings of the trade but a blue patterned sweatsuit, a purplish baseball cap, and large TV-shaped glasses with translucent grey frames.

For a man of seventy, with an ongoing history of arthritis (in the back as well as the hands) he moves with considerable grace and athleticism. Typical of goaltenders, he is not at his best on the open ice. However, when he backs his posterior into the familiar precincts of the net, he loosens, becomes cat-like, flicking out an arm, a leg, gliding out to cut an angle – in all, creating a distinct impression that he might yet have a big-league save or two left in his account.

When John was finished on the ice, we adjourned to the arena office for the first of three conversations that I would enjoy with him over the next few weeks. To spend any time at all with John is to gain a memorable sense of what a gracious and unassuming man he is – an eminently forgiving soul who apparently does not have it in him to say anything negative even about such obvious miscreants as his former boss, the late Harold Ballard, whom John refers to respectfully as "Mr. Ballard." Nor does he have anything unflattering to say about any of his old ice antagonists, including John Ferguson of the Canadiens, who on several occasions during playoff series in the sixties made it his business to create misery for John, if not to crack his skull, by crashing the Leaf goal crease, stick and elbows flailing. The worst indictment John can muster against Ferguson is to say he

wasn't sure Fergy was "being truthful" when, after slam-
ming John at full speed, he'd claimed he'd been unable to
stop. John's sense of absolution was such that one night,
when it appeared Ferguson had been injured near the Leaf
net, he rushed to him and cushioned his head with a goal
glove. "After the game," he recalls, "Imlach bawled me out
something fierce. He said, 'If you wanta stay on this hockey
club, Bower, don't go coddling the enemy.'"

In reality, John was not one to coddle the enemy, or even
his own teammates. The benignly avuncular personality
that governed his life out of uniform was balanced by
intensely competitive instincts on the ice. He is famous
among teammates for playing as hard in practice as in
games. Even during shooting drills, he refused to leave
pucks behind him in the net, where they remained
symbols of his (albeit fleeting) insufficiency. If he sensed
one of his defencemen had let him down in some way, he
was not beyond embarrassing the delinquent by refusing to
feed him the puck, even when he was the nearest and most
obvious target for it.

All of this contributed to the composite of John's image
and popularity. Not only was he "the most courageous
bloody goalie ever to strap on a pair'a pads," he was fever-
ish in his desire to succeed, a guy who could, and eventually did, bring home the Cup. Moreover, he was a kind of
grandfather figure, a psychological soft touch, who we as
fans could relate to in a familiar, homey sort of way that
was not part of our link to younger, slicker, perhaps more
glamorous stars. From the time John joined the Leafs
during his thirty-fifth year, we ascribed to him the mantle
of Methuselah, seeming to cherish his longevity and
endurance in the same way baseball fans became endeared
to the great fastball pitcher Nolan Ryan as he ripened into
middle age. Indeed, the older Johnny got, the better we
liked it, perhaps seeing in his advanced years something of

our own best hopes against mortality. While he admits to fibbing to the Leafs about his age, telling them he was a mere thirty-three when they drafted him from the Cleveland Barons, there were perpetual rumours (undoubtedly started by the likes of ourselves) that he was much older – say, forty-five or fifty, or, toward the end of his career, even fifty-five or sixty. His compelling endurance was embodied in his grandfatherly face, his benevolent smile and eyes, and to a lesser degree in the old-fashioned haircut, white-walls running back over his ears and around to the nape of his neck.

What we were not so much aware of as John aged was the remarkable bodily strength that permitted him to carry on as younger players stumbled from the stage (Punch Imlach once called him the greatest athlete in the world). Even today, to see John in a T-shirt and shorts is to gain an instant appreciation of his remarkable physique. He is thick with muscle through the neck, shoulders, and torso. His thighs are the size of twenty-pound bags of potatoes, his forearms as big around as fenceposts. From years of playing the game, his hands are preternaturally muscular. "See here," he says, pointing out deep linear scars on his palms, a result of ten-year-old surgery to correct the ruinous effects of his arthritis. His face is fleshy and well-crinkled from smiling, his eyes buried so deeply in surrounding tissue that it is difficult to tell what colour they are. Considering that he has been hit by dozens of pucks and sticks and taken hundreds of stitches in the face, the scars around his eyes, nose, and mouth are surprisingly difficult to decipher. "They've gotten buried in the wrinkles," laughs Nancy, while John credits their relative insignificance to the cocoa butter with which he habitually massaged his wounds once they had begun to heal.

He was born John William Bower in Prince Albert, Saskatchewan, a city of some thirty-four thousand people, on the North Saskatchewan River, 120 kilometres northeast of Saskatoon. The city is perhaps best-known as the home of John Diefenbaker (it has also been represented politically by prime ministers Wilfrid Laurier and Mackenzie King). Regionally, it is more commonly recognized as a milling and distribution centre for the Saskatchewan forest industry.

During prosperous times, John's father supported his wife and seven children by working in the "casing" room of the Burns meatpacking plant on the edge of town. During the Depression, however, the family survived largely on relief. "My dad would get the odd day's work on a farm," recalls John, "or he'd occasionally get work in Prince Albert National Park, north of the city – I think he made twenty-five cents a day up there."

John, who helped the family through the thirties by collecting and cashing in beer bottles, remembers Depression Christmases when, in temperatures of minus-forty Fahrenheit, a horse and wagon would pull up to the front door and deliver oranges and apples – in some years the only holiday treats the children got.

Saturday nights during those long Depression winters were brightened by Foster Hewitt's galvanic broadcasts of NHL games from Maple Leaf Gardens. "We'd gather up to the radio at 8 o'clock," says John, "and for the next hour and a half or so we were in another world."

John's hero in those days was a young goaltender with the Boston Bruins, Frankie "Mr. Zero" Brimsek, who had earned his nickname by shutting out the opposition in six of his first eight NHL games. "I'd tell people that some day *I* was going to be Mr. Zero!" says John, who by the age of nine or ten was preparing for the role by tending net on local rinks in a pair of felt boots that he describes as "pretty good protection." His stick was made from the

planks of old apple crates; his goal pads were Eaton's cata-
logues. "We made pucks," he says, "by sawing rounds off
the trunks of small trees."

At the age of eleven, he got his first skates, a pair of
hand-me-down dirigibles once worn by a local player named
Curly Kerr. "They were so big," says John, "I had to stuff
them with paper. But that was okay; it gave me extra
padding from the puck." It also afforded him a trifle of insulation against the tormenting cold of the northern outdoor
rinks. "I remember games," he says, "when the weather
was so bitter that, after ten minutes, we wouldn't be able to
feel our hands and feet. And, oh, they'd *ache* as they thawed
out." The cold was even worse for a goalie, John notes,
because of the relative inactivity of tending net.

At the age of sixteen, John was sufficiently skilled that
he earned a spot with the Prince Albert Black Hawks, the
local Junior-A team. By this time, however, the war had
begun, and during the summer of 1941, amid a flurry of
local recruitment, the athletic teenager iced his hockey
ambitions and joined the army, claiming to be eighteen,
the minimum age for enlistment. "My dad was so mad,"
he says, "he threatened to tell them I wasn't old enough. I
cried my heart out; I wanted to go. I told him they'd never
send me overseas." But after a year of training in Vernon,
B.C. – a year in which he played goal for the local army
hockey team – John was indeed sent overseas, to a base in
Horsham, England, to await mobilization. "There was a
good army hockey team nearby at Guildford," he recalls,
"except I couldn't make it, because they already had the
Leafs' goalie Turk Broda playing for them."

John was not in Horsham long when the arthritis that
would torture him for decades began gradually to cripple
his hands. It was not what kept him out of the raid on
Dieppe, but it was severe enough that he did not, in the
end, see action.

He returned to Prince Albert in 1944, played a final year of junior hockey, and landed what he describes as "a great job as a boilermaker's helper" with the Canadian National Railway. "We'd cool down the engine boilers," he says, "then get inside them, and if there were any leaks we'd weld them up." As far as John's family was concerned, he was fixed for life. But his dreams of a career in hockey were far from dead, and he continued to work slavishly to develop his by-now exceptional skills as a goaltender.

In early 1945, the effort paid off when he was scouted and drafted by the Cleveland Barons, a venerable American Hockey League franchise, which was being rebuilt and was in need of new talent. "I wasn't sure I was quite ready," he says. "But the scout Hub Wilson told me he thought I could make it. So I said, 'I'll try.' And he said, 'You'll have to sign a contract.' I said, 'I will?' I didn't even know what a hockey contract was – or where Cleveland was! Hub said, 'I'm going to give you fifty dollars to sign this paper.' I said, *'Fifty dollars!'* Till then, the most I'd received to play hockey was a five-cent soft drink and a ten-cent hamburger. So I signed."

From the beginning, John's father had been resistant to his son's athletic ambitions, at times going so far as to take away his goal stick. "He wanted me to do something useful," says John. And now, as before the war, he was reluctant to let John leave Prince Albert. "When I got the fifty dollars," says John, "I remember I came home, and he said, 'Where did you get this?' And I said, 'The man gave it to me.' And he said, 'Nobody gives anybody that much money to play hockey.' I said, 'I had to sign a paper to get it.' He said, 'Where's the paper?' I said, 'He took it with him!' He said, 'Are ya *sure* somebody gave you that money?' He thought I must have stolen it."

In September of that year, when a letter came from the Cleveland Barons, containing a rail ticket to the club's training site in southern Ontario and five dollars for meals en route, John's father could do little else but accompany his son to the train station and, however reluctantly, see him off.

John played his first year in Cleveland for seventeen hundred dollars, lived on half of that, and brought the other half home to Prince Albert.

Before his second season, Bun Cook, a one-time all-star with the New York Rangers, took over as coach. He immediately endeavoured to modernize John's goaltending style. "He tried to teach me to play the angles," recalls John, "telling me to come out and so on, and I didn't know what he was talking about. I said, 'I can't do that; I'm used to staying in my crease.' He said, 'That won't work up here; you've gotta come out.' So I would, and I'd let pucks in, and I got really downhearted. I never thought I'd last." But what he lacked in technique, John more than made up for in perseverance. "I'd spend hours and hours working at it on my own," he says. "I'd come out one side, back in, then out the other. Down to my knees, back up. I was still determined to make it to the National Hockey League, get my name on the Stanley Cup."

In those days, however, there were only six NHL goaltenders, and they were not easily displaced. And as the years ticked by, and minor-league honours accrued to him, John seemed no closer to getting to where he so much wanted to be.

Throughout his career in Cleveland, he returned yearly to Saskatchewan during the off-season. In July 1948, while working as an assistant golf pro at Waskasiu, in Prince Albert National Park, he met a young woman from Saskatoon who was vacationing in the park. "I was up at the golf course watching one day," recalls Nancy, "and this young fella came up to me and said, 'Miss, you're standing too close to the tee – would you stand back!' A few days later we got introduced, then we met down in the village, and he asked me out. At that time, the golf pro at Waskasiu was another professional hockey player named Johnny Chad, and John picked me up in Johnny Chad's car. There was no place to go, of course, so he just showed me around the park. He knew it well from the days when his dad had worked up there during the thirties."

The two were married in Cleveland that November, and when Nancy's parents left the city to return to Saskatoon a few days after the wedding, she got her first real taste of the loneliness of the long-distance hockey wife. "John had already gone on the road," she says, "and there I was in a big strange city by myself. I don't know what I would have done that winter if I hadn't loved hockey. I'd followed it as a girl on the prairies, and in all the years John played, I never missed a game if I could help it."

On the ice, John continued to accumulate accolades, but he admits to becoming quietly, increasingly frustrated with his lot in the minor leagues. "I'd think, boy, eight or nine years have gone by. Surely, some of these NHL guys'll be retiring soon."

In 1953, he got what he now calls "his big break" – a try-out with the New York Rangers, who invited him to their training camp and rewarded him with the starting goaltender's job. By his own matter-of-fact estimation, he had "a terrific year," playing in all seventy games and allowing twenty-nine fewer goals than Gump Worsley had allowed the previous season.

That summer, however, John came as close to complacency as he would come during his twenty-six years as a pro. "I had some extra money," he allows, "so I didn't take a job and consequently didn't get much exercise. I didn't stop eating, of course, and by the time I got back to training camp, I was about twenty pounds over my playing weight of 180." When he had trouble reducing, coach Phil Watson, as vindictive and reviled a man as ever coached in the NHL, demoted him to the Rangers' farm club in Vancouver and reinstalled Gump Worsley as his goaltender.

"It was *very* discouraging for John," says Nancy, "especially after he'd played so well. . . . The only good thing about the demotion was that at least we got sent to a decent city. We lived in a suite in the Lucky Strike Motel right in downtown Vancouver. In New York, we'd been in an apartment on Long Island; we'd both just hated it. The only thing I look back on with any pleasure about New York is that our son, John Jr., was born there."

Despite his discouragement, John Sr. was by no means cowed by the seeming hopelessness of his situation. "I still didn't have my name on the Stanley Cup," he says, "and I'd realized by this time that I was pretty much as good as any of the other goalies. If I kept fighting, I figured I could get back."

The following year, he was traded to the Rhode Island Reds of the AHL, but returned to Cleveland for the 1957–58 season. Meanwhile, in Toronto, Punch Imlach, the recently appointed manager of the Toronto Maple Leafs, was searching for a goaltender capable of anchoring the team that was beginning to come together at Maple Leaf Gardens. "During the spring of 1958, he sent his chief scout, Bob Davidson, to Cleveland to have a look at me," says John. "Mr. Imlach had seen me play when he coached in Springfield. I was hot against him in the playoffs one year, so he knew what I could do."

At the end of the season, the Leafs drafted the aging goaltender and during the summer invited him to camp. But with his long-awaited ascension at hand, John felt a sorely ironic pang of indecision. "Suddenly, I wasn't sure I wanted to go," he says. "I wasn't sure I could help them.

I told our manager, Jim Hendy, 'I'm thirty-four years old (I'd told the Leafs I was younger); I think I may be past the point of starting over.'"

But Imlach was persuasive about steering his new ward into a Maple Leaf jersey. And when the time came, John was equally persuasive about convincing his new boss that he was an NHL goaltender.

With the Leaf camp behind him, he would never play another game in the minors. Over the next thirty-three years – twelve as a player, twenty-one as a Leaf scout – he would see the best and the worst that big-league hockey can offer. But in those early years, he had ample reason to feel good about life with the Leafs. For one thing, he was Imlach's kind of player. While Imlach himself could be testy and capricious, he had no use for players of his own temperament, preferring trenchmen, soldiers, men whose feet were firmly in contact with the planet. "What I want," he once said, "is a guy who will *play* for me" – in other words a guy who would accept without question the stingy, defensive conformity that defined Punch's brilliance as a coach.

The true Imlach players were the likes of Bob Baun, Bert Olmstead, Dave Keon, George Armstrong, Bob Pulford, Tim Horton . . . and, of course, Johnny Bower. Imlach was a goaltender's coach, and the Leafs had the personnel to be a goaltender's team. "A goalie's best friends are some big mobile defencemen," says John. Indeed, the team's regular defencemen – two veterans, Allan Stanley and Tim Horton, and two extraordinary youngsters, Bob Baun and Carl Brewer – were as fine a quartet of blueliners as the modern game has seen. When a fifth all-star defenceman, Red Kelly, joined the team in 1960, Imlach enjoyed the luxury of being able to use him as a centreman.

Even in that first season of 1958–59, John could sense that he had sold his future to the right buyer. "We had a great blend of young guys and veterans," he says, "and Imlach was smart. He analyzed everybody; he knew how to get the best out of them." Through the first half of the season, the Leafs had done little to convince their fans that they had forsaken their long-held lease on the league crawl-space. But in mid-winter, Imlach fired his coach Billy Reay and established himself behind the bench, repeatedly promising anyone who would listen that his team would be present when the playdowns for the Cup began. His airy assurances may even have hinted at the finals or the Cup itself. "My guys are gonna rise up like Lazarus," he announced to a caucus of reporters in early January 1959. "In fact if Lazarus isn't under contract, I might like to sign him for the stretch run." The sportswriters and fans loved it. They'd endured ten years of a team that founder Conn Smythe had compared to jellyfish, and even the *prediction* of a playoff spot was more exciting, and made better press, than no playoffs at all.

And, sure enough, during the last few weeks of that "Cinderella" year, the Maple Leafs began to stir, then to rise precipitously. The record shows that between March 14 and March 22, they won four games in a row, climbing from seven points back of the last playoff spot to within a point of the swooning fourth-place New York Rangers. On the last night of the season, still one point out of a playoff position, the team wheeled into Detroit for a fateful game with the Red Wings, who had recently replaced the Leafs at the bottom of the NHL food chain. Behind 2–0 at the end of the first period, and with owner Stafford Smythe gloomily allowing that the season was over (between periods, he went so far as to congratulate Punch on "a pretty good year") the team quickened to prophetic impulse. By the end of the second period they had tied the game, 4–4.

By the time they left the Motor City that night, they were a playoff team, as promised.

Ten days later, they finished off the Boston Bruins in the semi-final, before conceding the final to the Canadiens, an extraordinarily strong team in the second last year of a five-season run on the Cup. "Even though we lost," says John, "it was a pretty heady experience; it sharpened up our appetite for winning."

The 1961–62 season was headier yet, as the Leafs, with an all-but-unbeatable Johnny Bower in net, won their first Stanley Cup in eleven years. For their fans, it was as if some once-great aristocracy, some long-deposed embodiment of their pride and well-being, had been rightfully, triumphally restored. For Johnny Bower, it was the fulfilment of his Depression-era dream. "Oh, it was wonderful," he says quietly. "Really, I never thought I'd be around to see it."

The team again won Cups in 1963 and 1964, but perhaps the greatest of their championships came in 1967, a year in which they finished twenty points behind the first-place Blackhawks and in which the team's veteran players were beginning to look increasingly like outpatients from the geriatric ward (a couple of years later, comedian Johnny Wayne would observe that they were the only team in the history of pro sport to have their dynasty ended by prostate problems). "One of the things that made the last win so nice," says John, "was that we knew the team was going to have to be rebuilt, and quite a number of us weren't going to be playing much longer, at least not together. Plus, with expansion coming that summer, I think maybe some of the guys felt they'd won the last real Stanley Cup."

What no one foresaw was the brutal rapidity with which the Maple Leaf organization would deteriorate. At age forty-three, John himself would go on to play three more years. But by the time training camp opened the following summer, five veteran regulars, including Baun, Kelly, and

Eddie Shack, had moved on. Within a year, five more were gone, among them Allan Stanley and Frank Mahovlich. Two years later, Punch himself would be history (he would return to the Leafs in 1979 after a decade in Buffalo, but by that time both his ego and attitudes had become far too brittle for the exigencies of the contemporary game).

Within a year of John's retirement in 1970, only Dave Keon and Ron Ellis were still in the old uniform – in fact, the old uniform itself had been transformed, updated.

During the forty years of the franchise's history, it had been run with a purposeful hand, first by its founder Conn Smythe and, after 1958, by a trio of owners that included Conn's son Stafford, John Bassett, the owner of the Toronto *Telegram*, and Harold Ballard who, until the late fifties, had been manager of the Toronto Marlboroughs Junior-A team. By 1972, however, Bassett had been bought out, Stafford Smythe had died, and Ballard had gained control of both the hockey team and its home at Carlton and Church streets. His ascendancy introduced the darkest period in the Gardens' history, an eighteen-year farce that began with Ballard being sent to prison for tax evasion (he served nearly a year) and ended with his death in 1990.

Between these notable events, the organization sank into disgrace. Except for brief periods of modest success, the team became a chronic loser. Players and Gardens employees were often shabbily treated, and the building deteriorated to the point where, for several years during the eighties, large plastic sheets had to be suspended from the rafters to catch the drips that came through the decaying roof.

Ballard's parsimonious habits and bloated ego became a public joke. Building superintendent Wayne Gillespie recalls that, one day, Ballard inquired as to how many cucumbers would fit in the 30,000-gallon brine tank – a holding vessel for the salt water and toxic chemicals that are pumped out at sub-zero temperature through the refrigeration pipes beneath the ice. "He said he wanted to make dill pickles to sell at games. He'd dream up these schemes – anything to make a buck – then he'd forget about them."

On another occasion Ballard got Gardens employees to help him make imprints of his hands and feet in the concrete beneath centre ice. The prints, accompanied by a brass inscription, were originally filled with epoxy, which created inconsistencies in the quality of the ice above them. For that reason, the epoxy was removed and the imprints filled with concrete at the first opportunity following Ballard's death.

It was into the wearisome fiasco of the Ballard years that John was hired as a talent scout and part-time goaltending coach following his retirement in 1970. But if he was in any way dissatisfied with the instability of the Leaf organization in years to come, he was not one to complain about it. "I'm sure he saw things he didn't care for from time to time, particularly regarding the management of the team," says Nancy. "But by and large he was happy just to be able to stay in the game when so many of his teammates were pushed out of it. Even during his last year as a player, we'd had no idea he was going to be offered work with the Leafs. So really we'd been prepared for a much tougher time after he retired. As it turned out, the transition was really very smooth."

Nancy is a gracious, articulate woman, with a sense of humour and a thoughtful, caring mien. If she had one cavil about John's role as a scout, it was that, after all the years of travel – years in which she had done a good deal of childrearing on her own – her husband was back on the road. "By this time John Jr. was sixteen, our daughter Cindy was twelve, and Barbara was ten," she says, "so, we were through the toughest years, but still it would have been nice to have John home a little more, to have a little extra help driving the kids to hockey games and skating lessons and so on. But at least we had him through the summer months."

For twenty years, until his second retirement in 1990, John travelled the skies and highways of the continent, sitting through games in sometimes drafty arenas, bedding down in whatever accommodation was most convenient, filing expense-account forms and of course endless reports on the assets and liabilities of this young defenceman, that young goaltender, occasionally a player who had gone unnoticed and had been ripening gradually in some obscure senior or college league. Scouting is a job fuelled by vast amounts of coffee, generally in styrofoam cups, by cheese-burgers, doughnuts, and breakfasts on the run. "I went wherever I was told," says John, who acknowledges that, toward the end, the travel became increasingly tiresome. "You see a game in one town or city," he says, "and early the next morning, or even the same night, you're on a bus or a plane to another town, a game, a meal, another hotel, maybe a rent-a-car, back on the road again. Sometimes I'd go weeks at a time, right across the prairies, or through the Maritimes."

During the early eighties, John and his daughter Cindy, who was once a competitive figure skater, decided that enough was not enough and founded a two-week annual goaltending and skating instruction program called the Johnny Bower Goalie School. The Bowers are an exceptionally close family, and, today, three genera-tions of them are involved in the thriving mid-summer enterprise. They cater to forty goalies a week during the school's two-week run in early August – twenty young-sters (as wide as they are high, in their goalie gear) and twenty older netminders, many of them midget-level or junior prospects. To see the lot of them, masked, lumpish, and diligent, on the same sheet of ice – the smallest of them barely able to skate in their bulky gear – is to get a sense of some futuristic defence force, a new-age children's brigade, under the tutelage of a wise old Master of the Wars.

At an average evening session, John is likely to be found teaching in one corner of the rink, or at one goal, while John Jr., now forty years old, works in another. Cindy is in yet another area, teaching skating technique, while her husband, Jim, assists with the goalies, and John's teenage grandsons, Bruce and John III, work where they are needed. Nancy is the school's administrative co-ordinator, as well as its all-purpose grandma and on-site ambassador (in the interest of family harmony, she points out that daughter Barb and her husband, Terry, should also be mentioned as contributors to the school, as should grandchildren Kelly, Dale, Staci, and Alison). In all, there is an upbeat, well-lit atmosphere about the school, a progressive aura light-years removed from the intimations of Gothic carnage that dwelt in the crease half a century ago, when John made his stand in the AHL (today's goalies have scar-free faces and their own teeth). "The only thing about goaltending that hasn't changed," smiles John, "is that you still have to stop the puck. And most of these kids have better technique at ten than I had at twenty."

Apart from teaching with her dad, Cindy operates power-skating clinics, working with players at all levels of the game, including NHL stars such as Rick Tocchet and Ron Francis. Away from the rink, John Jr. works for PetroCanada in Burlington. A one-time defenceman in Toronto-area junior hockey, he was drafted by the Washington Capitals in 1974 but never turned pro. "When he was a boy," notes John, "I urged him not to be a goalie. I thought there'd be less pressure on him if he wasn't always being compared to me. He was a good defenceman, but he didn't quite have the skating, and now, sometimes,

I think I should have let him fulfil his ambitions as a goalie; he might have made it."

A few weeks after I had visited John at Teen Ranch, I spent a day with him and Nancy at the north Mississauga town-house that they have occupied since they moved from their home in Etobicoke eight years ago. Despite its being part of an extensive suburban complex, there is a village atmos-phere about the place. The front door bears the Bowers' name, plus a welcome sign and a decorative straw hat, and the main-floor living room is an old-world amalgam of comfortable furniture, porcelain ornaments, and pastoral art. A copy of Millet's "The Gleaners" hangs on one wall, a dreamy prairie watercolour on another. Family photos hang here and there, and a mounted hockey card depicting John in his rookie season with the New York Rangers sits on a low table. The room's only other reminder of hockey is a glistening silver samovar given to John by the manage-ment of the Maple Leafs after the 1967 Stanley Cup cham-pionship.

On this day in August, Nancy is pleased to point out a pot of stunted but determined sunflowers that have bloomed unexpectedly on the fenced patio out back.

The upstairs office and downstairs den are well-endowed remembrances of John's lengthy and storied career. The den is crowded with framed photographs – here of John testing a Christmas turkey during his days in Cleveland; here fishing with Gordie Howe in northern Saskatchewan; at a party celebrating his Vezina Trophy in 1966; at Toronto City Hall after winning the Stanley Cup in 1962; here wearing the Cup upturned on his head. Two small models of hockey's most famous trophy stand on a shelf in the corner not far from a replicated version of the Hap Holmes Memorial Trophy, which John twice won as the AHL's all-star goaltender during the fifties. Nearby is the Les Cunningham Trophy, awarded to John in 1956 and '57 as the AHL's Most Valuable Player. As he picks up the trophy for examination, he accidentally snaps the sculptured metal hockey player from its pinnacle ("I'll have to get some super glue," he mutters).

Most of John's goaltending equipment is in the Hockey Hall of Fame, but his gloves are here: the leather blocker, with its burnished tract of maple-coloured leather, and the trapper, heavier than expected, and grizzled to the point that it suggests some item of failed taxidermy or post-expressionist art. More photos hang across the room; John skating with the children at a Maple Leaf Christmas party; with Dave Keon in the Leafs' dressing room; in an official photo of the Leafs of the early eighties (a shot in which Harold Ballard's dog, the luckless mascot, T. C. Puck, appears front, centre, and serious). John pauses at a photo of his army hockey team from Vernon, B.C., winners of the "Coy Cup" in 1942. He peers at it with the benefit of his glasses, attempting to bring individuals into focus. "A lot of these guys never made it back," he says almost to himself.

A tour of the upstairs office reveals, among other keepsakes, framed letters from both Pierre Trudeau and John Diefenbaker, congratulating John on his election to the Hockey Hall of Fame in 1976. Elsewhere hangs an antique litho, dated 1873, showing a group of men playing roller hockey, a sport thought to have been invented during the past decade. The jewel of the room is a framed 45-rpm recording of "Honky the Christmas Goose," sung by "Johnny Bower, Little John and the Rinky Dinks." The disc, which is still played at Christmas on Toronto radio stations, was recorded by Capital Records on November 20, 1965, just a few hours, recalls Nancy, before "the big blackout," an electrical power failure that shut down much of eastern North America. "Really, John didn't want to do the thing," she laughs. "He'd been asked to, and he'd agreed, but I remember him grumbling away about how he couldn't sing, it was gonna sound awful, this and that. Now, we're trying to get the rights back so we can reproduce it."

Since 1990, when John retired as a scout, the Mississauga townhouse has been little more than a port-of-call for the Bowers, a way-station between their six-month "summers" at the cottage they have owned for twenty-six years near Bobcaygeon, Ontario, and their lengthy winter vacations in Fort Myers, Florida. It also functions as a telephone-answering centre through which they control, among other things, John's freelance teaching engagements, registration for the goalie school, and the numerous card-show and charity appearances John is invited to make. "Last year I probably did forty card shows," he says. "I go all over Canada, sometimes into the States – just signing my name, reminiscing with the fans. It's easier than stopping pucks." Since late 1993, John has also done promotional work for an up-market street-hockey net called "Goal-Eeze."

Asked about the challenges of retirement, John responds immediately that the only difficulty he's encountered is that time seems to "whiz by" too quickly. "Up at the cottage, I'll get up in the morning, do a little fishing, and it's noon hour. You cut a few weeds, and it's the long weekend. Then the summer's over. It never went that fast when I was playing."

When it is suggested lightheartedly that, to slow down the clock, he might return to the game that knocked out his teeth and put 250 stitches in his face, he smiles and explains that, during the last game he played – a 1988 charity contest in which he was a reluctant participant – he'd had "a very strong feeling" that injury was imminent and that he should not have been on the ice. He says, "I wouldn't play today to save my life."

And yet he is still very much a goaltender. He notes that, at times, he finds himself pondering old foes, old performances – or dreaming about them. "Sometimes," he says, "it's as if I can still feel the pads on my legs. When I'm watching the playoffs, I'll move with the goalie, twitch a shoulder or an arm, kick out a leg. Making the save from the easy chair."

"I'm trying to design a headstone shaped like a goaltender," jokes Nancy.

Asked if his musings on the past include regrets, John is predictably noncommittal. "I might have one or two," he says softly. "But they're not very significant."

Nancy is more direct. "I think John feels he probably could have been paid a little better," she says. She reflects for a moment and adds, "I sometimes imagine that if we'd had even one year at a quarter the salary some of these guys are paid today, we'd have been set for life. In John's day, you had to prove yourself for two or three years just to get a tiny raise."

"I had to prove myself for *twenty-six* years," says John. "We worked hard, and we have our scars and our arthritis to prove it. But I have no grudges. It's been a dream. I started out in felt boots and ended up winning four Stanley Cups."

Which somewhere down the line just might be a fitting inscription for that goalie-shaped headstone.

BOBBY SMITH

## PRESSURE TO PERFORM

FIRST, A FEW FACTS:

• Until the age of eighteen, he was Bob Smith, at which point his mother, sensing the name was too plain for an athlete of impending stardom, suggested he try "Bobby," a hockey player's dub in the tradition of Orr, Hull, and Clarke. During his next game, he informed the announcer at the Ottawa Civic Centre that he wished to make the change. Asked why, he said, "Because my mother thinks it sounds better." "Bobby" he became.

• During his final year of high school, he played 110 games of junior hockey, half of them road games entailing round-trip bus rides of up to a thousand miles. He missed weeks of school and often attended class on three or four hours of sleep. He kept an A average throughout.

• In 1978, he set a junior scoring record (192 points) that has never been broken. (The following year, the Ontario Major Junior Hockey League enshrined his accomplishments by creating the Bobby Smith Award, given annually

211

to the player who, in the league's words, "best combines hockey excellence and academic achievement.")

• He was the first player chosen in the 1978 NHL entry draft and a few weeks later was given a quarter-million-dollar signing bonus by the Minnesota North Stars. He bought a sports car for himself, a sedan for his parents, and invested the rest.

• Eight months later he won the Calder Trophy as the NHL's rookie of the year.

• Eight years after that, in 1986, he scored the Stanley Cup-winning goal for the Montreal Canadiens.

• His NHL playoff totals, 64 goals, 96 assists, make him the ninth-greatest playoff scorer in the history of the game, tied with Gordie Howe and Mike Bossy, and ahead of Hall of Fame notables such as Stan Mikita, Phil Esposito, Guy Lafleur, Bobby Hull, Maurice Richard, and Frank Mahovlich.

• He says, "When I retired in 1993, I was told there'd be a tremendous void, a very deep sense of loss. But it just never happened. Not that I didn't have a burning passion for hockey. I sometimes look back and think: Hockey wasn't something I did, it was something I *was*. For thirty years, I lived and breathed and dreamed it. But even knowing how attached a player can get to it, I have little patience for guys who can't accept that it's over when it is. Of course it's over! Did they think they could play forever? As my kids say, 'Get a life!' . . . I guess a big part of my dealing with the loss of it was exactly that: knowing that I *had* a life, that I was capable of doing something else."

On a Friday afternoon in late April 1995, Bobby is seated at a pint-sized desk, in a frumpy classroom, in a nondescript building, at the heart of the campus of the University of Minnesota, in central Minneapolis–St. Paul. He is here for one of his two weekly political science classes (this one focuses on American foreign policy, the other on the arcane workings of the U.S. Supreme Court). Up front, the professor, an unflappable thirty-something woman in a mauve knitted dress, is rattling through a summary of the nuances and nightmares of the Carter and Reagan administrations. Her coffee mug, on the desk beside her, bears the inscription COFFEE FROM HELL, while the blackboard behind is a dusty collage of the scribbled names and touchstones of a decade of American foreign policy: Khomeini, Samoza, Iran, hostages, helicopter crash, Star Wars, the Persian Gulf, Afghanistan, Nicaragua. In the upper corner of the blackboard is the terse question: "DOES YOUR JOB SUCK? Earn over $1,800/month and get college credits too!"

In his bluejeans and deck shoes, Bobby has a casually collegian look that is not out of sync with the sartorial ambience of the classroom. But he is by no means fully camouflaged among his fellow students. For one thing, at thirty-seven, he is nearly twice the age of some of them (he is twice the size of others). What's more, he is carrying an old-fashioned top-opening briefcase, a most serious holster, not at all the sort of thing one would expect to see in the hands of, say, the young man two seats over, with the three earrings and the Pink Floyd T-shirt, or the kid with the shaved temples and bleach-blond topknot – or any of the half-dozen young men in beat-up Nikes or hiking boots, wearing their baseball caps turned back-to-front. Even to the casual eye, Bob's avidity and sense of purpose are notable departures from the class norm. He listens intently to every question asked (but on this day asks none of his own) and seemingly takes more notes than the rest of the class combined (when the lecture ends, a fetching young woman in a leopard-print miniskirt tells him with obvious admiration, "I can't *believe* how much you write down!").

By and large, Bob's professors and fellow students are unaware of his exotic former life in that school of ultimate knocks, the National Hockey League. In the lecture hall and in his seminars, he is simply Robert Smith, student number 145635, one of forty-five thousand students on campus. "When I enrolled in September of '93," he says, "it had been in the papers that I was going to be in the business school here, so some people knew. But in my history and political science classes, there were maybe 325 people, so I was such an insignificant part of things that everybody left me alone, even if they knew I was there. The funny thing was that, on the last day of term before Christmas, a lot of them brought hockey cards that they wanted me to sign. It was kind of a nice moment – I mean, I'm happy to be an old hockey player, if that's what people want. But, really, my preference in class is to be just another student."

It is under the study lamp in the wee hours of the morning that Bob's red-eyed alter ego emerges, a metaphoric werewolf that has no interest whatever in being "just another student." There, in the lamplight where it counts, Bob is every bit as obsessive about his studies as he ever was about hockey or anything else he has done in nearly four decades on the planet. Which is no small claim. He is a guy, for example, who as a teenager in Ottawa quit all summer sports to concentrate on tennis, played eight hours a day, seven days a week, until he was the best player in the city – a guy who no longer plays tennis because he cannot play daily and refuses to brook defeat at the hands of players he would have beaten at the peak of his game. "I won't play golf either," he says. "I don't want to play a couple of times a summer and shoot 107. If I can't play every day, don't talk to me about it."

Bob applied the same radical standards to his hockey career, invariably attending training camp as fit and fixated as any player in the game, working constantly to increase strength and endurance, often training long after others had left the ice. "I remember early in my career being surprised that not everybody shared my convictions," he says with a wistful chuckle. "Teammates would head out to a bar after practice, or they'd go hunting or fishing or sailing; I remember guys saying things like, 'I wish I had time to go skiing,' and I'd think, what on earth would you want to do that for, or do any of these things, when you could be improving your game by concentrating on hockey? We'd be on the road, and I'd say, 'Who wants to go to such-and-such a place and have a burger and watch the Blackhawks and Pittsburgh, or whoever, on ESPN; I phoned ahead; they've got it.' And the response would be, 'Don't you want to get away from hockey?' And I'd think, well, no, I don't! Some guys would get knocked out of the playoffs and never watch a game after that. *They wouldn't know who won the Stanley Cup!* I could never understand how they could be so casual about this thing I was giving my life to."

Bob clearly remembers the night on which the North Stars were eliminated from the playoffs by the Toronto Maple Leafs during his first year with the team. "We chartered home from Toronto," he says, "and a lot of the guys were joking around, and I just felt *crushed*; I felt *terrible*. How could they be goofing around? I was just so *angry* at them, and disappointed in them. Here, the playoffs were starting, and we weren't going to be in them!"

Prior to the last game of the 1986 season, Bob sat in the dressing room at Madison Square Garden in New York, listening as a number of his Montreal teammates grumbled their dissatisfaction at having to play a game that meant nothing to either team's playoff prospects. "I said, 'Guys! We've got twenty-five players in the minors who'd die for a chance to play this game in Madison Square Garden!' I just never got to a point where I took any of it for granted." Or where he could tolerate giving the game anything less than his utmost. "A few months after I retired," he says, "I went out on a Wednesday night and played oldtimers hockey with some ex-North Stars and college players. I got home, and Beth said to me, 'How did you like it?' I said, 'I'm not going back.' She said, 'Whaddaya mean?' I said, 'I'm not going out there once a week, stepping on the puck, losing it off my stick – I couldn't even feel it on my stick! I had to be staring at it all the time.' She said, 'Look, that's crazy; you've just gotta relax and enjoy it – it's not the NHL.' I said, 'No, that's it.' If I couldn't play well, I didn't want to play."

"Eventually he did go back," says Beth, Bob's wife of thirteen years, "but not until he'd started skating four or five times a week on the outdoor rinks and felt his game was at a satisfactory level."

Even as a child, Bob was remarkably focused and resistant to diversionary activity. "I never had any toys," he says without a trace of regret. "In hockey season, I played hockey. Baseball season, baseball. Football season, football. I wasn't a well-rounded kid, not at all. And I'm not unhappy about that. Well-rounded kids are not going to make it to the NHL. If you're a kid with lots of interests – say, you like to read a book after school, watch a bit of TV, go to the mall, do some skiing, some basketball, go hunting in the fall with your dad – you're probably going to be a well-rounded adult, but forget about being a professional athlete. I remember hearing a Cheech and Chong song about a kid who was completely obsessed with basketball, didn't want to do anything else – that's the way I was. I heard Doc Rivers, the basketball player, say that, in Chicago, as a kid, he and his buddies were so fanatical about basketball that they'd shovel snow off the outdoor courts in the middle of winter so they could keep on playing. That's what it takes."

Bob acknowledges that, during an early phase of his hockey career, he allowed himself to believe that a diffused focus was permissible, even valuable, in the realm of friendship, if nowhere else. "But the longer I played," he notes, "the more I could see how guys were becoming increasingly fragmented in their social lives, building up big circles of friends from different walks of life, all sorts of business acquaintances, and I could have gone that route, too, but I didn't. I found that as I got older I just got closer and closer to the hockey circle. Part of that may have been an unconscious attempt to preserve my career by pouring everything into it. I know in the end I didn't leave much on the table. I put a lot into hockey, and I took a lot out. And that's why I'm at peace with not playing now. I mean, I've sat around with fellas twenty-eight or twenty-nine who say, 'If I had it to do over again, I'd take it a lot more seriously.' I think, *holy smokes*, what an awful thing to have to say at the end of your career! When I walked away, I had the satisfaction of knowing that I couldn't have given it more than I did. And when I'm finished at university, and eventually with business, or whatever I get into afterwards, I know I'll be able to say exactly the same thing – I couldn't have given more."

Ironically, where Bob's financial investments are concerned, his greatest satisfaction is in knowing that he could not have given *less* than he has. "I do monitor my investments," he says; but as in tennis or golf, which he refuses to play unless he can play six days a week, he sees no justification in spending three or four hours a week administering his portfolio when for a relatively small fee he can place it in the hands of brokers who, as he puts it, "give ten hours a day" to the management of their clients' stocks and bonds. "I've seen teammates go out and get broker's licences and proceed to dabble at managing their own money. I've also seen guys invest in restaurants or businesses that they know nothing about and can't spend any time at, and they end up losing. I mean, how many writers or actors do you know who have any real success working at their professions in their spare time? I used to say I'd *love* to compete against hockey players who only did it part-time; I'd eat them up!"

One notable exception to Bob's forthright pronouncements on dilettantism is that, for the last eight years of his career, he acted as his own agent in contract negotiations, the sort of action seen by some as tantamount to going into court without a lawyer, or into a hockey game without shin pads. "Actually, I don't think it ever cost me a cent," he says. "I mean, who knew better than I did what I wanted and what I had to offer? Besides, it gave me a different view of the business of hockey and of how a team is run from the management's perspective."

Bob's take on the business of the game was abetted more substantially by nine years of service as a vice-president of the NHL Players' Association – years in which he three times knocked billysticks with the wardens and wattlekind of the NHL Board of Governors in the interest of achieving collective-bargaining agreements.

Given his intelligence and attitude, it is hardly surprising that Bob's progress at university has been precipitous. He has taken classes winter and summer, without a break, since September 1993, and by mid-1996 will possess a Master's degree in Business Administration from the University of Minnesota's esteemed Carlson School of Business. "When he finishes," says Beth, "he'll basically have done four years in three."

Such an accomplishment, she is quick to point out, is not something that can be effected without extensive sacrifices and tolls. "Sometimes, it's been ridiculous," she laughs. "Bob will do hours and hours and hours and hours of work. He just kills himself doing the essays. But of course he doesn't want his name on anything that isn't his very best effort. Sometimes, he'll go for days, getting no more than four or five hours of sleep. I'll say, 'Bob, *get* six hours of sleep. Does it really matter?' And of course it does matter – at least to him. Otherwise, he wouldn't be doing it the way he is. And of course he wouldn't be getting straight A's, either."

Beth notes that, in two years of studying, Bob has been given only one substandard mark, a B-plus, awarded in a course that required him to work as part of a group to achieve his grade.

"What some people would find strange in hearing all this," she says, "is that you could observe Bob, even at some absolutely critical time in his school term, or at some other very demanding time in his life, and you probably wouldn't have a clue that he was under pressure. He's so controlled. After we got married, I used to love to yell and scream and slam the door, and he wouldn't even bat an eye or raise his voice. It took me years to teach him how to argue. In the sixteen years I've known Bob, I've never heard him say one thing he'd regret, never seen him make one wrong move."

Still others might find it strange that a man who has earned millions of dollars as a pro athlete and whose financial needs will be met until kingdom come would embrace the extraordinary pressures and perils not just of obtaining an advanced university degree in an almost impossibly brief period of time, but would do so under self-imposed standards of excellence that to the average onlooker would seem all but masochistic. What's more, he chose to return to school in the face of a coveted job offer in pro hockey that would have fulfilled one of his long-range (although publicly unspoken) ambitions: to work in

NHL management. "I may still end up in hockey," he allows. "But to go back to it with an M.B.A. in strategic management and finance, which is what I'll have when I graduate, is going to be far more advantageous, both for me and for the organization, than simply going back with a knowledge of the game."

Among his scholastic incentives, Bob also cites the possibility of gaining employment in some corporate endeavour unrelated to hockey, as well as a desire to better understand the performance of his personal investments. To divine the true nature of his academic aspirations, however, one would do well to aim the witching stick into more personal terrain, and as far back in time as the Great Depression, which, in Bob's estimation, has always been a substantial, if indirect, influence on both his habit of mind and his scholastic ambition. His parents, he explains, were children of the thirties, who, because they didn't go as far as they could have in school, ended up with an acute awareness of the importance of education. He says, "They passed this along so emphatically to my brother, my sisters, and me that even the *thought* of any of us not going on to university was absurd. It wasn't *if*, it was *where*. There were no options. At the dinner table it'd be, well, that was great that you got three goals last night, Bob; how did the math test go? And my sister's social studies essay was every bit as important as my hockey games. My younger sister was a Canadian tennis champion, so the fact that I was a hockey player didn't even dominate the family athletic scene."

Bob recalls being asked several years ago by his Montreal teammate Bob Gainey, "Well, what if one of the kids decided not to *go* to university?"

"The thought just seemed so foreign," shrugs Bob. "I said, 'It would be the equivalent of announcing at the age of seventeen that you'd decided to run off and join the French Foreign Legion.'"

Which, as far as Bob's parents were concerned, was more or less the equivalent of what he did. He says, "It was especially disturbing to my mother when my hockey ability became apparent and she realized I'd probably be leaving school at a certain point to pursue a hockey career." She was equally disturbed by the image of the pro game, which, as Bob points out, was populated at the time by high-living and well-publicized free-wheelers such as Derek Sanderson. "She was so concerned about it all," he says, "that at one point she went out and did some research and came back and told me that once every six to eight years a superstar came along – it was Rocket, Howe, Hull, Orr. She said, 'It looks like this young fellow Lafleur is going to be next.' Then she said, 'If you can be next, I think you should go ahead with it. If not, you're wasting your time; you'll regret your involvement with this game.'"

What Jeanne Smith could not have foreseen was that, between the time she spoke during the early 1970s and the time Bob signed his first NHL contract in 1978, the economics of the game would be changed so dramatically by the emergence of the World Hockey Association (which exploded salaries by competing intrepidly to sign NHL players) that even players far less talented than her son would readily become millionaires in the profession she mistrusted. "When I finished high school," says Bob, "somebody offered me a quarter of a million to write my name on a piece of paper and a whole bunch more to play, and that was just too much to walk away from. But, you know, in all the years I played, I never lost sight of my original intention to go to university. It was very much a piece of unfinished business, and I never felt I'd be in any way satisfied with myself as a human being until I'd done it." Bob feels now that, in small part, his return to school is also an example to his children, Ryan, aged ten, Megan, seven, and Daniel, six. "I don't want them asking me ten years from now, 'Dad, if it's so important, how come you didn't do it?' People also tell me, 'Oh, it's such a good example for other players.' And to a degree I accept the validity of that. On the other hand, I think it's one of the most selfish things I've ever done. I mean, sometimes it seems far less a sacrifice than an indulgence, a kind of abdication of my responsibilities as a husband and parent."

While Bob has undoubtedly been a successful self-representative in contract and business negotiations, he is not necessarily his own best agent in the area of image management. He is remarkably free of self-doubts and self-deceptions and thereby inclined to reveal things about himself that men or women with less confidence in their views might tend to play down. His bristling accounts of the no-frills commitment with which he has approached his career, schooling, and recreation create an impression sometimes of rigidity or narrowness, at other times of exaggerated self-focus. What Bob does not convey accurately or convincingly about himself (Beth ascribes it to modesty) is that, week in, week out, his rigorous agenda is tempered by personal and community commitments that consume oodles of time and attention and whose conceptual base would seem to lie less in the precepts of the Carlson School of Business or the NHLPA than in the progressive poetics of the New Testament. "You'll never hear him talking about how much charity work he does," says Beth. "But the phone just rings off the hook around here – people calling to ask for an appearance or contribution of some sort, because they know he won't say no. We're always going to fundraising events and dinners, and Bob's invariably the first to show up. He just feels there's so much good he can do because he was a hockey player, and he takes it as a responsibility, whether it's helping raise money or visiting hospitals, or simply writing a letter to a fan or talking nicely to a child on the street."

While many pro athletes are prepared to donate an auto-graphed photo or stick to any of the hundreds of charity auctions that regularly solicit their contributions, Bob routinely offers a half-day of his time and talent as a hockey-clinic instructor, to be awarded to the highest bidder. "He knows it raises a lot more money if he shows up personally for these things," says Beth. "He's got at least five or six clinics promised for this summer." He was at one time the honorary chairman of the Minnesota Children's Cancer Research Fund, which raises a million dollars a year for research at the University of Minnesota, and is now on that organization's board of directors. "Not long ago," says Beth, "somebody called asking if he'd help raise money to buy a special van for a single mother of two kids with some very debilitating disease, and of course he pitched right in. Sometimes I tell him that, since the North Stars left town, I think he's the only hockey player left in Minneapolis."

During March 1995, Bob was involved in a benefit dinner for the one-time North Star Bill Goldsworthy, who had recently been diagnosed with AIDS. "A lot of guys flew in," says Bob. "Darryl Sittler, some old teammates: Cesare Maniago, Barry Gibbs, Henry Boucha, Dennis Hextall, Lou Nanne, Jean-Paul Parise, Jude Drouin, lots of hockey exec-utives. I took some neighbours and local coaches. Goldy was gone from the North Stars when I got there, but he used to scout for them; I'd see him around. We raised a fair bit of money, but you know this sort of thing can be equally important as a morale booster and, in this instance, a reminder to the outside world that when help is needed, you help – that you don't start categorizing people in need as 'acceptably' or 'unacceptably' needy, based on what disease or disability they might have."

Discussion of the event and of Goldsworthy's illness

and wide-margined life style prompted Bob's opinion that it is a mistake to attempt to make role models of athletes, and that they should not be thought of, or held accountable, as moral or social examples. While Bob himself has not shied away from responsibility as a behavioural model, he is adamant that the onus for showing children and young people how to best conduct their lives should be part of everyone's contract with society, not just that of the pro athlete. "If you've got something to give, give it," he says. "Muhammad Ali said, 'If you're looking for a role model, and he isn't sitting at the dinner table, you've got problems.' The whole notion of being a role model is really pretty complex. I mean, I try to show a positive face, and to encourage kids to feel good about themselves, to make good use of their talents, and so on, but by no means do I feel every kid should conduct himself the way I did as a kid. I was extremely single-minded, and that just isn't going to work for everybody."

Bob's life as a single-minded kid began on February 12, 1958, in North Sydney, Nova Scotia. But to hear him talk about his childhood, you might imagine it had begun a couple of years earlier, when his parents and older siblings, were living on Sable Island off the southwest tip of Nova Scotia, where for two years Bob's father was a radio operator for the federal government. As he sits in his study, describing his beginnings, Bob turns to the shelves behind his desk and brings out dozens of black-and-white photos, not of North Sydney or of later stops along the way, but of life on Sable Island, a life to which he has seemingly staked some romantic prenatal claim. Here's a photo of his sisters and brother in the sand dunes, here at the seashore, here with the famous island ponies.

By the time Bob was born, the family had moved to the

mainland, and, by the time he was two, had moved on to Ottawa, where his dad continued his career with the federal Department of Communications.

Bob describes his upbringing in Ottawa's west-end suburbs as "typically middle class." But his three years of junior hockey with the Ottawa 67's were anything but typical. "At the time," he says, "the trick of combining hockey and school, keeping an A average, and so on, really didn't seem such a big deal. It's only in looking back that I can see how much discipline and time management it must have taken. A lot of the guys would sleep on the bus, play cards, that sort of thing, when we were on the road, whereas I'd always feel I had to be studying, reading textbooks, getting ready for exams. We'd get home from, say, Niagara Falls at 5 in the morning, and my parents would have to kick me out of bed a few hours later. I'd get home from school the same day, do some homework, drive down to the rink for a practice or a game, and away we'd go again. Those were big-league games, too, 7:30 to 11, and I was the top scorer on the team, so I'd be on the ice a lot. I'd just be exhausted at the end of a day, and of course there'd always be an English essay due the next morning, or a chemistry test, or something. But it was good for me. I learned a lot about discipline."

Bob also learned enough hockey that, by 1978, his final year as a junior, he was the most accomplished twenty-year-old and the most attractive professional prospect in North America. He possessed extraordinary scoring and playmaking skills, and at six-foot-four, 210 pounds, was not a player who was likely to be intimidated by the relentless savagery of NHL play. "More than any other pro sport," he said recently, "hockey is a war. In football, you see players helping one another up. In baseball, they chat away at first base. In hockey, you get unfeigned animosity; it's barbaric. In fact, one of the things I've always liked best about it is that it's a test of a person's courage, and to be successful at it, it's not enough to be a good skater and shooter – you have to be able to withstand the violence and the intimidation."

Bob allows that, at times, his preferred method for dealing with the game's primitive component was "just to get right into it." While not known as a fighter, by his own estimation he never retreated from a fight, and acknowledges having played an infrequent part in the ongoing verbal battles that paralleled (and sometimes provoked) the more obvious physical antipathies between teams. "Sometimes the spoken stuff was nothing more than an attempt to break the other guy's concentration," he says, "but sometimes it was outright intimidation. I remember play-off games in which guys would be yelling the most brutal stuff imaginable at one another during the warm-up; it'd be, 'Hey, Modano, I'm gonna break your arm tonight! I'm gonna be right there with ya when ya get the puck, and I'm gonna break your arm!' . . . My own response to that sort of thing was always just, 'I'll be there! I'll be the guy with the puck! You'll know where to find me!'" Bob laughs aloud in recalling what he refers to as "the more personal stuff, comments on the way a guy looks, and so on. I remember one night somebody got onto me about an article that had been written about me – 'I see ya did this and that! You must really be something special!' I said, 'Who read that to ya?' . . . Doug Risebrough ripped into me one night, and I said, 'Still yappin', eh, Doug? That's what ya always did best!' Oh, he was mad. I remember a night when the Red Wings had some new guy in their line-up; it was obvious he wasn't going to last long, and Jack Carlson yells at him, 'Don't give up your day job, Buddy!' I mean, really, there was no end to that sort of thing. It went on all the time. Most of it was just ridiculous, like Chris Nilan asking Tim Hunter during a playoff game if he got his nose in a joke shop. Tim says, 'Boy, that's a really original line; I've never heard anything like that before!' The trick was to say just enough to irritate the guy, break his concentration, maybe intimidate him a bit, but not enough to get him cranked up. Really, though, I wasn't into it to any great degree. I preferred beating the guy on the ice."

Which, more often than not, was what Bob did. His first four years in Minnesota were distinguished by a steady escalation in personal productivity and by a leadership role in the team's rise from the lowest level of the league basement in 1978 to the Stanley Cup finals in 1981. During the 1981–82 season, Bob set a North Stars scoring record of 114 points.

At the end of his first season in Minnesota, he returned to Ottawa for summer courses at the University of Ottawa, where he had studied during his final year of junior. There, he met a slim, dark-eyed science student from Montreal, who three years hence would become his bride. "When I started dating Bob," says Beth, "I remember my parents were like, oh, my goodness, not a hockey player! All the money and the crazy life style. So he got kind of a strange reception when he met them. But he was just so different from what they'd expected. I mean, a polite guy with lots to say, and an interest in education, and so on. They changed their minds pretty quickly."

Beth is an intelligent, hospitable woman who, over the years, has provided a balance for the ambition and perfectionism that have played such significant roles in the composite of her husband's personality. "I'm always saying, 'Relax, Bob, what's the difference?' And what *is* the difference? When Bob would get into a scoring slump in Montreal, he'd think it was the end of the world, and I'd say, 'Walk across the street to the children's hospital and look around. *There* are people with problems.' I have that attitude. I don't tend to worry about things the way he does."

In 1983, after Bob's fourth season with the North Stars, he and Beth were married in Ottawa, and moved into a house Bob owned in suburban Minneapolis – "just as Bob's career was beginning to disintegrate down here," she says. The agent of that disintegration was a short-sighted (and ultimately short-tenured) coach named Bill Mahoney, hired by the North Stars in 1983 and gone forever from the NHL by the middle of the following season. "This guy came in and decided he'd show everyone who was boss, starting with Bob," Beth explains. In the process, he cut back substantially on Bob's playing time and instituted an unimaginative offensive style that did not lend itself to his all-star centreman's capabilities, or, in Bob's view, to winning. "I put up with it for a while," says Bob, "but at that age I was pretty impatient, and eventually I just said, 'Enough. Trade me to a team that appreciates me, or I'll quit and go back to school.'"

The team took him at his word, and for both Bob and Beth, the resulting trade to the Canadiens was made partly in heaven, partly in heaven's twin city, Montreal, where Beth had been born and raised, where Bob was as close to home as the NHL could position him in those days, and where the home-town club shared Bob's longstanding compulsion toward excellence. "When my professors start talking about what makes a successful business or corporation," says Bob, "I often find myself thinking about the Canadiens. I mean, besides being the most successful athletic organization in the history of pro sport, they're as well managed business-wise as any corporation in North America. At school, we talk a lot about how a first-rate business will build up a kind of folklore around itself – Rolls-Royce, Coca-Cola, whoever – and the Canadiens have done that so brilliantly. They've created this notion of the Canadiens as family, with ancestry, traditions, pride, responsibilities, all of that. And when you put on the

uniform, you become a part of it. And it's convincing. You
believe in it. I mean, it's not just something somebody tells
you about; it's in the record book; it's part of the building!
You go into the Forum when it's empty and the lights are
down, and you'd swear sometimes that the old voices and
ghosts are right there with you. In the dressing room,
above the stalls, there are pictures of all the great Hall of
Fame players – they're painted in such a way that their
eyes follow you around the room as you move. So, you're
sitting there putting your equipment on before a big game,
and all the old greats are looking right down at you, pro-
jecting this message that you'd better do your part. I
remember Bobby Clarke saying to me once that the
Canadiens have an advantage over every other team. And
they do – in this belief that they're special. . . . For me, just
to see the older guys coming around was a thrill: Dickie
Moore, Jean Béliveau, Jacques Plante, occasionally the
Rocket or Henri. Heck, it was a thrill to be on the same ice
as guys like Guy Lafleur and Larry Robinson. I loved
Montreal; I mean, there I was, in the prime of my career, in
the greatest hockey city in the world, with the greatest
organization, close enough to home that my dad could
come down for games, all my games on television, Beth in
her home city. . . . In terms of my role as a player, it was
just nice to be with a team where I was only one of twenty
guys; we had Lafleur, Gainey, Robinson, lots of good
players, when I got there. In Minnesota, I'd been more or
less the marquee guy – a lot of pressure."

In spite of his enthusiasm for the Canadiens' organization, Bob acknowledges that its ethos and attitudes are not
for everyone. "What you have to remember," he says, "is
that, in exchange for what they offer a player, they want a
certain return – some respect for the organization, some
conformity to the standards; and not every player is either
willing or able to give that. You have to buy into it, and

some guys don't. Even some of the greats were disaffected in the end – Lafleur, Geoffrion, the Rocket. They just didn't quite fit the mould."

Bob notes that, apart from the *team's* expectations of its players, the city imposes its own intense pressure on the hockey club. "Losing is a civic disgrace in Montreal!" he laughs. "And, I mean, there's just *so much media attention* that, if you do lose, there's no place to hide. The media in Montreal can make a player's or a coach's life so absolutely miserable that, in the end, the team has no choice but to move him out of town."

Bob and Beth were barely off the plane from Minnesota when they were introduced to the Canadiens' way of doing things. "The general manager, Serge Savard, and the president, Ron Corey, were there to meet us," says Bob. "My dad and brother were there; lots of media. We were driven downtown to a press conference. It was just so obvious I was welcome. . . . When Mark Napier and Keith Acton, the guys I'd been traded for, got to Minneapolis, there was nobody to meet them; they had to locate their bags, lug their sticks and stuff around, figure out how to get to their hotel, then to the rink – a completely different reception."

It was a measure of his commitment to the new team and culture that Bob enrolled immediately in French classes and was soon fluent enough in the language to communicate comfortably with his francophone teammates and with French journalists and broadcasters. But by his own admission, he did not immediately feel comfortable with the grand Montreal traditions. "It wasn't until after we won the Cup in 1986 that I felt I was really a part of all that," he says. "Before that, I kind of felt that my teammates and I were the black-sheep team. My first year in particular was bad; we set a record for losses at the Forum; we were the first Canadiens team with a losing record against this or that expansion team; I was the leading scorer that year, and

I had the fewest points of any leading scorer ever, and on it went. But we did win two playoff rounds that year and ended on a high note. And by the end of the eighties, we were among the best teams in the league every year."

During his years in Montreal, Bob confirmed his reputation as one of the most reliable and productive playoff performers in the history of the game. As the checking tightened and the post-season goaltending improved, his offensive skills seemed to blossom in inverse proportion. During a fifteen-year career, he scored 64 playoff goals and had 96 assists. "I used to feel tremendous pressure in the playoffs," he says. "I remember thinking, if only we can just get through this first round, there'll only be eight teams left; then if only we can get through *this* round, and so on. I felt a huge responsibility to the team, because I knew my offence would be counted on. I guess maybe that's why I was able to do as well as I did. With any team I ever played on, I used to look around the dressing room before playoff games and pick out the guys I could really count on. And I wanted guys to be able to count on me. This guy might not score tonight, but he's going to be giving it all he has. I guess I've always been quite proud of the way I played in the playoffs. It's a mark of your value to the team, and to the team as a business. And that was significant when it came time to negotiate a contract. A team nets maybe $800,000 per home playoff date, but the team has to keep advancing to keep bringing that in. At contract time, I was the guy who could help your team advance."

In 1991, a year after his departure from the Canadiens, Bob helped the Minnesota North Stars advance all the way to the Stanley Cup finals, scoring five game-winning playoff goals, to tie a record held jointly by two other renowned playoff scorers, Jari Kurri and Mike Bossy. His return to Minneapolis the previous summer had been every bit as calculated as his departure seven years earlier.

The Canadiens had acquired Denis Savard during the off-season, and, seeing that his playing time would be restricted by the acquisition of another first-line centre-man, Bob approached Serge Savard and requested a trade. Initially, Savard was unwilling to comply, but eventually his resistance waned, and in June 1990 Bob was reunited with his one-time teammate Bob Gainey, who was by this time coaching in Minnesota.

Notwithstanding his sensational playoff performance of 1991, Bob's last three seasons with the Stars were marked by a gradual decline in productivity. During his final season, 1992–93, he played just forty-five games, adding a modest five goals and seven assists to his lifetime totals. The team missed the playoffs for the first time in five years.

On April 20, 1993, within days of his last game in uniform, Bob announced his retirement from hockey.

Four months later, he was back in school, a thirty-five-year-old rookie, under self-imposed pressure to perform.


At the conclusion of his class in American foreign policy, Bob and I sat through a lecture on the functions and frailties of the U.S. Supreme Court. We then took a walk around the University of Minnesota campus, a varied amalgam of brick, stone, and green space, bordering the Mississippi River, which snakes through the Twin Cities, swollen at this time of year by spring run-off from its head-waters in north-central Minnesota. On a bridge that joins sections of the campus on opposite sides of the river, Bob told me that if he had not become a hockey player, he would quite likely have become a doctor. "I've said that before," he smiled, "and seen it reported that I was in pre-med school or on my way to a medical degree when I was playing hockey. After a certain point in my career, I'd seen so many false reports about myself that I stopped trying to correct them."

From the university, we drove south toward Eden Prairie, an affluent suburb in the southwest corner of Minneapolis, where Bob, Beth, and their children have made their home since returning to Minnesota in 1990. In the car, on the 35W freeway, Bob explained that his enrolment in business studies had been influenced by his curiosity about the ups and downs of the investments he had made during his years as a hockey player. "You get interested in the stock market," he said, "and then in how companies make a profit by providing a service or product better than anybody else, and then in what kind of management has to be there to keep a company growing and keep its *position* in the market. Should it be diversifying? consolidating? I find it all fascinating."

The more time you spend with Bob, however, the more you're inclined to believe that his professed fascination with business will never quite supplant the deeper fascination that he clearly still feels for the challenges, drama, and rewards of the game of hockey. When the notion is put to him in more or less those terms, he demurs briefly and reiterates an earlier thought that when he graduates in 1996 he'll explore business and corporate possibilities in the Twin Cities. "But I'll admit," he says, "that the kicks you might get in hockey management would be hard to replicate in any other business endeavour. I talked to Bob Gainey about this last year. We agreed that the typical business executive just couldn't get the same thrill seeing his company's product in the window of, say, a hardware store that a hockey person can get out of seeing the team he's put together go on a tear in the Stanley Cup playoffs. Really, the idea of helping build a winning hockey team is very enticing to me. You've got such different intangibles than you have in merely trying to put together an investment portfolio. I guess ideally if I were to return to hockey, I'd be able to contribute to the hockey side of things and would have enough of a feel for the business side that I could help the team make some money. The opportunity has to be there of course."

And one senses that it will be. Sooner or later.

In the meantime, there is a demanding slate of studies to pursue, essays and exams to write, and a personal agenda replete with family, recreational, and charitable engagements. There is also a more esoteric commitment to private betterment. Contrary to Bob's depiction of himself as career-focused to the point of narrow-mindedness, he has undoubtedly worked as hard as any player to develop a multi-dimensional inner life. During his last year with the Stars, he took a university correspondence course in, of all things, Russian geography. "He has a book under his arm all the time," says Beth. "These days it's usually a text-book, but it used to be a novel, a political book, whatever." Bob expresses a literary preference for history and biography and enjoys "just about anything on Winston Churchill or the Second World War." He has an interest in contemporary art, and is an aficionado of the paintings of the famous American realist Andrew Wyeth, several of whose prints and one of whose original watercolours hang in the Smith's expansive home in Eden Prairie. It is a small badge of distinction with Bob that, during a visit to Wyeth's studio in Chadds Ford, Pennsylvania, in 1980, he was invited to have a glass of wine with the artist and his wife, in the Wyeths' home. Despite claiming that he has centred his social life on the hockey world, he has also, over the years, found time and energy to make and maintain a number of exceptional friendships that extend far beyond the borders of sport.

It is readily apparent, however, that Bob's deepest and most heartfelt responsibility is toward his family. "In spite of everything else that's going on," says Beth, "the kids are the centre of his world." He devotes large portions of every weekend, and several evenings a week, to their recreational activities, and during the past winter often took six-year-old Daniel for a couple of hours of outdoor skating on weekday mornings, before dropping him off at kindergarten, then returning home to study.

"I used to watch him with the boys," says Beth, "and I'd worry that he was going to become this pushy sports father. Then he started coaching Ryan's hockey team, and he bent over backwards *not* to push him, or show any favouritism, or even offer any criticism for fear of seeming too negative. And I said, 'Bob, you don't have to criticize him, but you can teach him.' Now, he's gotten a lot better, and he *can* teach him. I guess it's obvious that Bob thinks sports are really important. This summer, Ryan's going to play some golf. Last summer it was tennis. He's in basketball, too. All three kids are on soccer teams. We're not going to push hockey more than any other sport. Really, I've never seen Bob get upset at Ryan for how he played a sport. He's getting a lot like his own parents – more concerned about how the kids do in school than on the ice or field."

Beth contends that Bob is "by far the biggest kid" in the Smith family. "He'll organize these *huge* games of shinny on the neighbourhood pond," she says. "He'll have half the subdivision out there. Even the fathers come out when he gets a street-hockey game going. We've had kids come to the door asking, 'Can Bobby come out and play?' I tell them, 'No, he's got to do his homework.'"

On the way home from classes in winter, Bob will often stop at a favourite outdoor rink, put his skates on, and get into a pick-up hockey game. "Sometimes I take the kids over," he says. "They go on one sheet of ice, I go on another with older guys – they always make me play into the wind."

"He'll get home just drenched," says Beth, "but with a big smile on his face. When he's got Daniel with him, the poor little guy'll be so exhausted he can hardly stay awake for supper. . . . During his last year with the Stars, Bob would phone when he was on the road, and his first question would be, 'What's the ice on the pond look like? Are there any cracks?'"

One day in January 1995 Bob stopped for a pick-up game on the way home from class and stayed so long that he got frostbite in his feet. "By the time he got home," says Beth, "his toes were turning black! I said, 'Bob, you're thirty-seven years old. How could you not know it was time to quit?'"

"The problem," says Bob, "is that you're so absorbed when you're out there, you don't really know *anything*. Something inside you just wants to keep on playing."

Asked what that "something" might be, Bob reflects for a moment and says, "I guess it's in the motion and speed – swooping around with the wind rushing past. I've always truly believed that there's something intrinsic about hockey that makes it better than any other sport. I mean, when you're running and you stop pumping your legs, you stop moving. In skating when you stop, you keep on gliding. On the big surface, with the wind behind you, you really do feel you could go forever."

"Some day," says Beth, "he's going to come home with a great big smile frozen on his face."

And that, Bob suggests, is as good an incentive as any to keep on playing.